Freedom and Borders

Freedom and Borders: A Theory of Citizenship for the Age of Globalization

BY

DARIO MAZZOLA

University of Geneva, Switzerland
University of Bergen, Norway

emerald
PUBLISHING

United Kingdom – North America – Japan – India – Malaysia – China

Emerald Publishing Limited
Emerald Publishing, Floor 5, Northspring, 21-23 Wellington Street, Leeds LS1 4DL

First edition 2025

Open Access

The ebook edition of this title is Open Access and is freely available to read online

British Library Cataloguing in Publication Data
A catalogue record for this book is available from the British Library

ISBN: 978-1-80117-994-2 (Print)
ISBN: 978-1-80117-990-4 (Online)
ISBN: 978-1-80117-993-5 (Epub)

Printed and bound by CPI Group (UK) Ltd, Croydon, CR0 4YY

INVESTOR IN PEOPLE

To Fabiola and Eleanor, citizens of the world, and to the memory of Professor Geeta Chowdhry, who taught that justice reaches as far as humanity.

Epigraph

[S]o long as I may keep my mind directed ever to the sight of kindred things on high, what difference does it make to me what soil I tread upon? –Seneca[1]

---

[1]*De Consolatione ad Helviam*. Translated by John W. Basore. Loeb Classical Library 254. Cambridge, MA: Harvard University Press, 1932. P. 442.

Contents

Contents

About the Author

Dario Mazzola is a political theorist currently working as a researcher at the University of Bergen. He holds a BA and MA in Philosophy from the University of Pavia and a PhD in Philosophy and Human Sciences from the University of Milan. Dario has published on a variety of subjects, especially in political, social, and moral philosophy, and is specialized in the political and moral theory of migration and in the ethics of international relations and affairs. Articles by and about him have appeared on newspapers and scientific blogs in Italy, Norway, Switzerland, the United Kingdom, and China. Beginning in February 2024, Dario works on a project funded by the Swiss National Science Foundation at the University of Geneva, where he is also a lecturer in Methodology of Political Theory.

Acknowledgments

This is a book about giving every human being their due. It is therefore especially regrettable that I have to violate this principle on the very first page. I will be unable to thank all who deserve it, but I made the hard choice of being unequally just toward a few rather than equally unjust toward all.

In the early years of this project, at the University of Pavia Ian Carter, Emanuela Ceva, Luca Fonnesu, and the late Salvatore Veca greatly encouraged and contributed to this project with their insights and feedback. I also thank Federico Faroldi and Enrico Grosso for their friendly support as well as for the philosophical discussions. At Northern Arizona University, Christopher Griffin, John Hultgren, Matt Evans, and Andrew Nuno, each in their specific fields, all gave me directions over crucial issues. A special thank you to the activist group No More Deaths, who illustrated to me the situation at the border. Valeria Ottonelli and Gershon Shafir also offered commentaries to working papers.

The late Geeta Chowdhry lavished her kind mentorship and extraordinary intellect and knowledge over a rudimental version of this work, in the last year of her life. The greatest hope I can put in this book is to participate, with its modest contribution, in her immense legacy.

At the University of Milan, my PhD advisor Marco Geuna provided guidance to issue in another monograph, but that also influenced this book. I as well thank all my colleagues from the PhD school in Philosophy and Human Sciences for supporting my research – and making my spare time worthwhile.

I too thank all the colleagues at the University of Bergen and Geneva who provided support and in particular Matteo Gianni and Esma Baycan-Herzog. I am grateful to the students I taught at these institutions and, especially, the ones I met during a visit to the MINT program of the Graduate Institute of International and Development Studies on a gracious invite by Davide Rodogno. Questions and comments preciously enriched this work, but the IHEID students helped me uniquely by reporting views from their diverse international backgrounds.

David Kretz deserves my gratitude for the encouraging assessment he provided on an earlier draft of this book and for suggesting precious bibliographical references.

A sincere acknowledgment is also due to the excellent team at Emerald Publishing for having scouted and endorsed this book: Hazel Goodes, Abinaya Chinnasamy, Lydia Cutmore, Lauren Kammerdiener, Katy Maters, and Shanmathi Priya, all persevered with incredible tact and professionalism, even when I was sending more extension requests than pages. They own a large share of merit if this book is seeing the light after a pandemic, a war, a change of job and country, a marriage, or a child (just to name some of the circumstances, from terrible to marvelous, of the last four years).

Finally, a heartfelt thank you to my wife Fabiola and my daughter Eleanor: you conferred greater purpose to the book and to the author, and neither would be the same without you.

Geneva, February 28, 2024

Chapter 1

Introduction: Theorizing Citizenship in Critical Times

Our purpose is to consider what form of political community is best of all for those who are most able to realize their ideal of life. We must therefore examine not only this but other constitutions, both such as actually exist in well-governed states, and any theoretical forms which are held in esteem; that what is good and useful may be brought to light. And let no one suppose that in seeking for something beyond them we at all want to philosophize at the expense of truth; we only undertake this enquiry because all the constitutions with which we are acquainted are faulty.

And also for the sake of mere life... mankind meet together and maintain the political community. –Aristotle[1]

1.1 Theorizing Citizenship

In a nutshell, the argument of this book is that citizenship can be understood as a compact of normative relations determined by a specific interpretation and realization of the human condition: the elements of this interpretation and realization that are shared across countries, nations, and cultures, together with the elements of politics and law that are globally established, provide the substance for a form of global citizenship that already exists. There is, however, an imbalance between the subjective value and dignity of the human person as it has been recognized, especially with the development of the legal and ethical culture of human rights since the end of

---

[1]Aristotle, *The Politics of Aristotle*, trans. into English with introduction, marginal analysis, essays, notes and indices by B. Jowett (Oxford, Clarendon Press, 1885), 2 vols.

Freedom and Borders, 1–10
Copyright © 2025 Dario Mazzola.
Published by Emerald Publishing Limited. This work is published under the Creative Commons Attribution (CC BY 4.0) licence. Anyone may reproduce, distribute, translate and create derivative works of this work (for both commercial and non-commercial purposes), subject to full attribution to the original publication and authors. The full terms of this licence may be seen at http://creativecommons.org/licences/by/4.0/legalcode
doi:10.1108/978-1-80117-990-420241001

the last World War, and the objective implementation of that citizenship through equitable, cooperative, and effective global institutions to integrate and harmonize states and their sovereignty. In other words, there is an asymmetry between what I call subjective and objective global citizenship, as well as between this latter and objective domestic citizenship (what other scholars have described as "the citizenship gap"). The normative horizon I defer to solve these gaps is an integral – both positive and negative – conception of world peace.

Other crucial points of this book are summed up in the following sections of this Introduction. Before articulating them, it is important to make explicit some changes in perspective and awareness that have found expression in this last version of the work and which are useful to frame and interpret it.

This book is indeed a research study on national and global citizenship that started about 12 years ago. In the meantime, the state of the political world has been revolutionized: what is perhaps more important, the direction of its movement has changed radically.

First, in the original study, I presented global citizenship in such a way that a reader could have derived the impression I was theorizing about a "world state" or a global confederation. In this book, I have taken care to make it explicit that I reject any rigid version of the "domestic analogy" – the idea that just as citizens are ruled over by a state, a superstate can and should rule over other states. This clarification has made the argument more realistic and gives me the occasion to further specify that the idea of a "world state," however, pursued, under present and foreseeable conditions is too close to extreme imperialism and colonialism to be plausible or desirable.

Second, in the first version I (moderately) suggested that the European Union (EU) could serve as a model. While there still is a mention of such an analogy, I have now specified that I mean this only in very general terms. Broadly speaking, states lack the cultural, social, and economic similarities together with the historical motivations (including a long list of mutually devastating wars) that led to the creation of the Union. Furthermore, the European project entered a crisis in the last decade, with an important member unprecedentedly seceding, expansion stopping, plus stalemates in its organisms requiring unanimity and other issues. It is therefore the case to clarify that as this Union of several nation-states differs greatly from a state, all the more should the union or community of humankind.

Third, I have abandoned any reference to "direct global democracy." Initially, I considered the idea that objective global citizenship could be realized with global assemblies to be elected in parallel to national institutions, without making this the fulcrum of my vision. Now, not only have I removed this but I have also to reject conceptions of direct global democracy of the kind of Daniele Archibugi and David Held's. I have come to suspect that the chasm between the individual and lofty global institutions would be too large for such democracy to be workable and substantial. As shown by the democratic deficit that is already affecting the EU – and some large centralized countries – I am now more inclined to think that intermediary bodies and a cultural and geosocial dimension that remains understandable for individuals are needed. Hence why I see a constructive role for the nation-state in serving as the step up in the ladder to conduce to full global citizenship, without of course exceeding to the point of reserving all responsibility for the state alone.

Fourth, and perhaps most importantly: in the original version, although without endorsing it, I left room open for what I now believe to be a serious theoretical mistake. The model I provided – even if less than others one can encounter in the literature over the topic – seemed to suggest that the national, local, and other cultures and institutions on the one hand, and human rights on the other hand, were simply two different "layers" or "levels" that should be distinguished and contrasted. Thereby, human rights could have served as an independent touchstone to assess the legitimacy of the state and the appropriateness of a given national citizenship. I went so far as to suggest that states should repress violations of human rights, endorse national rights, and tolerate nonnational rights. This schematism might be feasible and reasonable in some cases. Yet in general, such a view is flawed by two serious mistakes. First, it is not only true that in the overwhelming majority of cases, rights of all sorts – human or national – are realized by institutions from the state level down. It is also true that national rights are often indistinguishable from human rights. Take the rules regulating traffic. In some countries, one must drive on the left rather than the right side of the road. This might appear as the most trivial and arbitrary matter of "national" preference, and in a sense, it is so, but if someone violated this convention, it would nonetheless jeopardize rights to life and safety among others which are certainly human rights. This banal example should illustrate in a simple and straightforward way that the abstract and general conception of human rights is necessarily realized in this or that way that is practically incompatible with some alternatives. Sure, theoretically, one can separate preferences over the direction of traffic from rights to life, safety, and movement. But practically, they here coincide. And the problem highlighted by this trivial example becomes only more serious in more complex and divisive matters.

The second mistake is not at the practical, but rather at the epistemic level. Human rights *need* to be interpreted through the lenses of this or that specific ideology, philosophy, and culture. Any individual philosopher who would sweepingly reply to this with *that philosopher*'s account of "objective, universal, and culturally neutral rights" would both miss and validate this point. Are polygamy or the death penalty a violation of the human right to equality and the human right to life? Nations, just like individuals, disagree. Independently of whether one is a relativist or believes in absolute moral injunctions, which is irrelevant to this matter, widespread and extensive disagreements over such issues are mere facts of life. While there are many moral and legal principles all cultures can and do agree on, any conception of "human rights" needs to be interpreted and integrated through this or that specific culture. It is sufficient to look at the history of its drafting to prove that the formulation of human rights we presently have is biased toward Western culture: yet had it not been left somewhat open to *all* cultures, nations would have rejected it (as some do in theory or, more frequently, in practice).

The problem of the controversy of some quasiuniversal norms was already recognized in the classic history of international morals and law, as shown in the distinction between the "primary" and "secondary" precepts of Natural Law. It was the persuasion of many theorists in the Middle Ages and early modernity that while the former could be agreed upon by all nations, the latter were more difficult to demonstrate, and while it was considered possible to adjudicate them definitively by reason, this adjudication was bound to remain precarious and controversial. To deny that there are and will be foreseeably such disagreements is to support a theory of moral absolutism that is not only unrealistic and unworkable but very dangerous, as it lends legitimacy to a range of crusades and other practices of intolerance even on matters that have been known to be debatable along centuries if not millennia of ideological and practical pluralism. This theoretical mistake, on the political plane, gives way to "Western (or other) globalism" and "clashes of civilizations" which are from the moral perspective unnecessary if not damaging and from the historical perspective desperately indefensible.

Hopefully, these four interpretive keys help frame and understand the content of this work, which I now summarize.

1.2 What This Book *Is*

This book offers a theory and analysis of national and global citizenship, including a historical account and a consideration of related concepts: especially rights, peace, and freedom.

The core question of this book is what citizenship is and how it applies to the global era and condition (hence the title[2]).

In Chapter 1, as citizenship is classically considered to be a composite of rights and duties, in order to answer the central question, I analyze the meaning, foundation, working, and limits of these normative relations. In my theory, the view that rights possess an autonomous substance is unpersuasive for the objections I recall there. Three ways out are then presented. The first is the sociological (but also analytical, historical, and political) recognition that rights consist of *normative overlaps* abstracted from their comprehensive systems of origin. The second is the indication that there *is* a way to provide a transversal, transcultural foundation through a philosophical anthropology applied to human nature. The third is the furthering of the intercultural and interphilosophical debate that originated the concept and list of human rights, to begin with, and that still supports them indirectly (through their "local" underpinnings). It is important to stress that these three ways are complementary and mutually supportive and by no means alternative, even if they indicate autonomous lines of inquiry: the first of them, descriptive; the second, transhistorical and universalist; the third, historicist and particularist. Furthermore, I emphasize the importance of *duties* as a counterpart to rights to obtain a substantial normative

---

[2]Incidentally, I realize some will frown upon the mentioning of the "era of globalization", as it is commonly believed that the last decades saw the rise of deglobalization or at least a decline in global integration. While these perspectives have certainly great merit, and without detailing the conceptual debate on what globalization truly is or the empirical debates about how many tons of commodities are shipped how far (for this see Josh Zumbrun, "Is Globalization in Decline? A New Number Contradicts the Consensus". *The Wall Street Journal*, 03.11.2023), I simply point out that *a certain form* of globalization has ended, while interconnectedness could even be on the rise.

configuration both at the national and international levels. I then summarize the rights and duties of which global citizenship consists, using the Universal Declaration as a sample. I proceed with the identification of global citizenship as a form of political recognition or "the right to have rights." I tangentially discuss some basic principles of prominent theories of global justice and how they affect this new theory. I continue by arguing that global citizenship has been, is being, and will be developed in a dialectic manner, by addressing violations and filling gaps, and that the protagonists of this dynamic are above all the victims. I conclude Chapter 1 with some preliminary observations on peace as the guiding goal for citizenship, both national and global.

In Chapter 2, I summarize the history of Western citizenship by highlighting some key elements together with the performative dimension of modern nationalism. I then review some elements of citizenship and introduce the distinction between subjective and objective citizenship to analyze what is still lacking in the realization of the global human rights regime. I conclude by covering some additional features of global citizenship, including the kind of rights it principally consists of, and the role of citizenship as latitudinal citizenship.

Chapter 3 opens with a comprehensive conceptualization of citizenship by distinguishing its *requirements* or criterion, its *content* (the specific rights and duties and other normative relationships each particular citizenship consists of), and its *rationale*, that is the guiding principles that determine the other two elements. I notice how the *essence* of citizenship is, in a sense, its *rationale*, since this is what distinguishes any individual example from the others. With the introduction of peace, conceived as the equitable integration of freedom, as the guiding principle for the development of national and global citizenship alike, the core theoretical contribution of this work is almost complete. I finally discuss two theories of nationalism and special ties as an opportunity to further detail the relationship between national and global citizenship.

In general, every chapter consists of one or two core theoretical and analytical themes (Chapter 1: *rights*; Chapter 2: *citizenship* objective and subjective, national and global, introduced by a historical account; Chapter 3: *peace*: the conceptual analysis of the three main components of citizenship and the relationship between peace, freedom, and equality with a focus on the first). Each is followed by brief considerations of prominent philosophical problems and standpoints on the matter that help tease out the details (Chapter 1: global justice; coercion, and redistribution; the dialectic of citizenship; "abject cosmopolitanism." Chapter 2: latitudinal citizenship; globalizing T. H. Marshall's theory of citizenship as an "equal floor." Chapter 3: reconciling nationalism and global citizenship in the theories of David Miller, Robert E. Goodin, and mine). The Conclusion simply recapitulates some claims and stresses implications.

1.3 What (and Whom) This Book Is *For*

The book addresses students and scholars with an interest in national and global citizenship and the related themes listed in the previous section. It is meant to serve both as a basic introduction and as an original theoretical contribution. In some cases, the distinction between the two is intuitive: the first paragraphs on rights and the short history of citizenship are almost compilatory, even if some original considerations are interspersed as it always happens, and the perspective under which they are presented is itself rather innovative. On the other hand, the reconceptualizations of rights and citizenship are original proposals. Of course, the discussions of other philosophical standpoints fall on a middle ground in-between these two poles. Hopefully, these distinctions will help students and scholars in political and legal theory, philosophy, and political science, as well as those in law, international relations, history, and sociology, to find and extract from this book what interests them the most.

The book serves also as a springboard or intermediate step toward a broader research program, as sketched in the next session.

1.4 What This Book Is *Not*

Definitions require distinctions and exclusions: here, I mention what is *not* included in the book.

As mentioned, the theory of citizenship advanced here suggests no less than three further research questions, which do not find a comprehensive response in this book.

First, a philosophical anthropology based on an interdisciplinary study of human nature that draws from cultural anthropology, biology, psychology, neuroscience, sociology, and other fields would help identify human invariances to support universal human rights and duties.

Second, an intercultural, intertraditional, interphilosophical, and of course international debate over ethics, politics, and law should complement the previous line of inquiry. If one reflects on it, it is rather surprising how short a consultation preceded the drafting of the Universal Declaration (and other such documents), and how rare and neglected these encounters are, even in a moment when global tensions and incomprehensions would make them literally vital. Few universities offer courses and projects on Christian, Islamic, Confucian, Communist, Hindu, Buddhist, aboriginal, and native ethics, politics, and law, and on the ways these converge or diverge, despite the importance of developing a common discourse.

Third, an important counterpart to this argument would be a similar conceptual/historical exploration of sovereignty. I left this out, together with a methodological consideration of the relationship between the empirical and the normative, and many other problems. The critiques of the theories I consider are also very concise. I hope to address some of these related issues in future articles: I am certain it would have been impossible to do so here, on penalty of making the book too tortuous and long and diluting its focus.

Fourth, this work in political theory is certainly more *theoretical* than *political*. It focuses on aspects of citizenship, rights, and the like which are largely abstracted from time and context. The implications and political counterparts of this theory are conspicuously absent from this work. I have elaborated on some of these in my other monograph, which has already appeared as a PhD thesis on *The*

Migrant Crisis and Philosophy of Migration: Reality, Realism, Ethics (already publicly available through the AIR online repository) and is being reworked as a book. However, that is a standalone research study, and I have not made connections to this background research too explicitly. Other political aspects are mentioned sparsely in this work, and I expound on them briefly in the next section.

1.5 The Politics of Global Citizenship

In revisiting the earliest materials for this work, I noticed at least two anticipations.

The first was rather positive: I noticed that David Frydrych shares my view on the sterility of the debate between will and interest theory (of rights) among others. Even more, Frydrych has provided thorough and documented arguments on the point that serve as indispensable references for the general critiques I included in this work as well as in its predecessor of a decade ago.

The second anticipation made me decidedly less happy. In what is now note 85 of Chapter 3, I had written since the first version that the current global system was unbalanced and incomplete, despite its pillars having emerged after the Second World War precisely with that purpose (including the United Nations (UN) and the human rights regime); this unbalancement exposed us to the risk of a Third World War.

As I write, French President Emmanuel Macron and United States Defense Secretary Lloyd Austin, just like the Russian leadership, are discussing the prospects of a possible direct confrontation between Russia and North Atlantic Treaty Organization (NATO) depending on the development of the conflict in Ukraine.[3]

The recognition that the misfunctioning of the global political system could have led us to war, as it did, is not the only political import of the theses advanced here, and the attentive reader will recognize it. However, in this book, I do not discuss, say, which world order would be more appropriate for the development of global citizenship. A unipolar model is historically outdated, but I leave it to the reader to determine whether my account better resonates with an "anarchical society" (as in the English School theory of International Relations) or a "community of a shared future" (as in the official Chinese vision for global affairs), with the G7's perspective or with the Brazil, Russia, India, China, and South Africa (BRICS'), or with any other actual standpoint or process in international relations and politics.

---

[3][Lloyd Austin]: "And quite frankly, if Ukraine falls, I really believe that NATO will be in a fight with Russia"; Aila Slisco, "NATO Will Be Drawn Into War With Russia If Ukraine Loses: Lloyd Austin". *Newsweek*, Published February 29, 2024.
[Emmanuel Macron]: "Il n'y a pas de consensus aujourd'hui pour envoyer de manière officielle, assumée et endossée des troupes au sol. Mais en dynamique, rien ne doit être exclu. Nous ferons tout ce qu'il faut pour que la Russie ne puisse pas gagner cette guerre". "Guerre en Ukraine: Emmanuel Macron appelle à un « sursaut » pour assurer la « défaite » de la Russie". *Le Monde* avec AFP, published online the 27.02.24.

What I do claim more or less explicitly is that the UN and related agencies, with all their incompleteness and defects,[4] remain the pillars of a system and an order based on their Charter and international law. In fact, I have reworked my own conception of the legitimization of states through human rights to better align with such commonsensical and authoritative principles.

However, I do also claim that there is an important deficit in democratic participation in such institutions: and as I said, by this I do not mean direct democratic participation (e.g. voting for representatives in the UN Assembly) but rather a proportionate, reasonable, and fair representation of states, including from the Global South. It should suffice to mention the blatant example of the UN Security Council, where 3 out of 5 permanent members have their capitals in Europe, and 2 have less than 100 million inhabitants. At the same time, states with a population of hundreds of millions or more than a billion are excluded, irrespectively of the fact that they fought the Second World War on the right side. Such unbalances are present at all levels and branches of the system, and they must be eliminated to make it fully legitimate, sustainable, and effective. So is the irresponsibility with which some powerful states breach international law and carry out military aggressions, occupations, and even war crimes and crimes against humanity without facing the slightest repercussion and irrespectively of the opinion of the overwhelming majority of the world, which is often voiced in the General Assembly.

Another heated political point that I touched on is global justice. As I suggest in the discussion in Chapter 1, and sparsely in the book, the classic two-tiered model is problematic for a number of reasons. It tends to assume that radical economic inequality is somewhat justified by the differential coercion exercised against citizens and noncitizens. Depending on the specific theory, such inequality is defended absolutely or conditional on a threshold of sufficiency. On the other hand, respect for human rights is considered decisive in determining whether states are legitimate or have a right to interfere through armed forces on the territory of others.

Such a double model is inconsistent and risks serving ideological purposes for a number of factors. First of all, there is no clear-cut divide between "human rights" and "economy," between "legitimacy" and "redistributive justice." Radical impoverishment prevents states from ensuring the human rights of their citizens, and it is often caused not by the sovereign choices of the same states – all the least of their populations – but rather by the unbalanced workings of the global economic and financial system. These very inequalities insist on military, technological, cultural, and crucially, historical ones, as they serve as extensions of colonialism and hierarchical relations. Second, coercion is neither independent from the economic sphere – withdrawing humanitarian aid on which a country is dependent to feed its citizens, or sanctioning it economically, is powerfully coercive – nor reserved for nationals. Hybrid and classic conflicts are only the most blatant examples of how a state can coerce another: intelligence and

---

[4]Consider, for example, the current paralysis of the WTO.

aggressive diplomacy are less apparent but sometimes just as effective means. Third, no clear threshold can be set, either in terms of economic necessity or in terms of violations of human rights. Even some of the richest countries host crowds of homeless on their streets, and it is hard to compare and weigh, say, relatively subtle but systematic legal discriminations against a minority on the one hand and the execution of the death penalty against minors through cruel and dehumanizing means on the other. Where is the measure to weigh the one against the other and tell objectively when a threshold has been crossed? Fourth, what should be the tribunal or authority to judge on such cases? International courts such as the International Court of Justice (ICJ) and International Criminal Court (ICC) are obviously limited – by states who do not recognize their jurisdictions, for instance, and have a hard time enforcing their verdicts. The global community organized in the UN and through other means would be the best candidate: but as mentioned, these institutions are often disregarded or paralyzed. It is also a common misconception that the UN could exercise any vertical, top-down authority or coercion over states, while in reality, they are no "superstate" at all, but rather a horizontal venue where states converge to interact and take binding and nonbinding decisions over one another: as Bibiano Fernández Osorio y Tafall pithily explained: "the United Nations are not better or worse than the countries represented there."[5]

In short, the danger of some interpretations of global justice theory is to leave us with an incoherent world, where scandalous inequalities and mechanisms of systematic oppression or domination are tolerated and even condoned as an inevitable but regrettable side effect of "global liberalism," while unilateral, inconsistent and arbitrary interpretations of what count as too numerous and too grave violations of human rights allow the most powerful states to discipline the weakest through violence. There is no need to spell out further the extent to which such claims can be put to ideological purposes.

As I mentioned in Chapter 1, our best hopes against the perils of these dys-regulations lie in the globally destitute: the stateless, the migrant, the refugee, the oppressed, the poor, and the exploited at the individual level. At the collective level, in the groups and organizations, often marginal or despised, that struggle against neocolonial shackles and bring about a world where the safety and liberty of every and each community are respected independently of its riches and geographical location.

I therefore see as symbolically considerable developments, again in these very days, that the Brazilian presidency of the G20 has called for a global tax on wealth, an idea already advanced by Thomas Piketty.[6] Scandalous inequalities and bossing around by individuals and corporations are in fact among the gravest challenges against global citizenship in the current era. In a world where Wall Street's "Magnificent Seven" (Microsoft, Apple, Alphabet, Amazon, Nvidia,

---

[5]Bibiano Fernández Osorio y Tafall, interviewed at 1:23:39 of *Attila 74,* by Michael Cacoyannis. https://www.youtube.com/watch?v=NuSLtNoP_cQ
[6]Maria Eloisa Capurro and Andrew Rosati. "Taxing the Super-Rich Is Brazil's G-20 Plan for Climate, Hunger". *Bloomberg,* 18.04.24.

Meta, and Tesla) just reached a market capitalization of $13 trillion, the equivalent of the GDP of Europe's four largest economies (Germany, the United Kingdom, France, and Italy), where inequality of wealth and power is so rampant, existential threats to global and domestic justice, equality, democracy, and freedom are both neglected and unescapable.[7]

Historically, liberalism suffers from a blind spot when it comes to private domination. Born to fight the privileges and powers of premodern authorities – state, religion, and community – liberalism typically disregards the domination exerted by private actors and groups, especially in a capitalist system. Yet there is little moral difference between the forced labor enchained by the emperor in a galley and the exploited child who is beaten up in a workshop, or who is told that exploitation is the virtuous alternative to starvation. Likewise, the radical thinker censored by the Inquisition can be compared with the uncomfortable view that is conveniently controlled and hidden by Google's algorithm. Just like the physical world, politics suffers *horror vacui* ("terror of a vacuum"): a void in power is almost invariably filled. And globalization has given the occasion to the most powerful states and other actors, to grow in the place of former national boundaries, and exploit the fall of geographical borders as well as the fluidity and flexibility of rules to regulate the international and supranational space, if not their lack of enforcement or absence altogether. Hence why I hold that sovereignty is not always to be seen negatively: not when exerted in the interest of the people or by the resistants to colonial domination.

It is the utmost task of the present and future generations to address the classic problem of reconciling a diversity of national communities without neglecting these new challenges so that every human being can finally live as a dignified global citizen in "freedom, justice, and peace." This book provides no ready-made recipe. Yet by the insights of the political theory of citizenship it offers, I hope it will play its due part in the service to the common end.

---

[7]Piero Cingari. "US Magnificent Seven Rival Europe's Top Four Economies: A Sign of Overvaluation?" *Euronews*, 06.02.24.

Chapter 2

Fundamental Rights: The Right to Have Rights

> The representatives [...] have resolved to set forth, in a solemn Declaration, the natural, unalienable and sacred rights of man. –Declaration of Human and Civic Rights of 26 August 1789

> We hold these truths to be self-evident, that all men [...] are endowed [..] with certain unalienable Rights. –The Declaration of Independence

> *Natural rights* is simple nonsense: natural and imprescriptible rights, rhetorical nonsense -nonsense upon stilts. –Jeremy Bentham[1]

> There are no such rights, and belief in them is one with belief in witches and unicorns. –Alasdair MacIntyre[2]

2.1 What Is a Right?

Citizenship seems intuitively distinct from rights for at least two reasons. The former is that, in this age, rights have been unbundled from the framework of the nation-state, as the expression "human rights" itself suggests. The latter is that the notion of rights, both at the local and universal level, has been thus represented as unproblematic to displace any in-depth discussion of it from the context of

---

[1]*Nonsense upon Stilts (Routledge Revivals) Bentham, Burke and Marx on the Rights of Man.* Edited By Jeremy Waldron (London: Routledge, 1987).
[2]Alasdair MacIntyre, *After Virtue. A Study in Moral Theory* (Notre Dame: Notre Dame University Press, 2007).

---

debates over the nature and form of citizenship. In this work, both assumptions are reversed. Citizenship is considered not in opposition, but on a continuum between the local or national level and the human or universal one. And respectively, the concept of "right" is recognized in all its complexity and problems, in a way that makes it impossible for a notion of citizenship to rest securely on it without calling it into question.

It is here possible to draw a parallel between rights and citizenship. To say that both go unquestioned in daily life is an understatement. People cheer for the national team and suppose, even require others to be inflamed by patriotic passions as they see the national colors.[3] People invoke rights and are angered when they see these ignored or violated. How are these rights defined? It is hard to say. A supporter of the Second Amendment claimed to me that the reason why "the right to keep and bear guns" should not be questioned is that "it is a right: if you take it away, what else are you seizing next?" This example from a trivial conversation displays with remarkable ingenuity the circularity of the argument: rights are sacred because[...] they are rights. Likewise, the quintessential importance of citizenship and nationality – the two terms will be used interchangeably here – is rooted just in that: that nationality is sacred. Both are hard to spell out. Americans want to see "America First." But why? And what is "America" and who belongs to it? Likewise, rights ought to be respected. But why? And how are they defined? Wherefrom are they taken, in other words?

The connection between the two questions will become clearer as we reflect on the classic definition of citizenship as an assemblage of rights (and duties) and will notice that citizenship is usually and normally the main legal *cum* political *cum* social device to implement them.

However, this book will not provide a definite answer to the question of "what is a right" or where rights come from. This is for a number of reasons, in order of relevance.

First, the question could be itself misconstrued: as we will see, entire civilizations have been built and thrived without the concept of a "right," and this has been the case in the classic eras of Western civilization as well.

Second, a theory of morality and justice would lead us astray from the inquiry into the nature of citizenship, while a preliminary and limited consideration of its problems needs not.

Third and finally, under the conditions of value pluralism and ideological diversity we find in Western societies, and above all, with the perspective of global or world citizenship that is taken in this work, any answer, no matter how sound, that can be provided – indeed included the many sound answers that *have* been provided – is bound to be rejected on this or that perspective. A question more fitting to this

---

[3]The "Tebbit Test" briefly recalled by David Miller. (2008). "Immigrants, Nations and Citizenship." *The Journal of Political Philosophy*, 16(4), 372 would have cheered the English team into a requirement for the candidates to citizenship, and Samuel P. Huntington cites the fact that Mexican-American booed the US soccer team as a symptom of their threatening the national identity (Huntington. "The Hispanic Challenge." *Foreign Policy,* March/April, 2004, p. 37). More recently, see the debates around "taking the knee" at the intersection between sport, civil rights, and national identities.

inquiry is as follows: "What conception of rights is workable, how should we understand rights to put them to use *under these conditions* of radical value pluralism and cultural diversity?"

When we speak of a pragmatic, or implementable, conception of rights, it is necessary to further qualify this objective: what is needed is a conception that has *some* employment, but one should not be overoptimistic about the weight that can be exerted by it. In looking for it, two different directions need to be explored. The former is the status quo of the debate over rights. The latter is a number of acquisitions about and around rights that while falling short of yielding a closing answer to the question of "what is a right" do indeed help to bring it into focus.

2.1.1 The Form of Rights

The formal structure and definition of rights are perhaps the most solid springboard from within a debate where everything is contestable. This should offer at least a general matrix into which the question of citizenship, like many others, can be translated. Furthermore, any indication we can gain about the structure of rights should constrain answers to more substantial questions, in the same way as the description of a shell or a dwelling can reveal something about the content or the inhabitant. This formal inquiry is of course still open to the radical objection – uselessness/emptiness – that comes with the rejection of the very idea of a right to be considered later on.

A formal description of the kind we are looking for has been offered by the American jurist and legal philosopher Wesley Newcomb Hohfeld approximately one century ago, as he published his seminal essay on *Fundamental Legal Conceptions* in 1919.

> Rights are entitlements (not) to perform certain actions, or (not) to
> be in certain states, or entitlements that others (not) perform
> certain actions and/or (not) be in certain states.[4]

We will leave aside the problem of clarifying what "entitlements" are as the term is hopefully more self-explanatory than right. All rights can be described as "Hohfeldian incidents," that is, they pertain to one of the categories helpfully clarified by Hohfeld and named after him.[5]

---

[4]Leif Wenar, "Rights", in Zalta, E.N. (ed.) *The Stanford Encyclopedia of Philosophy* (Fall 2011 Edition). http://plato.stanford.edu/archives/fall2011/entries/rights/.
[5]Wesley Hohfeld, *Fundamental Legal Conceptions*, Cook, W. (ed.) (New Haven: Yale University Press, 1919). My description of the Hohfeldian incidents relies primarily on Leif Wenar. (2005). "The Nature of Rights." *Philosophy and Public Affairs*, 33, 223–253. The author specifies that his version is slightly different from the original scheme proposed by Hohfeld.

The simplest of these incidents is the *privilege,* namely an exemption from a general duty. It can be written in a general form such as

"A has a Y right to phi" implies "A has no Y duty not to phi".[6]

Examples of privileges are police carrying guns and border guards asking for documents, or, to come to our subject, the statement "Citizens have a general legal and moral right to return to their own country without a visa," where this means that they have no legal or moral duty not to do so.

The second Hohfeldian incident is the *claim,* which is correlative to an obligation of someone toward the person who bears the right in question:[7]

"A has a Y right that B phi" implies "B has a Y duty to A to phi".

In this way, we say that "Citizens have a right to be provided help and information by their embassy when they are undergoing special difficulties abroad," or we make the complementary (technically speaking: "correlative") statement that "Embassies have a duty to support their own nationals when these are under circumstances of special needs." Most ordinarily, very young children unquestionably have legal and moral claim rights to be taken care of by their parents and/or guardians and tutors: these imply correlative duties on the part of the latter.

These two simplest or "first-order" Hohfeldian incidents share the linguistic forms of the "second-order" incidents, the entitlements that alter the normative situation of oneself or another: that is, what oneself or another has an entitlement to be, do, or be done to. The "second-order" incidents are in turn divisible into *powers* and *immunities.*

---

[6]Y stands for a category of right, such as "legal" (the primary object of Hohfeld's account), "moral," "epistemic" and so on. In this work, I deal prevalently with moral and legal rights. I also stress that the different dimensions are often linked, and that sometimes the boundaries between the one and the other are blurred. For instance, human rights are considered by some not to be rights in the strictly legal sense.

[7]Privilege(/liberty)-rights usually exist in the "protective perimeter" of claim-rights (Herbert L. A. Hart, *Essays on Bentham* (Oxford: Oxford University Press, 1982), p. 171). The *logical* definition of privilege does not imply any accompanying claim or correlated duty, but a *political* theory deals with something more than mere logic. According to Hart, liberty-rights are appropriately understood as "rights" only when their exercise is protected (ibid., p. 173). Only in a world like Thomas Hobbes's state of nature we can imagine "entirely naked" liberty-rights, but again, this represents "little more than a logical possibility": "In society as we know it, liberty-rights are usually associated with "protective" claim rights," and so with correlated duties. See Peter Jones, *Rights* (Macmillan: London, 1994), p. 20. Thus the liberty-right to breathe (lack of a duty not to breathe) is accompanied by the negative claim right not to be chocked (A has a right not to be chocked by B); the liberty right to free expression is paralleled by the negative claim-right not to be coercively silenced, etc.

The general form of *powers* is the following: "A has a Y right to phi." As we have just seen, this is the form of a *privilege*, but it indicates a *power* if by "phi" we mean to "change the rights and duties within a set of rules." Namely, "Joe has a moral/legal right to establish and/or waive rights and duties for Julie" is an example of a *power*: simply, in this scenario, and quite similarly to ordinary parlance, "Joe has *power* over Julie." Two parents have a moral and legal *power* to forbid their child from eating candies, within the set of rules that regulates parenting within any given society. As a consequence of their decision, the child would therefore lose the *privilege* to eat candies. Citizens have the legal *power* to vote for someone in a national election and thereby assign her the *power* to restrict or widen the requirements for naturalization, through her work in the legislature and within the limits set by the constitution.

In this last example, two *powers* are implied: the citizens' altering their representative's *power* by electing her to be a representative and the latter's *power* to participate in lawmaking which affects the citizens in turn. Note, however, that the "right to vote" signifies the *privilege* to express one's political preference, which does translate into *power* only under certain conditions – such as those required for a voted candidate to be elected. These intricacies – associations, overlaps, uncertainties, and ambiguities – are common in the analysis of rights and make confusion on the matter very likely, already on a purely formal perspective. Hohfeld provided a partial antidote: yet if his language might prove sophisticate even in court, applying it in everyday discussions is often utopian.

Moving on to the last Hohfeldian incident: the general form of *immunities* is in turn formally the same as that of *claims*. "A has a Y right that B phi." An *immunity* consists of the right (and the correlated duties) that someone's normative situation within a set of rules is *not* altered: for example, female citizens in many advanced democracies hold an *immunity* from being disenfranchised by virtue of their countries' constitutions.

It is difficult to come up with a right claim that falls beyond the reach of the Hohfeldian scheme: thanks to its lights, it became possible to recognize and signal the continuous switches in the meaning of the word "right," but as noted, Hohfeld's antidote was not a panacea. Any attempt at analyzing a right should nonetheless requires much effort and patience because of the complexity of our morals, our laws, our society, and our language. For instance, the right a mother has to decide the diet of her young child would involve constitutional *immunity* from having a particular kind of upbringing imposed by the state, the *power* to delegate the care of the child to relatives, schools, nurses, and nannies, the legal and moral duties not to threaten the health of infants by irresponsible choices and so forth.

The interconnectedness, richness, and complexities of rights, duties, and the institutional and conceptual cantilever and scaffolding can get vertiginous. In the past, I have argued that the apparently uncomplicated claim that refugees have rights implies a political conception of the international community that would have been deemed revolutionary for centuries in the long history of modern nation-states.[8]

Citizenship rights work like any other, and from a legal point of view, they connect the "ordinary" political authority of the community that enforces them to the multilayer legislation of international institutions and agreements. For example, a state of the EU must take into account national laws, standards agreed on by all the members of the Union and international treaties that reach even wider. Occasionally to regularly, it is of course problematic to understand what norms are in fact rights (and duties) and how rights should be ordered and applied: this is the everyday job of courts, and sometimes also a task for governments, parliaments, committees, and other such bodies. Beyond the legal sphere, *moral* rights can be no less pressing: a classic case in point is *Antigone*, Sophocles' play in which the protagonist is torn between the legal obligations against her brother, who has become a public enemy, and the moral obligations toward him. The story illustrates clashes between the legal and the moral, the personal and the political, the local and the universal (as "natural law" is supposedly borderless) at one time. Some theorists speak of prima facie rights to refer to the number of obligations that have to be taken into account at first sight but must be ordered and either enforced or trumped upon consideration. For instance, during a medical emergency, it is usually possible to drive in a way that would ordinarily be forbidden, and a state emergency can suspend or alter a large body of legislation, including *immunities*, as COVID-19 has shown.

Hohfeld and the scholars that followed him shaped an all-embracing tool for analyzing situations in which rights are disputed, and for clearing up their composite meaning, but this step toward the harmonization of moral and legal conflicts is far from being conclusive. Beyond the practical problem of reducing the complexity of aggregated, "molecular" rights, questions about rights' proper function remain theoretically as biting.

2.1.2 The Function of Rights

It is apparent that, despite its utility and range, what has been provided so far is more of a description than a definition: we know that rights are Hohfeldian incidents, but we still lack a most important exclusion of the Hohfeldian incidents that are not rights. Every whim and extravagant claim can be translated into Hohfeldian terms. The theory reported so far is inclusive and not exclusive, but the question of linguistic structure and substantive content must be asked independently. All dolphins are mammals, but not all mammals are dolphins: likewise, Astolfo's right to ride the hippogriff to the moon is certainly well construed in Hohfeldian terms, and based on the fiction, we might wonder whether it is a

---

[8]"Political Theory on Refugees," organized by the Netzwerk Flüchtlingsforschung in Augsburg on November 17–18, 2016. I have advanced the same point in my doctoral thesis: *The Migrant Crisis and Philosophy of Migration: Reality, Realism, Ethics* (2018), which is to appear as a monograph. In its currently available version, the claim opens the Introduction, at page 7: https://air.unimi.it/handle/2434/589308 (last accessed on 27/12/2023).

privilege, claim, power or *immunity* but what distinguishes this bogus construct – as well as any invalid right – from a genuine one?

On this matter, the wide to unanimous agreement one encounters when pondering the general convenience and applicability of the Hohfeldian account fades. Many have tried to give a further contribution by identifying one or more common features, but the debate is still ongoing and after about a century it seems impossible to secure stably any notable improvement, to the point that the very terms in which the question is posed are sometimes challenged.

There is a set of thus-called "monistic theories," meaning the theories that aspire to single out just *one* essential element as constitutive of a right. The most important theories in the field, at least in recent years, argued for the defensibility of one or the other comprehensive principle.

The *will* theory, in particular, focuses on the choice that a right gives to an individual entitled to it. The right-holder is in this perspective a "small sovereign" capable of limiting other people's wills through her decision.[9] It is already apparent from this interpretation that rights are directly connected to *sovereignty* and especially to *freedom,* as well as to propriety. Indeed, *claim* rights are often considered the paradigmatic form of rights, and propriety rights offer either a model or a historical source for rights in general. Per the "will theory," one's choice (an alternative name of the will theory is "choice theory") establishes duties for others. While sovereignty and freedom are key elements of this research, and it is, therefore, appropriate to stress their relationship and analogy to individual rights thus represented, neither the "will theory" nor its alternative is endorsed by the perspective put forward here.

The main rival for the will theory is the *interest* theory, which is based upon an assumption that is just as concise and straightforward: rights have the essential function of promoting someone's interests. Of course, this statement too must be analyzed carefully because no interest can constitute automatically a right. The development of interest theories has paid much attention to the problem of distinguishing what kind of interests has a normative relevance, and, conversely, which interests generate only prima facie rights that can be trumped by other norms.[10]

Behind the language of a "will" or "choice" theory of rights sometimes lies a normative assumption that is coupled with the descriptive analysis of the word "right"'s ordinary usage, but some argue that both theories should be in themselves "neutral"[11] in this respect.

---

[9]The metaphor is taken from H. L. A. Hart, *Essays on Bentham* (Oxford: Oxford University Press, 1982), p. 183.

[10]Event those who support the interest theory acknowledge that "there are cases in which rights and benefits *appear* not to be conjoined" (Jones, *Rights*, p. 30, my italics). It would be impossible to reconstruct the debate among interest theorists at length here: see Jones, especially pp. 26–36.

[11]"Will theorists and interest theorists have erred in adopting analyses framed to favor their commitments in normative theory. This has turned the debate between them into a proxy for the debate between Kantianism and welfarism. Yet this normative dispute cannot be resolved through a conceptual analysis of rights." Wenar, "The Nature of Rights," cited pp. 223–224.

There are also numerous and diverse pluralistic accounts of rights, as opposed to the main "monistic" ones recalled thus far. Pluralistic accounts tend to accept the complex and diverse set of normative phenomena ordered by Hohfeld rather than trying to reorganize or restrict them. Leif Wenar's "several functions" theory of rights matches the Hohfeldian incidents with a set of specific functions each one of them could perform, like exemption, protection, authorization, and so on. Hohfeldian incidents are thus taken to be rights only when they effectively play one or more of such roles.

Reaching even further, the "any-incident" theory of rights plainly suggests that all Hohfeldian incidents are rights. In this way, the problem becomes not that of distinguishing between incidents those which are actually rights but rather that of understanding the interaction between all these incidents.

Even if one of these theories turned out to be victorious, and achieved an endorsement as wide as the Hohfeldian formal scheme, the questions concerning the eventual normative validity of a single right would still be far from being fully answered. To wit: let us assume that the "interest theory" prevails. It is unclear whether any specific version of it would suffice to discriminate a normatively valid interest, say a private individual's interest in not having their government choose their partner, from an illegitimate one, say a thief's interest not to be investigated against. Any attempt at thus bridging a general theory of rights with its specific and detailed applications will necessarily turn into a general philosophy and view of society: and a normative loaded and specific one at it.

No one of these theorists is close, at least for the moment, to furnishing us with a practical test to distinguish between false and valid pretensions of having such and such rights. Each of them could be tempted to reply that as a part of his\her theory, there is in fact something similar to the test or the formula we are looking for, or some hint to it, but the sheer extent of the variations and differences between theories, and within theories, undermines the hope that this optimism is justified.

Neither the form nor the function of right is in and by itself a reason for its relevance and validity. Showing that a function is performed is one thing, and vindicating the legitimacy or effectiveness of such performance is quite another.

It must also be recognized that these theories have all arisen as *ex-post* interpretations, explanations, and perhaps even rationalizations of the conception of rights. The history and development of the general concept and its specific conceptions are relatively independent of them all.

Initially, I felt like this skeptical view was extreme and scarcely represented in the literature.[12] Yet about a decade after having first conceived it I see that first, no one theory of rights has emerged from the arena as triumphant, and second, David Frydrych has articulated the very same criticism in recent articles.[13]

---

[12]The thesis I defended at the University of Pavia under the same title in 2014.
[13]Frydrych, D. "The Theories of Rights Debate." *Jurisprudence*, 9(3), 566–588. https://doi.org/10.1080/20403313.2018.1451028; "The Case Against the Theories of Rights." *Oxford Journal of Legal Studies*, 40(2), 320–346 (2020).

What are we to do with all these theories, then? I believe the reply to be fourfold.

First, as suggested, the pluralistic and, to some extent, relativistic, arbitrary, and even accidental nature of what can come to constitute a "right" under specific circumstances should be recognized. The consequence is that of abandoning any attempt at providing a unitary neutral framework, as part of the utopian Enlightenment–liberal project to rewrite morality and law based on a principle or set of principles that can be attained rationally and in the abstract.

Second, these theories should nonetheless be known to extract some recurrences in the functions of rights, as well as to recognize their partial validity. There are indeed occasions in which a "will" is made into a right, such as marriages, contracts, and as the name suggests, wills. And there are also circumstances under which basic human "interests" are rendered into rights in the same way, e.g. the human need to eat translates into the right to food. This sober and limited theorizing can probably find its place. Interestingly, when societies that did not typically resort to Western-like conceptions of rights translated Western legal concepts into their languages, they fittingly recognized such plurality, as did the Chinese in speaking of "power, authority, interest."[14] A right can indeed be one or the other, or even be found at the border between the two – as it is difficult to distinguish nature from culture, it is sometimes unclear what is a "need" and what an "interest." Yet to rewrite the function of rights by restricting the focus on a principle such as "power," "authority," "will," or "interest," when exclusively conceived, will turn out to be impossible or misleading.

Thus, we have seen that, with rights, the form is unitary and systematic – the Hohfeldian scheme – and the function is pluralistic and diverse. In reviewing the *origins* of the idea of rights, the politics of their *justification*, and continuing the search for their *essence,* the controversial, refractory, elusive nature of rights is bound to become increasingly apparent.

---

[14]As mentioned in Danilo Zolo; *Globalisation: An Overview*, ECPR, Colchester 2007. Confront also with J. An and J. Sun. (September 22, 2022). "Translation Strategy of Legal Terms With Chinese Characteristics in Civil Code of the People's Republic of China Based on Skopos Theory." *PLoS One*, 17(9), e0273944. https://doi.org/10.1371/journal.pone.0273944. PMID: 36136970; PMCID: PMC9498954; Thomas-Walters, L. (2021). "The Complexities of Translating Legal Terms: Understanding Fa (法) and the Chinese Concept of Law." *Melbourne Asia Review*, 6. https://doi.org/10.37839/mar2652-550x6.18; Matulewska, A. (2019). "Legal and LSP Linguistics and Translation: Asian Languages' Perspectives." *International Journal for the Semiotics of Law – Revue Internationale De Sémiotique Juridique*, 32(1), 1–11. https://doi.org/10.1007/s11196-019-09602-x; Mannoni, M. (2019). Hefa Quanyi: "More than a Problem of Translation. Linguistic Evidence of Lawfully Limited Rights in China." *International Journal for the Semiotics of Law-Revue internationale de Sémiotique juridique*, 32, 29–46. https://doi.org/10.1007/s11196-018-9554-0.

2.1.3 The Origin of Rights

Rights occupy such a central role in today's morality and politics that it might be surprising to discover they are relatively recent as a concept. Unlike main and general ideas of law, morality, and politics, such as justice, good, and evil, and despite being now considered inextricably linked to these – a violation of a right is often considered a mere synonym of a breach of justice – the term and the concept was not employed, at least not in the modern sense, by societies such as ancient Greece and Rome, nor is it geographically universal even nowadays. There have been, there are, and there could yet emerge, worlds without rights. Granted, this does not mean that these societies were and are "rightless" in the sense of being immoral. If the ancient Greeks believed that refusing hospitality to a needy stranger was "against the gods," "against nature," or "against reason," that was as strong a reason to provide help as speaking of a "right to seek asylum."[15]

And yet, the very contingency of the notion of a "right" does not weaken its importance because rights characterize our society and its morality and politics in a way that reveals something distinctive of them.

There is some agreement in dating the birth of the concept of rights to the beginning of modernity, the Renaissance, or the late Middle Ages. During the first period, the term was used to point to the obligations of natural, religious, and canon law, as exemplified by the systems of Aquinas and Suárez. With Grotius, Pufendorf, and their contemporaries, the idea of rights is gradually detached from theism, religion, and faith, and the argument is advanced that, even if atheists were correct, the constraints of moral law would still be accessible to rational inquiry. The famous expression by which Grotius epitomizes this concept is *etsi Deus non daretur* (meaning: "even if God did not exist").[16]

John Locke, another prominent theorist of rights in modern history, established in this way the preeminence of rights to life, liberty, and property, without any implication on the nature of a *summum bonum,* or "highest good."

The age of the revolutions endowed with political and legal efficacy what until then were mostly advanced philosophical innovations. It is in this period that the rights vindicated were more and more frequently considered "human," for example in the French Declaration of the Rights of Man (1789). The turning points in the history of Anglophone countries, such as the great rebellions and revolutions in 17th-century England and the American Declaration of Independence in 1776, all have central roles in the history of the development of this concept. Arguably, they started with the 1215 *Magna Charta Libertatum* ("Great Charter of Liberties"), which limited the power of the English king and established the liberties and immunities of the subjects.

---

[15]See Raymond Geuss, *Philosophy and Real Politics* (Princeton and Oxford: Princeton University Press, 2008), pp. 60–70; cfr. also Geuss, *Reality and Its Dreams* (Cambridge: Harvard University Press, 2016). Geuss's historical account is in turn based on Peter Garnsey, *Thinking about Property: From Antiquity to the Age of Revolution* (Cambridge: Cambridge University Press, 2008).

[16]The concept, although in a slightly different phrasing, is included in *De jure belli ac pacis* (*The Law of War and Peace*), Grotius, 1625.

From the secularization, the politicization, and democratization of "rights" stemmed also their large expansion to the civil, economic, social, and political realms. These became the goals of the protests, revolts, and movements of the 19th and 20th centuries. The full development of modern nation-states, in particular with the adoption of ideologies of romantic origins in the 19th century, deeply impacted rights and citizenship. The status of citizenship with its rights and duties was then tightly linked to history, culture, ethnic origin, and political allegiance. In the meanwhile, a science-like bureaucracy was gradually put in charge of interpreting and applying rights. The entire system of Western bourgeoise nation-states came to a culmination and at the same time to a crisis with colonialism and the ultra-nationalism that fueled the world wars.

With the United Nations Universal Declaration (UD) in 1948 and the two Covenants of 1966 the history of rights touched its apex: an almost universally agreed-on list of moral precepts was finalized and became publicly known all around the globe. These developments also stimulated debates and processes with a focus on measurement, implementation, and enforcement. Several decades after the Declarations and Protocols, their legacies are normatively paramount, but their practical import has been disputed.[17]

Feasibility, good faith, and implementation are not the only problems for this sort of documents, as will be expounded upon in the next section. Other issues are the lexical ordering, harmonization, and interpretation of the rights they contain. The list of rights issued in 1948 is composed of 30 articles, reaching from such different matters as the entitlement to rest and leisure (Art. 24) and to health (Art. 25) to the right to take part in government (Art. 21). Yet such heterogeneous lists also go without any overarching principle to order their normative injunctions. Even more importantly, and contrary to national laws and constitutions, the interpretive and enforcing bodies of such declarations are usually underspecified, if anything at all is mentioned about them. The vagueness of such enunciations is especially evident about contentious issues, for instance, when different states and communities argue over the definition of "family" everyone has a right to (Art. 16). And generally, no indication is given as to what Hohfeldian incidents is denoted by a right, which opens up the space to argue about whether the right to health or to work and the like do in fact demand government intervention or are mere liberties the government should not infringe upon.

And as we generally welcome the extension of rights to such vast spheres as the environment or the animal realm, philosophers like Norberto Bobbio have denounced the risks that, in a context marked by difficulties in theorizing, as well as by massive and even ordinary violations of some of the most basic and uncontroversial human rights, this extension of rights risks translating into inflation of rights.[18]

---

[17]It is contentious that the development of human rights declarations and even treaties has bettered lives for human beings. See Jan Eckel, *The Ambivalence of Good: Human Rights in International Politics since the 1940s* (Oxford: Oxford University Press, 2019); see also Oona A. Hathaway. (2002). "Do Human Rights Treaties Make a Difference?" *The Yale Law Journal*, 111(8), 1935–2042. JSTOR. https://doi.org/10.2307/797642. Accessed December 28, 2023.

[18]Norberto Bobbio, *The Age of Rights* (New Jersey: Wiley, 1996).

2.1.4 The Justification of Rights

In February 1947, under the leadership of former US First Lady Eleanor Roosevelt, Pen-Chun Chang, and Charles Malik started working on a draft for the "International Bill of Human Rights."[19] The UN Secretariat then assigned responsibility for coordinating a preliminary draft to John Humphrey, and further to representatives from Australia, China, Chile, France, Lebanon, the US, the UK, and the Union of Soviet Socialist Republics.

UNESCO was one of the most active international bodies to join that enterprise, by assembling committees and surveying leading thinkers from Mohandas Gandhi to Aldous Huxley.[20] It should be remembered that the members of the UN were then a fraction of today's, and as apparent from the list of representatives, the committee was pretty much dominated by Western thought. Even some of the spokespersons for the Global South were in reality much Westernized: the Lebanese Charles Malik, for instance, was a Christian who held relatively traditional views, and Pen-Chun Chang, the Chinese representative, came from Taiwan – continental China not being represented at the UN back then – and later taught at the University of Chicago before passing away at his house in New Jersey. Nonetheless, as Western thought is by itself very pluralistic, finding convergences should have proven difficult. The fact that it was less such than expected is epitomized in an oft-quoted laconic sentence by the French Thomist philosopher Jacques Maritain: "We agree about the rights but on condition no one asks us why."[21] In this view, Maritain displays an optimism about the merging of the traditional and the modern, of the partisan and the transversal, that resisted unshaken at least until his last book.[22]

This statement expresses as explicitly as possible the interpretation of "rights" that is accepted here. Rights are seen, descriptively, but also understood, theoretically, as "normative intersections" (intersections between normative systems that are then abstracted from these latter): as a content of the "overlapping consensus" that was later to be defended in the work of the great political theorist John Rawls. Rights can be part of any traditional social system, including a collectivist one, as long as there is an individualist impulse, and there are practical necessities regarding the regulation of the relationship between the individual and the collective. Thus, the possible birth of the concept of rights in the debates among orders of Franciscan monks – as to whether any property should be

---

[19] https://www.un.org/en/about-us/udhr/drafters-of-the-declaration#:~:text=In%20Febr uary%201947%2C%20a%20group,Secretariat%27s%20Division%20for%20Human%20 Rights

[20] https://www.unesco.org/en/udhr#:~:text=UNESCO%20was%20the%20first%20UN,in% 20a%20spirit%20of%20brotherhood

[21] Mary Ann Glendon, *A World Made New: Eleanor Roosvelt and the UD of Human Rights* (New York: Random House, 2001), p. 77.

[22] A less optimistic tone is found in Jacques Maritain, *The Peasant of the Garonne, An Old Layman Questions Himself about the Present Time*, trans. Michael Cuddihy and Elizabeth Hughes (New York: Holt, Rinehart and Winston, 1968).

allowed, for example, and within which limits – is illustrative.[23] Yet rights in their most interesting forms – rights treated as freestanding and autonomous or even primary entities of sorts – arise as a necessity when a plurality of social and moral systems interact or clash. For the practical needs of living together – under religious civil wars, in diverse societies, in international organizations and diplomacy – arises then the need for moral and legal parlance that is able to abstract individual normative injunctions from any given worldview or broad and controversial system of justification. In this function of minimizers of conflicts, rights and the accompanying ideologies are necessarily opaque, ambiguous, ambivalent: any specification that is not strictly necessary to signal and strengthen agreement must be postponed to further debate, to the court, to a decision by the law of the stronger or, if the disagreement does not threaten civil order, to perpetual confusion and no decision at all.[24]

The liberal–modern constitutions are all examples, to varying degrees, of how such a doctrine and practice can justify itself, and work: they are, at the same time, a display of its limitations. Indeed, as there is no possibility of synthesizing the basic systems – socialism and liberalism, say, or Protestantism and Catholicism, or the combination of these four with additional doctrines such as in the case of Germany – the abstraction of neutral ad hoc, even *à la carte* moral–legal principles such as the right to life and property becomes necessary. As Ernst-Wolfgang Böckenförde explained with unique clarity:

> The liberal, secularized state draws its life from presuppositions it cannot itself guarantee. This is the great risk it has made for the sake of liberty. On the one hand, as a liberal state it can only survive if the freedom it grants to its citizens is regulated from within, out of the moral substance of the individual and the homogeneity of society. On the other hand, it cannot seek to guarantee these inner regulatory forces by its own efforts – that is to say, with the instruments of legal coercion and authoritative command – without abandoning its liberalness.[25]

---

[23]See Geuss and Garnsey quoted above.

[24]Michael Freeden. (2005). "What Should the 'Political' in Political Theory Explore?" *The Journal of Political Philosophy*, 13, 113–134.

[25]Ernst-Wolfgang Böckenförde, *Constitutional and Political Theory: Selected Writings,* Edited by Mirjam Künkler and Tine Stein (Oxford: Oxford University Press, 2017), Vol. II, p. 45. Confront with the debate on this "dilemma" or "paradox": Joseph Ratzinger, Jürgen Habermas, *The Dialectics of Secularization: On Reason and Religion* (San Francisco: Ignatius Press, 2007). I have heard a similar formulation recently, by the famous IR theorist John Mearsheimer: "My basic view is that liberalism alone does not provide the necessary glue to hold society together. Liberalism is predicated on the assumption that people cannot agree about first principles: and this is why liberalism preaches tolerance. The reason you have to have tolerance to make a liberal society work is because people do not agree about important questions involving the good life. So in any liberal society you are going to have centrifugal forces that tend to pull that

Rights, in the sense employed in the Western, pluralistic liberal democracies of advanced modernity, correspond to this dualism. They are abstracted from their cultural substrate into the neutral institution of the state. But they cannot survive or be justified on their own. In order to be filled with normative force, or just be defined specifically enough to warrant implementation, they need to be seen through the lenses of this or that specific political theory – academic philosophies have propounded a variety of them, often without securing agreement broad enough to make them socially relevant – of this or that political ideology – environmentalism, say, or nationalism – of this or that religion or comprehensive worldview – such as Islam or Marxism.

Rights are therefore unsaturated, abstracted normative injunctions presented in a neutral form. They presuppose or even require interpretations and enforcement by external agencies. They are not self-motivating or self-justified or freestanding.

The constitutions and, more loosely, the political and legal arrangements of the modern age generally reflect the underlying social and ideological pluralism: the fight between Catholicism, Anglicanism, and increasingly other Protestant and less conformist doctrines in Great Britain; the emancipation of the Jews, religious tolerance, and a substrate of theism in the case of the French Revolution; a broad variety of conceptions to be protected by the First Amendment in the US. It is, however, in the constitutions that are born out of the Second World War, and with internationalism and a significant amount of social diversity in mind, that this "overlapping consensus" and its corresponding *corpus* of rights as normative intersections are apparent. In that age, a specific spectrum of ideologies – those explicitly and most closely corresponding to Nazi-Fascism – was eliminated: not through philosophical debate, but through military annihilation. Correspondingly, an international consensus was to emerge and, over time, constrain and eventually disqualify remnants such as racial discrimination in the US and the *apartheid* regime in South Africa.

---

society apart. And the question then becomes: what provides the glue to hold the liberal society together? And nationalism is a very important glue because nationalism says that all of the people, you know, in Australia, they are part of a nation, they are part of a tribe, they have something in common, and that something should hold them together in the face of those centrifugal forces." Interview with (Australian former Deputy Prime Minister) John Anderson, released on December 8, 2023, minute 11 and 50 seconds and following (https://www.youtube.com/watch?v=huDriv7IAa0). Compare in particular Mearsheimer's expression ("people cannot agree about first principles") with Maritain's view ("we all agree on rights as long as we do not ask why"). Maritain's "whys" are Mearsheimer's "first principles" and pluralism on this coupled with the unanimity of regulations to be established by law is what grounds Böckenförde's paradox. I hold that while Mearsheimer's diagnosis is accurate, his solution is unhelpful. Nationalism means as many different things as there are nations in the world: his own explanation that nationalism "tells people that they have something in common" exposes the risk that nationalism could be wishful thinking or shallow or that what people do indeed have in common be irrelevant or relatively less important or even negative and problematic. Furthermore, knowing to have "something in common" does not provide any social glue in and by itself, no more than knowing to have humanity in common has taught people to get along and transcend nations.

Let us consider briefly a document that is coeval to the UD: the Constitution of Italy, which came into force in the same year, on January 1, 1948. At the time the constituent, assembly was composed of several opponents of the previous Fascist regime. Between them, we find figures as diverse, if not opposed, as Alcide De Gaspari, leader of the Catholic Christian Democratic party, and Palmiro Togliatti, the Communist politician whose close connections to the Soviets led these latter to name a Russian city after him. At the time, for an orthodox Catholic, the endorsement of Communism was a ground for excommunication while for orthodox communists, Catholic beliefs were a reactionary ideology and the "opium of the people." In principle, it would not be exaggerated to wonder what rights, if any, could have been agreed upon coming from such distant ends of the ideological gamut. Despite these deep clefts, the Constitution was drafted, and rights that so peculiarly marked the political culture of Italy like the social protection of the workers were recognized and enforced by both sides. In general, the Constitution and the rights it enunciates are examples of overlaps (and compromises) between ideologies as diverse as political Catholicism, communism, socialism, liberalism, republicanism, etc (Fig. 2.1).

The convergence on the democratic character of the republic, on popular sovereignty, on the right to work, and its central importance in the construction of the political community, all give place to divergences as soon as the rights derived therefrom are detailed, applied, or even interpreted.

A much more complex and broad overlap is obtained between and among the ideologies, worldviews, and cultures that came together for the drafting of the UN UD of 1948. The differences between such a global perspective and the case of a

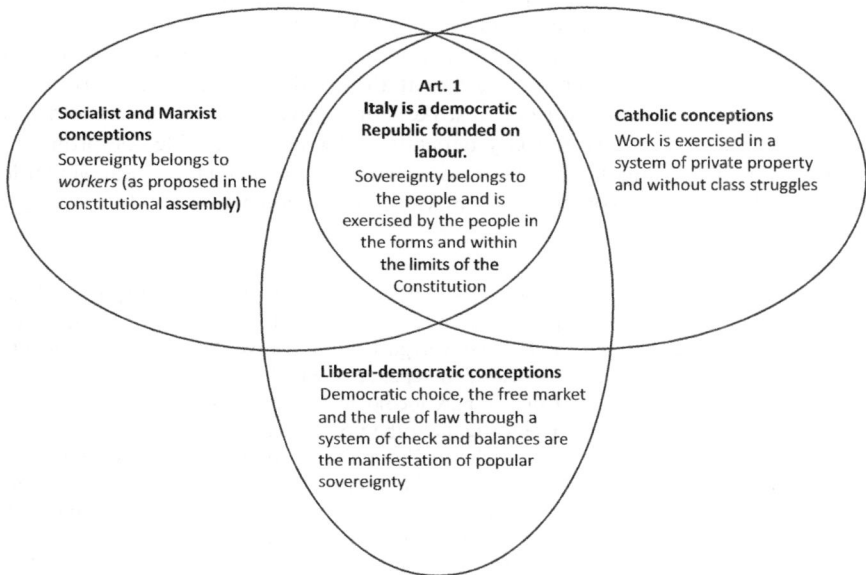

Socialist and Marxist conceptions
Sovereignty belongs to *workers* (as proposed in the constitutional assembly)

Art. 1
Italy is a democratic Republic founded on labour.
Sovereignty belongs to the people and is exercised by the people in the forms and within the limits of the Constitution

Catholic conceptions
Work is exercised in a system of private property and without class struggles

Liberal-democratic conceptions
Democratic choice, the free market and the rule of law through a system of check and balances are the manifestation of popular sovereignty

Fig. 2.1.   Overlapping Political Ideologies and Worldviews Compromise in the Italian Constitution.

nation-state like Italy are, on the one hand, the increased diversity and distance between the ideological and cultural components, and on the other, the absence of a political body to regulate the main aspects of the life of a people. The UN UD simply provides a general orientation in addition to already developed national institutions, and to orient them. Yet the challenge and possibility of articulating an agreed-upon set of "rights" remain the same.

In other words, the hermeneutic suggestion is simply to take rights at face value: as the outcomes of encounters, confrontations, and negotiations between otherwise disparate if not irreconcilable doctrines. Such compromises are not justified or legitimized by definition, but merely as pragmatic agreements aimed at finding a peaceful coexistence. They are functions of the broader normative landscape, and interpreting them independently would be as difficult as interpreting the fluctuation of the stock market independently from the economic, social, and political variables that are reflected in it.

The political and ideological convenience of an appeal to rights is therefore especially evident under conditions of pluralism and democracy, where consensus – even if broad or based upon misunderstandings – opens the doors to power.

The empirically testable counterpart to this account is some degree of tension between "rights" and any systematic moral philosophy are by definition irreducibly in tension. Any attempt at reworking a normative system "the other way round," that is to say, by starting from rights as departing blocks and arriving at general principles, would run the risk of being obliterated by contemporary changes in the very set of rights that are considered.[26] More radically, rights that are meant to work as compromises cease to make sense when considered independently: in the previous example of the democratic republic of Italy, a moderate right to strike would have been eliminated by both a conservative, social Catholic understanding of the relations of production and a radical communist theory of class struggle. Yet while no right to strike at all would make more sense from one perspective and an unlimited right to strike – or to revolution – from the other, a moderate right to strike is perfectly understandable as a workable compromise.

This understanding is therefore admittedly vague.[27] Rights, like versatile bricks and sticks, find someplace in many kinds of constructions. In fact, very

---

[26]A similar, bottom-up approach is preferred by James Griffin, *On Human Rights* (Oxford: Oxford University Press, 2008), p. 29. Griffin recalls and rejects top-down approaches such as the principle of utility and the Kantian categorical imperative: but these were already attempts at securing a rationalistic, neutral, independent and objective normative consensus on their own, and not the kind of complex ideological *and* socio-political-cultural-legal structures that historically gave rise to rights in the first place.

[27]I do not rule out in principle that a richer philosophical account could one day win such broad consensus to become the basis for a global moral and legal system. Yet: this seems very unlikely under present conditions, and such an account would require something both thicker and thinner than contemporary theories of rights. Indeed, philosophical theories usually propound views that are much more minimal, say, of the modern natural law conception that was at the basis of international law; at the same time, such conception was admittedly underspecified, and worked by leaving a large leeway to customs and other

few philosophies or political ideologies argued that depriving people of their livelihood and of a fair and reliable judiciary are fundamental principles of justice: those who did so, like Nazi-Fascism, have been wiped away from the table of history, and it is by no accident that only after they were the attempt at articulating international law and morality received a renewed impulse.[28] Counter-intuitive doctrines that cannot reserve even a small place for rights to life, freedom, basic bodily well-being, etc., however expressed and phrased, are doomed to disappear in a sort of "natural selection of ideas" or of their proponents. Such doctrines ought of course to be resisted: contrary to Jonathan Quong, the reply to Nazism does not need to be a bullet.[29] Indeed, most of the time – in education, for instance – we do not reply to Nazis by shooting. The theoretical point is very simple: it is easy to show how Nazism is self-contradictory and unsustainable: based on logic, common sense, any scientifically and factually informed conception of human nature, or the main system of thoughts that enjoys the respect of humanity. But the practical aggressiveness of such ideologies makes the advancing of theoretical points

---

forms of ideological and normative complementation, in a way that a rigid sanctioning of specific rights cannot do. Also, I doubt that such a conception can plausibly be derived by reversing the perspective: that is, by starting from rights abstracted from the struggles and contexts they emerged from. To the contrary, it would require, I suspect, a philosophy, and possibly an anthropology and other interdisciplinary foundations, that could only be taken from already existing inquiries. I do not engage in such task myself here, as my goal is first of all to offer an understanding of normativity as it is presently available, and as it would be a much more demanding and very different inquiry from what is possible and appropriate here.

[28]Some normative systems can justify more or less persuasively such deprivations in some cases, or even in many cases, but very few would argue for "anti-rights" of the kind of "a right to be judged unfairly," "a right do discrimination and arbitrary violence," "a right to domination and subjection" etcetera. As noted, Nazi-Fascist and similar extremist regimes realized this theoretical possibility to some extent. In general, one is more often confronted with the problem of a state of exception or emergency, or with withdrawal of rights in specific and rare cases, such as incarceration. Marginal cases and exceptions can be nonetheless explained and justified in many ways, but they are not assumed as norms (that is to say, as fundamental rights). There is no society where prison is the norm and freedom is the exception: only by force, and not theoretically, could such a society be established, and it would not spread far in space or in time.

[29]Jonathan Quong, "Introduction", *Liberalism Without Perfection* (Oxford, 2010; online edn., Oxford Academic, January 1, 2011). https://doi.org/10.1093/acprof:oso/9780199 594870.003.0001. Accessed December 30, 2023. "I therefore agree with Burton Dreben when he says, 'sometimes I am asked, when I go around speaking for Rawls, What do you say to an Adolf Hitler – The answer is [nothing]. You shoot him" See also: Burton Dreben. "On Rawls and Political Liberalism." In Samuel Freeman (ed.) *The Cambridge Companion to Rawls*, Cambridge Companions to Philosophy (Cambridge: Cambridge University Press, 2002) 316–346.

often naïve and irrelevant, and at times even counterproductive. After all, a good argument *can* be coupled with a good bullet when strictly needed.[30]

It is philosophically more interesting to consider (1) the rejections of conceptions of rights and (2) more radical rejections of *normativity* in and by itself, such as nihilism (or radical skepticism).

2.1.5 The Rejection of Rights

21st century readers from Western countries might be surprised to know that the very concept of rights has been radically criticized: and not necessarily by extreme or fringe thinkers, but by leading philosophers, including some writing in the tradition of the Enlightenment. As each of these critiques is extremely complex, and for the present argument there is no need to delve into any details, we will not consider them closely. Interested readers can refer to the sources directly. Here, it will suffice to recall the main points and show that these disparate writers display in fact a certain convergence.

Jeremy Bentham, the founding father of utilitarianism, took issue with one of the earliest declarations of rights: the French Declaration of the Rights of Man and Citizen. In his powerful text *Anarchical Fallacies*, Bentham shows that the list of rights cannot be interpreted literally and that it offers a fragmented, piecemeal view of normativity.[31] Although Bentham is a writer of the Enlightenment and he shares the rationalistic, humanistic, and democratic assumptions of the Declaration, he considers such a list of rights devoid of any unifying principle to be more problematic than advantageous to moral and legal progress. It is possible to conceive of some form of reconciliation between Bentham's utilitarianism and a list of rights: for instance, in some version of "rule utilitarianism." However, his monistic focus on the sole principle of utility forced Bentham to argue against the project.

A counterpart to Bentham's critique is the surprisingly converging thesis by the conservative English thinker Edmund Burke. Of course, Burke's problem was not that rights should be ordered and harmonized through reference to a unifying principle such as "utility." On the contrary, to Burke, any such unification sounded worse than simplistic and utopian. In the *Reflections on the Revolution in France*, he makes it clear that he prefers his "rights of an Englishman" to the rights of "man and citizen" *simpliciter*. It is only through the complexities of

---

[30]The speech against the Nazi *Neue Ordnung* by Franklin Delano Roosevelt is both an empirical account *and* an argument, and it works especially well as an argument as it corresponds to an empirical account: "Yes, these men and their hypnotized followers call this a new order. It is not new and it is not order. For order among Nations presupposes something enduring – some system of justice under which individuals, over a long period of time, are willing to live." https://www.presidency.ucsb.edu/documents/address-the-annual-dinner-white-house-correspondents-association.

[31]A version of Jeremy Bentham's *Anarchical Fallacies* can be found in his online *opera omnia*, volume II: https://oll.libertyfund.org/title/bowring-the-works-of-jeremy-bentham-vol-2.

history and culture that the general principles of natural law – whose classical conception Burke draws directly from Cicero – can be realistically and reasonably implemented. Rights are meaningless and dangerous without these: without institutions, precedents, prejudices, and wisdom, such as assemblies, courts (both royal and judicial), pulpits, debates, police forces, communities, families, history, and traditions.

Very distant from Burke, a second authority in the progressive tradition that rejects the very concept of rights is Karl Marx. In *The Jewish Question*, Marx rejects the thesis of those who support formal emancipation for the Jews, arguing that substantial discrimination and alienation will not be alleviated by the removal of their legal counterparts. More generally, here and in the rest of his philosophy, Marx considers the idea of subjective rights to be part of the ideology of individualism and capitalism: indeed, the quintessential right, which serves as a model for all rights, is the right to property. It is perhaps the most famous and central claim of Marx's philosophy that private property is a form of alienation. Marx rejects rights on a deeper level than Bentham: for Bentham, rights are, as he says, *fallacies*. They are logically inconsistent and linguistically vague and misleading: the plane of Bentham's critique is logic and the philosophy of language, even if, at the level of principle, his systematic views of normativity are incompatible with the fragmented repository of the Declaration. For Marx, rights are the manifestation of an erroneous anthropology: one in which human beings are narcissistically focused on their possessions – "*I have* a right to this and that. . ." – rather than on their social nature and interdependence.

A much more radical and, to a certain extent, qualitatively different critique is articulated by Friedrich Nietzsche. In the works of his maturity, and clearly in the *Thus Spoke Zarathustra,* Nietzsche exposes the emptiness of Western normativity, revolving around an idea of God that was by then already outdated. Modern individuals must now reckon with the heroic task of a "revaluation of all values." Duties and rights are now based not on *I ought*, but on *I will*. Science, progress, religion[. . .] All the guiding principles of Western civilization have been deprived of their mystic sacredness – in a *Twilight of the Idols*, and have become, in and by themselves, unable to sustain individual and social behavior.[32]

Nietzsche's impassioned rebuttal was to return in the form of scientific detachment and analytic rigor in the writings of Axel Anders Theodor Hägerström, and the school of "realists" that drew from him. Hägerström surveyed as large a sample of Greek and Roman laws as materially possible in his

---

[32]Alasdair MacIntyre, *After Virtue. A Study in Moral Theory* (Notre Dame: Notre Dame University Press, 2007), p. 113. According to the interpretation given by Alasdair MacIntyre, Nietzsche is to be considered the "Kamehameha II" of the Western tradition. Kamehameha II was the Hawaiian king who abolished the taboos without facing any resistance, as they were the relics of superstitions whose origins had been forgotten long before.

search for "the essence of all law."[33] The result he found was that *all law has no essence at all*. Hägerström could only recognize, in his characteristic sobriety, that rights as social facts present themselves as "actual forces, which exist quite apart from our natural powers; forces which belong to another world than that of nature, and which legislation or other forms of lawgiving merely liberate." In other words, right and duty would amount to superstitions. The reviewers who complained because his monumental study of legal antiquities prevented Hägerström from spelling out *his* normative theory more fully seem not to appreciate the implications of such discovery in full.

A number of contemporary philosophers have built upon these critiques or added their own and sometimes both.

Alasdair's MacIntyre skepticism about rights has three main sources. MacIntyre's initial philosophical position was that of (analytical) Marxism, and he appropriated the rejection of liberal individualist anthropology and its normative implications that we have seen in Marx. Later in his career, and as his rejection of post-Enlightenment morality and politics evolved, MacIntyre rejected belief in rights as the like of a belief "in witches and unicorns." The terminology is similar to Hägerström, and MacIntyre draws extensively from the Nietzschean and postmodernist "tradition" to argue that all the Enlightenment's attempts to provide an independent justification for morality have failed. Yet MacIntyre does not embrace Nietzsche's nihilistic and super/post-humanistic perspectives. On the contrary, MacIntyre considers Nietzsche's life and theory as largely a *reductio ad absurdum*.[34] The superhuman is unachievable and the individual who sets out to the "revaluation of all values" is bound to become uncomprehensible and prisoner to the loneliness and burden of the feat.[35] If the Enlightenment project of a new foundation of morals based on rationalistic, ahistorical, universalistic premises fails and the very dissolution of that project in Nietzschean and postmodern thought is unlivable and offers no constructive alternative, what is the way out?

For MacIntyre, this consists of a return to the classical – Aristotelian and Thomist – the(le)ological view of human nature. MacIntyre references philosophy of science to argue that the most workable theory, however imperfect and flawed, is to be preferred.

A colleague of MacIntyre's takes a very different route. For Raymond Geuss, "no solace" is to be found in discredited, outdated theories from the Ancient and

---

[33]Ehrenzweig, Albert A. and Barna Horvath. (1954). "Review of *Inquiries into the Nature of Law and Morals*, by A. Hägerström, K. Olivecrona, & C. D. Broad." *The American Journal of Comparative Law*, 3(1), 117. JSTOR. https://doi.org/10.2307/837139. Accessed December 30, 2023.

[34]Alasdair MacIntyre, *Three Rival Versions of Moral Enquiry. Encyclopaedia, Genealogy and Tradition* (Notre Dame: University of Notre Dame Press, 1990).

[35]Both burden and loneliness are Nietzschean themes: see for instance the burden of the doctrine of the eternal return of the identical, and the loneliness that transpires from Nietzsche's poetry ("Pine and Lightning").

Middle Ages.[36] The rejection of the moralistic and unsubstantiated stance of normative ideologies can only issue in the mystic transcendence of *A World Without Why*. Similarly to Ludwig Wittgenstein, for Geuss the ethical is to be found in experience and existence. At the same time, Geuss discards the political theory that harkens back to Rawls as based on unargued "intuitions," and the corresponding parlance of rights as relying ultimately on assertion (poignant criticism of flat assertion was already found in Bentham).[37]

Two other contemporary critiques merit a brief mention. The former is Michael Ignatieff's denunciation of human rights as "politics and idolatry."[38] Far from arguing for their rejection, Ignatieff points out that the fetishism about (human rights), as exemplified by treating them as unquestionably authoritative and self-explanatory principles, is detrimental to the culture of rights itself. On a very distant political position, the conservative philosopher Mary Ann Glendon accepts rights but criticizes "rights talk" as too subjective, too self-centered, and too focused – as opposed to duties – on the receiving, passive end.[39]

2.1.6 *A Critical Redefinition of Universal Rights: Validity and Limits*

In order to proceed in spite of all the difficulties raised thus far, these objections need to be considered and, ideally, answered. In a sense, I will do so, and in another sense, I will not.

First, it should be noticed that these critiques are of three very different kinds. Jeremy Bentham and Karl Marx reject the language of rights, but they do propose an ethical–political source and organizing principle themselves: utilitarianism and communism respectively. As anticipated, the parlance of rights is especially foreign to, and at tension with, such standpoints, but it is not necessarily incompatible with them. Once it is established that a certain action maximizes utility, it is not entirely inappropriate to say that someone or everyone has a "right" that this or that action be performed; once the individualistic and sub-jective premises of capitalism are rejected, it still makes sense to declare that "the working class has a right to the collective ownership of the means of production." MacIntyre's critique is similar: he draws from classic Aristotelian–Thomism to defend normative positions that could easily be translated into the terminology of rights, with some correctives. The problem emphasized by MacIntyre is especially

---

[36]Alex Sager, "Review of Raymond Geuss, *A World Without Why*", August 3, 2014, *Marx and Philosophy Review of Books*. https://marxandphilosophy.org.uk/reviews/7882_a-world-without-why-review-by-alex-sager/. See also Raymond Geuss, *A World without Why* (Princeton and Oxford: Princeton University Press, 2014).

[37]Geuss, *Philosophy and Real Politics*, cited p. 70.

[38]Michael Ignatieff, "Human Rights as Politics, Human Rights as Idolatry", The Tanner Lectures on Human Values, Delivered at Princeton University, April 4–7, 2000 (available online at 495-7.qxd (utah.edu)).

[39]Mary Ann Glendon, *Rights Talk: The Impoverishment of Political Discourse* (New York: Free Press, 1991).

that of recognizing rights' derivative and atomistic nature. For him, rights can make sense only as part of larger embodied narratives – that is, of practices – which give them definite limits and temper them with duties. Even a minimal, "soft" form of Burkeanism could be accommodated to such more distant theories: all these doctrines require a tradition and a community to function. Therefore, while the communitarianism and traditionalism of Burke are certainly to be rejected by Marx, MacIntyre, and Bentham, a more moderate form that is displaced from the center of morality and is turned into a mere corollary of the respective doctrines seems to be more compatible with them.

Glendon and Ignatieff can be accommodated more easily: their problem is not to "unplug" rights from their liberal–universalistic justificatory source – even if Glendon would be sympathetic to such a move to some extent. They rather intend to correct the linguistic and social dangers of an unchecked language of rights. Glendon raises awareness of the risks involved in "rights talks," while Ignatieff advises against attributing to (human) rights a quasi-magic or religious power, or even a life of their own.

Yet all these theorists focus, in a way, on rights as the "shell" of normativity: as the form that is inadequate or incapable of expressing certain normative principles (utilitarianism, Marxism, Aristotelianism[. . .]) which they found to be correct.

Critiques of the Nietzschean kind are, of course, most difficult to address. And in a sense, I will not even attempt to do so. There is no dearth of updated reflections on the "sources of normativity."[40] Yet a substantial engagement with Nietzsche's nihilistic Prometheism, or Hägerström's scientific positivism – which practically amounts to a form of skepticism or normative indifference – is beyond the needs and scope of this work. It is sufficient to believe that *some* moral system is plausibly capable of resisting their objections. Their critiques prove fatal to rights and laws that are isolated from their sources: but without delving into the debate, it is *not* unreasonable to assume that *some* replies – possibly more than one – to their biting objections can successfully vindicate the coherence and effectiveness of a normative system.

Thus, perhaps surprisingly, I do not reject these critiques of rights but rather build on them. While there has been no space to consider these systems in detail as they would deserve, I would consider the core of their rejection of rights to be one and the same. I hope to have sufficiently explained why the rejection of rights does not, by any means, coincide with immorality or amorality. When the Native Americans condemned violence against family members as contrary to their customs, to nature, to the will of the spirits, to the common good, or on any other such grounds, they were acting just as morally as the 21st century New Yorker who orders not to violate the right to bodily integrity of this or that person. The former resorted to an entirely

---

[40]Roberto Redaelli and Andreas Funke (eds.) *Rethinking the Sources of Normativity*, special issue in *Etica & Politica/Ethics & Politics*, XXIII, 2021, 2.

different moral language that corresponded to just as different a worldview: but the moral substance is equivalent.

Thus, the theory of rights that I am offering assumes a different underpinning depending on the underlying theory that is plugged into it. But what is then its utility? Is such a position tantamount to radical relativism? Even at this broad and abstract level, the answer is at least twofold.

First, the theory should suffice to understand the meaning, implications, and limitations of debates and clashes over rights. It has therefore a hermeneutic–interpretive–explanatory function.

Second, the theory conceptualizes rights as a *lingua franca*, a neutral language that *can* be employed for intercultural communication and dialogue between different normative systems and worldviews, especially with a view to identifying possible overlaps and compromises. The theory adds information about the limits to such *lingua franca*. As it has been explained, it is precisely those overlaps and compromises that are then granted the status of rights, even if I hold that pro-jecting a life of their own on them could be misleading and practically problematic.

It is evident that rights thus understood cannot claim the centrality they are often granted in political debates and processes: they are neither freestanding nor invariably ultimate. I will later suggest complementing them with another normative incident that remains central in non-Western normative theories and ideologies and was more central to traditional Western normative thought as well: duties.[41] Yet even this addition does not solve all problems. Rights, duties, or a system that comprehends both still do not provide a workable moral (or legal) system.

Bentham is right: no coherent whole can be built on such fragmented, diverse, vague, general, and potentially conflicting injunctions (a "right to life," a "duty to help," a "right to self-defense," a "duty of non-interference"). At least not if taken *exclusively*. And Burke is right: it is not only abstract principles of the kind of Bentham's utilitarianism that can weave these frag-ments into a coherent whole: one needs at the very least historical experiences, institutions, and the shared life of a community for them to find their place and meaning. From a socio-political point of view, Burke is also generally right in stressing the importance of tradition, "prejudice" (in the sense he gives to the word), and conformism to strengthen normativity, even if the positive

---

[41]For the cruciality of duties in world ethics: Mangesh V. Nadkarni, "Ethics in Hinduism", in *Ethics for Our Times: Essays in Gandhian Perspective* (2nd edn.). (Oxford: Oxford University Press, 2014); Guojie Luo, "Introduction", in *Traditional Ethics and Contemporary Society of China* (Berlin: Springer, 2023); Peter Harvey, *An Introduction to Buddhist Ethics: Foundations, Values and Issues* (Cambridge: Cambridge University Press, 2012); Ataullah Siddiqui. (1997). "Ethics in Islam: Key Concepts and Contemporary Challenges." *Journal of Moral Education*, 26(4), 423–431. https://doi.org/10.1080/0305724970260403; Gyekye, Kwame, "African Ethics", in Edward N. Zalta (ed.) *The Stanford Encyclopedia of Philosophy* (Fall 2011 Edition). https://plato.stanford.edu/archives/fall2011/entries/african-ethics/.

lights he casts on these phenomena call for qualification, and to be beneficial they need to be coupled with the exercise of critical reasoning at the individual and collective level.

Marx is, I believe, right in claiming that the anthropology of liberal individualism is insufficient to ground normativity.[42] I also concur with his thesis that the language of rights, when employed acritically and without correctives, can have confusing and even alienating effects.[43] The extent to which this risks happening depends, however, on how individual subjective rights are arranged and importantly on how they are temperated with responsibilities and duties.[44]

MacIntyre is right that only from *within* a specific tradition and practice one can meaningfully understand and engage with any given theory and view of rights. It is, if not impossible, at least highly implausible to rebuild morality and law "upside down," so to speak: namely, by starting from rights cleansed of their sociocultural–historical–practical origins and backtracking toward some integrated neutral conception to replace their "partial" sources. A "view from nowhere," if only were it possible to obtain, would not guide some specific person in their search for just as specific somewhere: a "view from nowhere" leads nowhere. MacIntyre then offers a useful example of an attempt at complementing the parlance of rights with normative sources that integrate it: by his specific return to the Aristotelian-Thomist tradition, and by his general emphasis on traditions, narratives, and practices. The former will inevitably leave many dissatisfied: many will prefer Confucianism, Hinduism, Marxism, or some form of Enlightenment system (as MacIntyre notices), liberalism itself has turned into a tradition. But the latter is, I would believe, less problematic: most if not all Confucians, Marxists, and many liberals would recognize the central normative role of individual and collective histories and experiences (narratives), of their established modes of inquiry (traditions) and of their playing out empirically and experimentally in the pursuit of this or that good (practices).

Nietzsche is also right that, at least in some contexts, there is a socio-ideological crisis that has deprived many if not all traditionally endorsed normative injunctions of their authoritativeness and effectiveness: not only "God is dead" for a large share of the world's population, but so is "progress," "reason" and many other surrogates that the Enlightenment introduced in its place. As I have claimed, however, neither Nietzsche with his followers have been able to offer a workable alternative to ground individual and, especially, associated life

---

[42]For a "third-way" anthropology, between liberal pessimism and communitarian optimism about human nature, see Mario De Caro and Benedetta Giovanola. (January, 2017). Social Justice, Individualism, and Cooperation: Integrating Political Philosophy and Cognitive Sciences. *Teoria*, 37(2), 53–63.

[43]In Marx's view, rights were a symptom of workers' alienation and transformed every man in a "isolated monad... withdrawn behind his private interests and whims and separated from the community." Jeremy Waldron, *Nonsense Upon Stilts: Bentham, Burke, and Marx on the Rights of Man* (London: Methuen, 1987), p. 146.

[44]A responsibility-centered theoretical framework is evoked in Iris Marion Young. (2004). "Responsibility and Global Labor Justice." *The Journal of Political Philosophy*, 12(4), 365–388.

beyond their destructive critique, nor should it be assumed on principle that Nietzsche's genealogical deconstruction works the same with every and each (post-)Enlightenment normative system, with scientific projects explaining normativity such as evolutionary psychology and sociobiology, with the traditional Aristotelian-Thomist framework, with Marxism, with all the world's religions and non-theistic systems like Buddhism alike, and so on. Some people will continue to find Nietzsche convincing purely and simply, and by this, they will inevitably find themselves beyond right (and wrong). But others, both individuals and societies, will find in this or that version of the theories and worldviews I have just mentioned, in some combination of them, or in some development or interpretation of them, or in some other kind of normative sources I have not considered or of their own making, a reason to reject Nietzschean nihilism and to fill the parlance of rights with motivational and normative content.

Correspondingly, Hägerström's search for the essence of the law could well end with the finding that the law has *no* essence: because the essence of the law came (comes) from outside of the law itself. The Greek-Roman systems that he explored, for instance, offer a formidable conceptual and institutional machinery, but ultimately fail to make sense when abstracted from the concrete social conditions and the ideological worldviews that were associated with them.

While Geuss, as mentioned, is closer to Nietzsche than to MacIntyre in his rejection of such systematic strategies to solve the crisis of normativity, there are elements in his view that are to be accommodated. His critical understanding of rights is common to others: his analysis of the historical and institutional roots of a rights-based normativity is just as valid.[45] Finally, his "mystic" realization that normativity, and evaluation, cannot claim the entirety of, or even the centrality in human existence can complement this theoretical understanding most fittingly.

The final two criticisms are easiest to accommodate. Glendon's denunciation of the corrosiveness and groundlessness of "rights talks," with the implication that this would contribute to social disintegration, is consistent with the account I am here offering. Indeed, the interpretation of rights I have sketched, and its being historically and sociologically informed, is meant as a partial corrective.

The same can be claimed with regard to Ignatieff. While rights should not be simplistically reduced to politics and ideology, politics and ideology do play a crucial role in making rights emerge, and the very existence of the language and concept of rights has been explained above as a result of politics and ideology among other

---

[45]For the historical roots, see the already mentioned *Philosophy and Real Politics, Reality and Its Dreams; A World Without Why*. In his critique of Jurgen Habermas, Geuss advances most clearly his thesis that it is the electoral, liberal–democratic social context that provides the "magic" force to formulas such as rights and, in general, to debates and concepts as opposed to facts and institutions: "A Republic of Discussion", on *The Point*, June 18, 2019. https://thepointmag.com/politics/a-republic-of-discussion-habermas-at-ninety/.

factors. Therefore, even when talking about rights (and duties), as I will continue to do here, fetishizing these – "idolatry," as Ignatieff calls it – should be avoided.

The *democratic ethos* and institutions, based on votes and the formation of majorities, lead to the value of the broad appeal of general and abstract formulations.

The ideological history of Western societies, and others, in particular those characterized by *Abrahamitic religions*, lead to attribute a transformative power to "the Word," to the point of creating realities – as in the beginning of *Genesis* – or of constraining human behavior – as in the case of the Ten Commandments.

Individualism, philosophical and practical – for instance as dictated by the conditions of production of post-industrial societies – induces to privileging subjective "rights" that can be vindicated as a safeguard of an individual's interests and freedoms without any intrinsic and explicit link to this or that collective, organization, or ideology: "[R]ights language [. . .] presumes moral individualism and is nonsensical outside that assumption."[46]

The *pluralism* inherent in Western liberal democracies has led to focusing on the "overlapping consensus" between comprehensive doctrines, and to justifying and legitimizing politics based on this restricted common reference only.

While a more comprehensive analysis would be possible, these four factors explain much of the centrality and role of rights in the contemporary moral and legal language, especially in the West.

Yet the power of deliberation is limited. It is one thing to win over support for one policy: it is quite another to implement it. And as Fascism and other forms of demagoguery have shown, popular appeal and support do not automatically translate into moral and rational legitimacy. The same holds for rights (and duties) that are democratically established.

The power of "speech" in general – "rights talks" or others – is also limited. Once a right or a duty is sanctioned, it often takes at the very least education and understanding, and at most surveillance and coercion through force, to have them realized. This education and understanding, and these surveillance and coercion require in turn a culture and a way of living, together with a social and institutional apparatus. There is little hope of converting this world's "villains" simply by preaching "rights" to them, and there is no direct causal relationship between identifying and proclaiming a "right" and the real world being bettered or otherwise altered by this finding and proclamation.[47]

The power of individual-based right claims, while cherished by the culture and institutions of liberalism, can contribute to their success within these: yet, even in liberal societies, resources are not magically multiplied by the corresponding multiplication (inflation) of rights claims, and rights accorded to one may well translate into rights being taken from another, even if in a

---

[46]Michael Ignatieff, "Human Rights, Sovereignty, and Intervention", in Owen, N. (ed.) *Human Rights and Human Wrongs: The Oxford Amnesty Lectures 2001* (Oxford: Oxford University Press, 2003), p. 67.
[47]Assuming that such Manichean language of clearly distinguishable "right" and "wrong" sides is usefully applied.

way that is indirect and not immediately evident. Also, the continuous strengthening of individualism does not automatically translate into empowerment: it can also contribute to *anomie* – the concept sociologists employ to refer to the breakdown of shared social values. Once that one is used to articulate one's demands in the neutral, abstract, subjective form of "I have a right to x," one is also increasingly dishabituated to justify the same claims in terms of collective interests, histories, and ideologies, or even in more neutrally pragmatic terms. The risk is that of ending up as prisoners of "rights echo chambers," where the validation of one right rather than the other can only appear as arbitrary to any outsider, given the abandonment of normative languages and theories that are more encompassing and normatively deep. Rights individualism can end in rights solipsism. This is indeed a risk with the sort of atomization and polarization of political discourse we witness in the West.

Finally, pluralism and diversity are not achieved as a *fait* accompli, once and for all, and with their invaluable assets come a number of challenges. As Black Lives Matter, "culture wars," and other sociopolitical struggles in Europe and the US show us, even rights that were sanctioned to accommodate a broad range of identities and standpoints "neutrally" from the very beginning do occasionally become obsolete and untenable and, especially under conditions of material scarcity, there is no guarantee that a normative culture primarily focused on abstract rights (and duties) will suffice to support social cohesion in the long run. After all, such a culture where rights are normative centerpieces, rather than the appendage of broader normative theories and ideologies, is progressively taking shape as an unprecedented experiment. Its decisive emergence after the Second World War and with the cultural revolutions of the 1960s and 1970s does not afford enough data to predict its trajectory beyond a few generations.

As mentioned, rights are often complemented by other normative incidents (or relationships), such as responsibilities and, more classically, duties: fundamental, individual rights can therefore be linked to collective fundamental duties.[48,49]

---

[48]"Hohfeld himself says little on this issue but, since he presents rights and duties as correlatives and since his correlatives are supposed to work both ways, he would seem to hold that for every duty there is a corresponding claim-right." Jones, *Rights*, p. 26.

[49]To the purpose of this acknowledgment of the collective dimension of morality, and of a reassessment of the balance between the private and the public sphere, I take into consideration both the communitarian and the feminist critiques. For Carol Gilligan the language of rights mirrors the rigidness and assertiveness of the masculine voice (*In a Different Voice* (Cambridge: Harvard University Press, 2003)). Yet hopefully by presenting the defense of rights as a collective enterprise this confrontational feature of rights talk is somehow mitigated. Rights-language is usually employed to specify the benefits due to determinate individuals: however, the very existence of citizenship as a concept illustrates how this needs translating into a collective dimension. If a "duty designed to benefit individuals only as members of an undifferentiated collectivity" fails to give rise to a right

Before proceeding with a working list, let us resume, rephrase, and expand some definitions:

> A right: we use the word "right" to mean an obligation proposed by one or more normative system(s) that is widely accepted and/or institutionalized in our pluralistic society and is abstracted from its original and partisan (as opposed to "neutral") source(s).[50]

Fundamental rights:
• the rights that are presupposed by all the other rights.

(see Jones, p. 28), are rights then sufficient to analyze the relations between citizens, or, even further, between persons who are not part of a political society and are negotiating the conditions on which they are to enter into one or form it? Some consider rights and duties to be but two sides of a single relation (for example, see Christopher Arnold, "Analyses of Right", in Eugene Kamenka and Alice Erh-Soon Tay (eds.) *Human Rights* (London: Edward Arnold, 1978), pp. 74–86): my argument does not strictly require such an approach, but I would favor it. Here, it is sufficient to stress the interrelations between rights and duties, especially as regards human and citizen rights displayed in a scenario with collective agents (states, communities). A collective duty is distinguished from a universal duty by the fact that a collective duty cannot be discharged by an individual: for example, the duty to provide children with an education. This is not conceivable as a one-to-one relation, but implies a state-system or, at least, a community. Note that this distinction is not the same as the classical Kantian dichotomy between perfect and imperfect duties. For the complexities of this latter: Hope, Simon. (2023). "Perfect and Imperfect Duty: Unpacking Kant's Complex Distinction." *Kantian Review*, 28(1), 63–80. https://doi.org/10.1017/S1369415422000528. A collective duty can also be universal: see above, the duties implied by the Declaration. For examples of such duties, see the next section.

[50]By this "abstraction" I refer to the process through which an assertion that was originally part of a systematic reasoning or "comprehensive doctrine" is proposed and judged independently from it. As the coexistence of the interest theory and the will theory shows, one single entitlement can be considered a right for different reasons. In an extreme case, for no reason at all: the justification of rights that relies on their "self-evidence" implies that rights can simply be asserted. Imagine for example that a state accepts to give out to its citizens something similar to Philippe Van Parijs's "basic income." Suppose that this state does so because the cabinet agrees on a compromise between Van Parij's and other supportive theories. Then the entitlement to a basic income is defended by the bureaucracy and sanctioned by the judiciary more or less independently from Van Parijs's theory as well as any other, by adding other "neutral" reasons and insisting on the procedural legitimacy of the law itself. Basic income has become a right in consequence of the state's authority, that in a democracy is derived from the people's sovereignty.

- the rights more widely recognized and fully supported in a particular society at a certain time.
- the rights actually accepted as fundamental in our society.[51]

So when we say "This starving child has a right to be fed," we make an assertion that is equally open to interpretation as a way to "ease someone's unnecessary pain," in the utilitarian system, as obeying the imperative to behave according to a law that could be rationally universalized, in a Kantian form of deontologism, or as the Muslim, Christian and Hebrew theological precept to "feed the hungry poor," and so on. All this while avoiding the divisions that would arise in case we drew on a peculiar "comprehensive doctrine": divisions that will reappear as we try to specify further this right, the way it must be enforced, its (lack of) priority over my freedom to spend my money in resources according to my own needs and choices, etc. The moral attention is so switched from the subject, the duty-holder, to the right-holder, the one who is "benefited." As a consequence, the duties connected to rights, and the very recognition of rights themselves, sound impersonal: there is a right somewhere there, independently from my opinions, actions, or omissions.[52]

---

[51]These three conditions constitute a possible definition of fundamental rights which is not bound to any particular theory of rights but does not rule out any of them either. In this way, they are meant to explain the incoherence and fragmentation that is to some extent recognizable not only in rights-talk, but even in important political documents. These latter, indeed, do not endorse a singular, coherent philosophical system. I do not believe that this mainly descriptive definition of rights satisfies a critical question on the justification of morality: to the contrary, rights upheld by our society are to be called into question. In this thesis my aim is neither that of elaborating a coherent morality on my own nor that of constructing another theory of rights, but rather that of analyzing the way right language is employed, paying attention to academic debate, political institutions and practices, and everyday discussions together. Within this framework, that is the present moral and political scenario accepted in its pluralism and reordered through a particular (and therefore questionable) perspective, I hope to be able to advance challenges and suggestions. But any amelioration presupposes the reconstruction and the comprehension of the background, to which these definitions could contribute, provisional and tentative as they may be. As a consequence, both this definition and that of rights as "normative intersection" corresponds more to an attempt to definition given by a dictionary (neither arbitrary nor unique) than to geometrical axioms. In this particular sense, these three definitions are distinctively sufficient to give rise to a "fundamental right" in the acceptation of political declarations. Definition (1) is the only one which is essential to the concept of a "fundamental right" and I included it in this description of the political sense of "fundamental right" because of my belief that these two meanings tend to converge in practice, due to the rationality of the political process and of the people, that is its protagonist. My view is similar to what Beitz calls "the nonpartisan or restricted conception of human rights," but it is different in the fact that I take this as a *provisional* and *partial* understanding of human rights, an understanding which on its own would be insufficient to support my argument. This view, as Beitz remarks, displays some commonalities with Scanlon's and Rawls's. See Charles Beitz. (2001). "Human Rights as a Common Concern." *American Political Science Review*, 95(2), 269–282, especially note 3.

[52]The same happens when we speak of "a right to life," "a right to freedom" etc. without specifying who should do what in order to secure such rights. Indeed, one of the definitions

The practical simplicity of the proclamation of an atomistic right consists in its allowing us to abstract from any broader normative system. Consider a trivial example: someone jumps me in the queue at the checkout counter and I shout: "She does not have the right to do it!" This apparently unproblematic situation is morally complex and there is no universal doctrine or formula that can tell me a priori if my claim can be vindicated. Is the woman pregnant? Is she coming back after having exchanged a flawed item? Is her obligation to queue moral, in the sense that is merely based on the normative relationship between us; ethical, in the sense that it is regulated by a customary or written code in this and/or other supermarkets; legal, if potentially regulated by law: or all the three of them, or none? There are, normally, some conventions, some customs, some traditions, even some prejudices, or some procedures, that influence what we take to be (a) "right" in this as well as in more complex situations. These include emergency waivers and appeals for revisions of hitherto unchallenged precedents. Yet in a large if not majoritarian set of cases, nothing needs to be spelled out, or even considered consciously.

This example shows that everyday rights can also be found at the humble inter-section between habits and moral precepts or beliefs, or between different habits only. Usually, we see our customs as "rights" only when they are under attack; when some unusual individual or collective situation calls our presuppositions into question; or when we encounter disagreements and anarchy. No declaration included the liberty to breathe, even though there certainly is such a liberty, and air pollution might turn it into something worth spelling out.[53] By and large, dramatic moral/political normative reflections and debates tend to occur at moments of individual and col-lective crises. Adolescence serves as an example of when the individual transition between groups and statuses is accompanied by an evolution of morals: at the col-lective level, a civil war over the institution of slavery exemplifies a typical kind of crisis. Morals and rights become problematic when different civilizations meet also, as with the Greeks and the Asians at the beginning of the history of philosophy: e.g in the Third Book of Herodotus' *Histories* the Callatiae encounter the Greeks and display attitudes toward cannibalism and the burial of their deads. Finally, there are internal, ideological transformations of mentality, that it is difficult to reduce to corresponding social changes, such as when the British society secularizes and the crime of blasphemy is correspondingly abolished.

2.1.7 A Provisional List of Fundamental Rights and Duties

Let us now compile a list of basic rights and duties I will use as a basis for a theory of global citizenship, and as a touchstone to verify the legitimacy of national citizenship.

---

of citizenship I am advancing consists in the primary agency appointed to the enforcement of rights.

[53] In this sense privileges/liberties are called "defensive rights": they are usually invoked as defenses against external repression. Samuel Stoljar, *An Analysis of Rights* (London: Macmillan, 1984), p. 13. See Jones, *Rights*, p. 18.

It is only a working blueprint based on the Declaration of 1948, a core model for ethics and politics.

This document has been selected for many reasons. It proclaims rights: on the contrary to the Covenants, it is more oriented to defining principles than to pragmatic enforcement, in line with the present inquiry into general normative theory; it is concise, considering in 30 articles only many of the central moral and political issues of our times; it is internationally, even if not universally, accepted since it attracted a stable and large agreement. Instruments that have been developed in response to it, such as the 1990 Cairo Declaration on Human Rights in Islam and the 2004 Arab Charter on Human Rights, are possibly compatible with it, and translatable into it, at least on some interpretations.[54] Here is a workable summary:

According to the Declaration, all our societies recognize:

- *A duty to acknowledge and respect always every human being's dignity,* his or her moral value, and the active and passive obligations these impose. Human beings are entitled to realize their potentialities within moral limits, and no other limits (Articles 1, 2[...]).[55,56]

---

[54]I thank Alessadro Bussetti for having drawn my attention to these instruments in his analysis of their standing between universalism and relativism: an inquiry I cannot undertake myself here.

[55]*Duties* are literally mentioned in Art. 29 ("Everyone has *duties* to the community in which alone the free and full development of his personality is possible," emphasis added). In Art. 30, the close of the Declaration, duties are implied again: "Nothing in this Declaration may be interpreted as implying for any State, group or person any right to engage in any activity or to perform any act aimed at the destruction of any of the rights and freedoms set forth herein." By coupling this article with the previous ones, we deduce that states, groups and persons not only lack the power to annul universal rights and freedoms, which would plainly contradict the Declaration, but they are also *forced* not to do so, they lack the liberty to kill, oppress etc. Here "they have no right to" is synonym to "they have a duty not to." In this case, everyone would have a duty not to violate human rights: seemingly, the most reasonable interpretation of this article and of the entire Declaration. Some room is left to argue if everyone is always required to improve actively human rights: this seems implied by Article 28. According to the text of the Declaration, though, no doubt can arise on the collective commitment to such an improvement: states, societies, communities are bound to provide their members and subjects with the means to enjoy their rights and freedoms. See also Hugo Bedau's argument: "The emphasis on duties is meant to avoid leaving the defense of human rights in a vacuum, bereft of any moral significance for the specific conduct of others. But the duties are not intended to explain or generate rights: if anything, the rights are supposed to explain and generate the duties" ("International Human Rights," in Tom Regan and Donald van de Weer (eds.) *And Justice for All* (Totowa, 1983), p. 297). The issue is complex and I cannot spell it out at length here. I hope it is enough to restate my leading concern: I decided to present the duties which are correlative to the rights of the Declaration because I think citizenship has essentially to do with their enforcement. In fact, the citizen is entitled with those rights, but is also accountable for their protection, if anything as a member of a citizenry.

[56]"*All human beings* are born free and equal in dignity and rights." Art. 1; "*Everyone* is entitled to all the rights and freedoms set forth in this Declaration, without distinction of any kind[...]" Art. 2, and again "*everyone*[...]*everyone*" in the following articles with some

- *A duty to promote every human being's bodily and mental integrity*, to provide them with drinking, food, clothes, space, housing, health care, free time, rest, leisure, reasonable freedom of movement, and protection from illness, menace, torture, mutilation, aggression, detention within moral limits, and no other limits (Articles 2, 5, 9, 12, 14, 16, 17, 19, 22, 23, 24, 25).
- *A duty to institute, enforce, defend, and eventually reform or substitute a judiciary and the means needed to protect fairly and to strengthen every human being's rights and duties and to fairly compensate for their violation* within moral limits and no other limits (Articles 6, 8, 9, 10, 11, 12, 14, 15, 16, 19, 20, 22, 23).
- *A duty to institute, enforce, defend, and eventually reform or substitute global and local political institutions observing and strengthening fairly these duties and the corresponding rights*, within moral limits and no other limits (15, 21, 22, 23, 28).[57]
- *A duty to, at most, participate in, at least not to disrupt, and possibly, contribute to establishing a social and cultural life* that includes schools, families, associations, and trade unions, favoring art and science, and similar "higher" activities within moral limits and no other limits (Articles 16, 19, 20, 26, 27).[58]

This stipulatory yet central list calls for five clarifications.

To begin with, the first duty implies all the articles of the Declaration. In the dignity of the human being, we find the whole and complete set of rights that his or her "reason and conscience" can recognize and observe.[59] This very right, the "right to have rights" (and to have duties, and much more) is *the* fundamental right that translates into global citizenship (see next chapter). Arguably, all the rights and duties stem from an onto-bio-psychological foundation: that is, a possible attempt to circumvent the disagreements from which rights have been "extracted" would be by agreeing on a minimal, shared philosophical anthropology. However, this task would require much more work than the swift "philosophical diplomacy" that led to the drafting of the UD, and its outcome is not as guaranteed.

Second, as argued, a large part of normativity is *not* captured by rights or duties (or responsibilities, or the like). Individual and social benefits, as emphasized by all utilitarian theories, are here invisible. Also, duties and rights, even if sanctioned by (inter)national institutions, begin with one's own private environment and lived experience, as in a sort of expanding circle. Therefore, existentialism and virtue ethics have also captured other aspects of normativity. Also, by

---

exceptions (for example "Men and women of full age[...]" in Art. 16, with regards to marriage. My italics). Cf. next chapter.

[57]"Everyone is entitled to a social and international order in which the rights and freedoms set forth in this Declaration can be fully realized." Art. 28. In practice this *international order* probably entails international institutions, and being the rights declared equal, the UD presupposes a form of global citizenship, as I will better explain later. Cf. next chapter.

[58]In the sense of Abraham Maslow's "pyramids," with creativity, purpose etc. on top of basic physiological needs.

[59]Art. 1. For a more detailed discussion of the meaning of "dignity," see section 1.2.

defending one's bodily integrity, for example, by not polluting our common environment, or when promoting culture and education, one gains in turn a safer place to live in and a more stimulating community. As Martin Luther King powerfully argued: "Injustice anywhere is a threat to justice everywhere. We are caught in an inescapable network of mutuality, tied in a single garment of destiny. Whatever affects one directly, affects all indirectly." There is a complex web of *individual and common goods* that gives point and purpose to rights and duties: but no "declaration" or list will ever suffice to capture it. In this context, rights and duties can be conceptualized as different features, perhaps opposite ends, of a single normative structure: by abiding by my duty to respect others' rights I also defend my own.[60]

Third, a number of important, even fundamental issues are conspicuously absent from the UD. For instance, it presupposes sovereignty, and it says little to nothing to clarify how a system of sovereign states is to be organized in practice. As we will see, I consider this the typical example of how rights (and duties) need to be contextualized into, and complemented by, a real-world narrative with all its details, in order to become understandable.

Fourth, and relatedly, this scheme is open to a variety of readings. Where are religious freedom and freedom of expression to be placed, for instance? If rights and duties imply and support each other, one is to choose whether religion should fit into the first rank, in consideration of the spiritual dimension of human life and understanding dignity as a special relationship of humans to God – as in Islamic or Christian readings – or if it should be located among cultural rights and duties, as a humanist would more probably prefer. The same can be said of freedom of expression: if it stems from human rationality, as for example in Kant's thought, one cannot constrain it without directly offending human dignity.[61] Otherwise, it could also be considered to be indirectly protected by the fair judiciary (see the third set of duties) or to pertain to the freedoms necessary to the development of a good body politic (the fourth duty) or even, in some contexts, to that of art and science (the fifth). The majority of universal, general rights, though, like those mentioned in Article 16, are accomplished only if many different duties are observed: for example, family, which gives an important contribution to most people's bodily and physical health, to education, etc., is also "entitled to protection by society and the State." Namely, it should be recognized and defended by a fair judiciary and a well-ordered political system and so with all the complex intertwining of social and political life. These five main areas of duties and rights (1 – human dignity; 2 – bodily and mental integrity; 3 – the legal/moral sphere with its evaluative presuppositions; 4 – the institutional domain; 5 – the domain of "the civil": society and culture) are strictly interrelated as well.

---

[60]This is empirically true: yet in a conception such as Kant's, that puts universalizability and consistency at its core, it might even hold logically.

[61]This is true of *any* violation of fundamental rights, since I said they are grounded in human dignity. But what I am saying here is that a certain violation may also pertain more specifically to the sphere of judicial fairness etc. The question is, in other words, if these freedoms derive from human dignity or if they lie at the core of this very dignity.

Fifthly, while proclaiming rights can sound liberating, reminding duties can sound enslaving. How is one to live their life while oppressed by such demanding norms? A traditional distinction taken from Western moral philosophy proves useful: it is articulated in Thomas Aquinas' *Summa Theologiae* (II, II, Question 40, Article 1) and it has been adopted by his followers, including some forefathers of international law (for instance, in Francisco Suárez *De Legibus*).[62] There are, if any, only a few *negative* duties that hold always and in each case: do not kill innocents, etc. The majority of moral, even legal injunctions are to be realized conditionally: e.g. you "heal the sick" only if you work as a nurse, or when caring for your close ones. These precepts still hold *always* – they are generally valid – but not in *each* case. One does not need to feel compelled to enter a hospital and work whenever one sees one. The right (possibly even the duty, dictated by self-respect) to rest, leisure, and distraction, finds its proper place in this scheme of things.

2.1.8 Human Rights and Human Nature

Is the perspective I am offering boundlessly relativistic?[63] As stated, the purpose here is not directly that of working out an underpinning for (universal and fundamental rights). It is instead that of helping *understand* rights, and elucidating constraints that any justification will face, either in its construction or in its expression. However, before turning to other issues about the "right to have rights" and the dialectic of rights, I would like to provide a sketch – and nothing more than a sketch – of a way to establish such an underpinning in relation to human nature.

---

[62]This is not the only tool offered by traditional moral and political thought, and Thomism in particular, for a reflection on global citizenship. The distinction between primary and secondary precepts of the natural law is still valuable to make sense of normative pluralism and diversity and to manage it. See for instance Lawrence S. Cunningham (ed.), *Intractable Disputes about the Natural Law: Alasdair MacIntyre and Critics*, University of Notre Dame Press, Notre Dame (IN) 2009.

[63]For better or worse, I think that in this respect the definition suits much of the everyday usage of the word "right." One could argue that the definition is therefore useless. To this my answer is twofold. First, I suppose there are some constraints on this variation, which are based mostly on facts like the characteristics of human nature I am recalling here, and other constraints derived from the world as appraised by reason, reason itself, and so on. And second, the fact that a concept is variable, or a function of other concepts, does not make it necessarily useless. For instance, and to quote from Rawls' theory, an "overlapping consensus" could exist between much diverse "comprehensive doctrines." Being a subset, its content will vary according to the sets from whose intersections it results. Consider the vector addiction in physics: the direction and magnitude of the vectors are a matter of fact, but the rule (the parallelogram rule) through which we can estimate the result is of a conceptual nature and helps us explaining existing forces and predicting their outcome. It is worth remarking that this more "empirical" and "political" definition is not incompatible with other theories of rights to discern the genuine from the apparent ones. What I am trying to set forth here is only a standpoint for understanding political rights philosophically (namely, at a level of problematization and abstraction which is hardly available while debating politically).

There is, in fact, a large number of simple, undisputable truths rights can be built upon. To quote Iris Marion Young's argument against child labor and exploitation: "Exhaustion and the need to use the bathroom are cross-cultural experiences."[64] At the macro level, and in the long run, economic and social stability in a society that would not recognize or grant *any* right to workers would be doomed to collapse quickly. And the same holds with regard to many other human, fundamental rights, such as rights to life, a minimum of liberty, etc. While only comparative sociology and history can vindicate this argument, it seems at least worth considering in principle.

In the classic tradition of natural rights, divine law and the rationality of the created universe encompassed and sustained moral precepts. But in a much thinner sense, human rights are "natural" in the sense that they are shared by everybody simply by virtue of their humanity.[65] This is the "liberal" conception of "natural rights" or "natural duties," as formulated for example in *A Theory of Justice*.[66]

Some contemporaries have advanced other views of "natural" human rights, grounded in contemporary biology. Noam Chomsky, in a debate with Michel Foucault, suggested that one urgent task to be undertaken "is to try to create the vision of a future just society; that is to create, if you like, a humanistic social theory that is based, if possible, *on some firm and humane concept of the human essence or human nature*" (emphasis added).[67]

More recently Steven Pinker has again explored the implications of neuroscience for political and moral thought: the foundations of his views are nearly the same as Chomsky's, but the conclusions they draw are opposite, as one is a liberal, and the other a radical thinker.[68] In particular, Pinker challenges "the blank slate prejudice" which would affect modern philosophy at all levels – epistemological, normative,

---

[64]I. M. Young, "Responsibility and Global Justice", p. 108.

[65]In the "limited sense" circumscribed by Jones: "natural rights" are valid independently from any given social and legal institution, and they are possessed by humans "simply in their natural capacity as human beings." This sense differs from the more "substantial" one, that is historically preceding, in that it does not rely on a (theo/teleological) cosmology. See the discussion in Jones, *Rights*, pp. 79–82.

[66]John Rawls, *A Theory of Justice* (Harvard: Harvard University Press, 1971; revised edition 1999), pp. 98 "natural duties," also search for the many instances of "natural rights." "The argument for the two principles of justice does not assume that the parties have particular ends, but only that they desire certain primary goods. These are things that it is rational to want whatever else one wants. Thus given human nature, wanting them is part of being rational; and while each is presumed to have some conception of the good, nothing is known about his final ends." p. 223.

[67]Noam Chomsky, Michel Foucault, *The Chomsky-Foucault Debate On Human Nature* (New York: The New Press, 2006), p. 41. Note how Chomsky's conception of "natural" rights differs from Rawls both on the ethical and *meta*ethical level. See also my article: "Aristotelian Ethics and Darwinian Biology: Perspectives on Human Nature", in Sante Maletta and Damiano Simoncelli (eds.) *Practical Rationality and Human Difference* (Mimesis International, 2023).

[68]Michael D. Coe. "The Language Within Us." *The New York Times*; James McGilvray, "Chomsky versus Pinker on Human Nature and Politics." In: Edgley, A. (eds.) Noam

and so on. Linguistics provides some ground for theorizing a universal structure of human reasoning in that it has traced syntactic elements that are mirrored in neural circuits, and present themselves identically – or in a fixed set of variations – across all human societies and languages. If this linguistic homogeneity corresponds to a broader bio-neural–behavioral convergence, "human nature," namely a scientific account of culturally invariant features such as genes, the structure of the brains and bodies, and the like, would deserve attention by moral and political theorists, and potentially play a role in debating universal values, principles, and norms of conduct.[69] Even the Chomskyan scholars who focus prevalently on linguistics have noticed that principles such as "recursion" (namely the unique property of human languages, that makes it possible to combine a potentially illimited set of sentences) point to a unique relationship between human nature, infinity, and freedom.[70] More pragmatically, Pinker analyzes the results of comparative ethnography to conclude that many other relevant "cultural universal" exist besides grammatical rules embedded in the physiology of the human brain.[71] The "human universals" he cites from Donald E. Brown include items ranging from "conflicts, consultation to deal with" to "division of labor by age" (Donald E. Brown, "Human Universals," arranged in alphabetical order by *The Daily Omnivore*: https://thedailyomnivore.net/2014/08/21/human-universals/).[72]

Even supposing that it is possible in the first place, it is not easy to draw moral conclusions from such a list of anthropological facts. Tacking care of the sick is a human universal, but so is stealing and warfare: yet moral judgment about these could not be more diverging. Without a systematic approach, such as through a

---

Chomsky," in *Critical Explorations in Contemporary Political Thought* (London: Palgrave Macmillan, 2015). https://doi.org/10.1007/978-1-137-32021-6_7.

[69] See Chomsky's definition of *human nature*: "I would claim then that this instinctive knowledge, if you like, this schematism that makes it possible to derive complex and intricate knowledge on the basis of very partial data, is one fundamental constituent of human nature. In this case I think a fundamental constituent because of the role that language plays, not merely in communication, but also in expression of thought and interaction between persons; *and I assume that in other domains of human intelligence, in other domains of human cognition and behavior, something of the same sort must be true. Well, this collection, this mass of schematisms, innate organizing principles, which guides our social and intellectual and individual behavior*, that's what I mean to refer to by the concept of human nature." ibid., pp. 4–5 (my italics).

[70] Andrea Moro, *The Boundaries of Babel: The Brain and the Enigma of Impossible Languages* (Cambridge: MIT Press, 2008).

[71] Steven Pinker, *The Blank Slate: The Modern Denial of Human Nature* (London: The Penguin Press, 2002).

[72] Donald E. Brown, *Human Universals* (New York: McGraw-Hill, 1991); see also Brown's entry for "Human Universals" in *The MIT Encyclopedia of the Cognitive Sciences* (Cambridge: MIT Press, 1999), pp. 382–384. In the outset of this latter source Brown writes that "Human universals comprise those features of culture, society, language, behavior, and psyche for which there are no known exceptions to their existence in all ethnographically or historically recorded human societies." "Human universal" and "cultural universal" are synonyms, at least in my use (but also in the MIT entry).

scientifically informed philosophical anthropology, it is only possible to single out "certain features of our common humanity," or non-relative "spheres of experience," as Martha Nussbaum calls them.[73]

Still, this impressive bulk of commonalities shows at least that *there are some grounds for suspecting and establishing the existence of an identifiable human nature*. A successful attempt at deducting some moral implications may or may not follow: a look at the history of humanity, including the history of thought and global philosophies intent in articulating such that, yields at best mixed and resistible results. The mere existence of a "human nature" is a necessary condition to give legitimacy to this naturalistic view, but it is controversial whether it would also be sufficient. Chomsky, Pinker, and in a very different way also Nussbaum, though, have some strong arguments and facts on their side: since Book Eight of Aristotle's *Nichomachean Ethics*, indeed, it has been noticed that "Even when traveling abroad one can observe that a natural affinity and friendship exist between man and man universally."[74]

The experience of moral disagreement is also very common, and travelers can be struck by both: Herodotus' classic passage on cannibalism, already cited above, serves as a counterpart to Aristotle's quote. It is therefore easy to share in Rousseau's "surprise and disgust" while inquiring about the disproportionate divisions between those who believe in a natural law: indeed, a very narrow group of philosophers (and a much less significant number of people). And any attempt at specifying the content of human rights, and applying them, has indeed proved almost as divisive.[75,76] Nonetheless, this bookish confusion should not lead astray, nor should we welcome with excessive indulgence Rousseau's case against the consistency of moral and legal systems that successfully sustained civilization for millennia. Yes the customs of the peoples are disparate: but there is no country in the world where killing, stealing, lying, and raping are the norm rather than the exception. Whenever there is a written or oral normative code, these actions are generally and clearly forbidden, and this has been so for the vast majority of history. This is at least an invitation to hope that, in practice, an "overlapping consensus" or equivalent compromises about moral issues could be found, and that in theory, it should be possible to vindicate and ground it into a conception of human nature.

---

[73]Martha C. Nussbaum, "Non-Relative Virtues: An Aristotelian Approach", in Martha C. Nussbaum and Amartya Sen (eds.) *The Quality of Life* (Oxford: Oxford University Press, 1993). In her article Nussbaum does not rely much on anthropological observations, and not at all on neurosciences or linguistics. Aristotle's quote opens Nussbaum's article.

[74]The quote is from Harris Rackham's translation, on the online Perseus Digital Library (see Aristotle, *Nichomachean Ethics*, Harris Rackham (ed.) (Cambridge (MA)/London: Harvard University Press/Loeb Classical Library, 1926).

[75]Jean Jacques Rousseau, *The Social Contract and Discourses*, trans. G. D. H. Cole (London: Everyman, 1913), pp. 156–157.

[76]Jones, *Rights*, p. 97.

2.2 The Right to Have Rights

> To the extent that the purpose of the rule of law is to achieve some sort of shared liberty, the achievement of nondomination means that all must have some kind of status, if any are to have it. If that is the case, then this status cannot be derived from or acquired with some specific membership, say in a political community. –James Bohman[77]

2.2.1 Human Rights, Human Dignity, and the Global Polity

The classic foundation for human rights is dignity. This latter term has been criticized for its vagueness, but it finds a place in most philosophical discourses. Essentially, it has to do with *what a human is worthy of* (*dignus*, in Latin).[78] The question that is classically central in the domain of justice is what is owed to each person: to give "everyone one's due," as stated by a phrase variously employed by Cicero, Ulpian, and Justinian in the early days of Western jurisprudence. Its key component is the relevance and distinctiveness of being human, of what is owed to humanity as such. Human dignity so understood relates to the inherent value of personhood, its intrinsic moral relevance, which entitles one to a particular consideration as a member of a community spanning as widely as humankind. While much thinner and less politically organized than a nation-state in its explicit and enforced obligations, such a community would nonetheless be morally and ontologically preeminent. If one has human dignity, one possesses human rights, and the *right to have rights* that precede them and is presupposed by them.

In this context, dignity can be presented as "the right to have rights."[79] Hannah Arendt's formulation of this most fundamental right refers to the implied existence of a global polity since this right is not predicated on any specific particular

---

[77]James Bohman. (August, 2009). Living Without Freedom. Cosmopolitanism at Home and the Rule of Law. *Political Theory*, 37(4), 539–561.

[78]A discussion of the concept in relation to human rights is to be found in Griffin, *On Human Rights,* cited above, and more recently, in a conference given by Alasdair MacIntyre, who contrasted its secular, post World War II conception with classic Thomist doctrine. MacIntyre's discussion includes a critique of theories at the intersection between the two, such as personalism. Alasdair MacIntyre (De Nicola Center for Ethics and Culture). Plenary session of the 2021 Notre Dame Fall Conference. https://www.youtube.com/watch?v=V727AcOoogQ, last accessed 04/02/2024. Confront also with Andrea Sangiovanni, *Humanity Without Dignity, Moral Equality, Respect, and Human Rights* (Harvard: Harvard University Press, 2017).

[79]While the two concepts are usually seen as related but distinct in Hannah Arendt, this is precisely the title chosen by Christopher Menke, "Dignity as the right to have rights: human dignity in Hannah Arendt", in Düwell, M., Braarvig, J., Brownsword, R., Mieth, D. (eds.) *The Cambridge Handbook of Human Dignity: Interdisciplinary Perspectives* (Cambridge University Press; 2014), pp. 332–342.

political community.[80] Humans being "political animals," a person cannot fully exercise her rights if not as a member of an organized society. Many important articles of the Universal Declaration, such as Article One, which mentions dignity explicitly, and Article Six ("Everyone has a right to recognition everywhere as a person before the law"), are highly compatible with this idea of a non-disposable right to be respected as a human being at every relevant level (moral, legal, political).

The two occurrences of the term "right" in this formula have two different meanings: the first "right" lacks a particular addressee since "humanity as such" is, at present, something much more fluid than any nation-state. The paradox is that what appears to be morally more significant is hardly definable, while the apparatus that distinguishes between citizens and "others," and whose legitimacy

---

[80]"We became aware of the existence of *a right to have rights* [...] and a right to belong to some kind of organized community, only when millions of people emerged who had lost and could not regain these rights because of the new global political situation. The trouble is that this calamity arose not from any lack of civilization, backwardness, or mere tyranny, but, on the contrary, that it could not be repaired, because there was no longer any "uncivilized" spot on earth, because whether *we like it or not we have really started to live in One World. Only with a completely organized humanity could the loss of home and political status become identical with expulsion from humanity altogether.*" Hannah Arendt, *The Origins of Totalitarianism* (New York: Harcourt Brace, 1971), pp. 297–298, my italics. According to this quote, it seems that "humanity" in Arendt's vocabulary should be understood as implying both "the mankind" and the "human nature" (as the Oxford dictionary explains them: "human beings collectively" and "the state of being human"). Arendt excludes a third meaning of the word: "the quality of being humane; benevolence." So humanity (meaning 1 "human being collectively") is the addressee of the "right to have rights" claimed by each human being (one who possesses "the state of being human," meaning 2). Resolving this claim-right through normative/legal relations between individuals would be complex, or impossible altogether. A life cannot be fully human unless if it is lived in a community, and the relationship between a citizen and the citizenry cannot be replaced by the contingent relations between a citizen and her fellows considered individually. It is conceivable of someone opting out of one's, and therefore acquiring an almost complete immunity against it, but it would be impossible to opt out of humanity. As human, are naturally and inescapably entitled to its protection and to its coercion, when justly imposed. The right to have rights appears to be similar to the status of a rights-bearer (echoed in the condition required by Joseph Raz: X has a right "if and only if X *can have rights...*", *The Morality of Freedom* (Oxford: Clarendon Press, 1986), p. 166.). For the republican conception, see the discussion in J. Bohman. (2009). Living Without Freedom. Cosmopolitanism at Home and the Rule of Law. *Political Theory*, 37(4), 539–561. In particular on the relation between Philip Pettit's "legal status" and "the right to have rights": "For all their disagreement, Pettit and Arendt share a common presumption present in the republican tradition: that free status generally and legal status in particular derive from citizenship, from membership in a political community. But in the case of stateless persons and migrants without legal status, this presumption that legal status is derivative of civil status simply restates the problem and not the solution. We can get closer to a solution only if such legal status is unlinked from membership in a particular community for good republican reasons" (pp. 543–544).

is open to question, is well-identified and materially more forceful. Even nowadays, rights declared by international documents are not enforceable if not through national agencies: the extreme case of the controversial "responsibility to protect (R2P)" notoriously requires in practice that some state acts "on behalf of humanity." The most fundamental right is therefore very different and much less practically relevant than ordinary rights, and still needs to find its place in "a specific juridico-civil community of consociates who stand in a relation of reciprocal duty to one another."[81]

2.2.2 Cosmopolitan Norms From Global Violations

The global polity, the One World evoked in Arendt's analysis, is a matter of fact, a historical situation, rather than a political institution.[82] Arendt herself considers the modern nation-state the only purveyor of rights and the only context wherein the exercise of those rights is possible.[83] At the same time, though, the arbitrariness of the extension or limitation of membership, the wavering distinctions between subjects and strangers, are incompatible with a universal justification of rights. In this way the situation described by Arendt appears as a "paradox," a contradiction between the requirements of the respect for universal rights and the internal limits of political institutions. Even the "civic" criterion of membership she endorses is potentially exclusionary. Arendt also knows that nation-states are

---

[81]Seyla Benhabib, *The Rights of Others. Aliens, Residents and Citizens* (Cambridge: Cambridge University Press, 2004), p. 58. For a deeper discussion on the issue see all the second chapter "The right to have rights: Hannah Arendt on the contradictions of the nation-state."

[82]This historical situation reflects a moral fact: the equal concern due to every human being. But as long as humanity was divided by space and time, ancient societies lived in practice as they were separated universes. As Arendt puts it (see previous notes) "we *became aware...*" (emphasis added). It is not that the right to have rights came to existence thanks to globalization, but it was made clear and its requirements became inescapable due to the possibility each human being has to impact heavily, directly or indirectly, on someone else's life, even if the two live in the opposite corners of the world. Life in the atomic age has made this mutual moral belonging even more pressing.

[83]"The right that corresponds to this loss [that of a right to belong to some kind of organized community] and that was never even mentioned among the human rights cannot be expressed in the categories of the 18th century because they presume that rights spring immediately from the "nature" of man[...]the right to have rights, or the right of every individual to belong to humanity, should be guaranteed by humanity itself. It is by no means certain whether this is possible." Arendt, *The Origins of Totalitarianism*, p. 298. Frank Michelman has noted how this "right to have rights" does not challenge the existence of national institutions: these are the most likely addressees of claims to such a right: "The notion of a right to have rights arises out of the modern-statist conditions and is equivalent to the moral claim of a refugee or other stateless person to citizenship, or at least juridical personhood, within the social confines of some law-dispensing state" (Frank Michelman. "Parsing 'A right to Have Rights'" *Constellations*, 3(2) (October), 200–209, 203.

not to be considered a given, since they undergo frequent and radical transformations, or are even created anew.[84] She refuses the idea of a universal state sovereign as starkly as Kant. However, the possibilities of political evolution transcend the dualist alternative between central global governance and contemporary nation-states. Arendt's "experimental, fluid, and open reflections on how to constitute democratically sovereign communities, which did not follow the model of the nation-state, were not explored further," but they brilliantly alluded to a reality similar to the present.[85]

Indeed, as Benhabib claims, we have entered the era of "cosmopolitan norms of justice." This peculiar cosmopolitanism does not consist of a visionary utopia but is rooted in the conditions of global politics. The period in which states negotiated as the only legitimate agencies, the era of "international norms of justice," ended when states themselves became capable of losing their legitimacy in the eyes of citizens, especially if unfairly denaturalized. As citizens can be made non-citizens, a state may become a non-state. Of course, both of these incidents still occur in cases of emergency. Nowadays even democracy is limited by international norms and institutions.[86] Legitimacy has become a global question.

A "crime against humanity" is not the same of a crime against humanness: the former is a crime against all human beings, against the very existence of humanity itself.[87] A genocide is a criminal act against a whole community (since it is perpetrated against a whole ethnicity or nation) and by virtue of

---

[84]Hannah Arendt, "Zionism Reconsidered", in Ron H. Feldman (ed.) *The Jew as Pariah: Jewish Identity and Politics in the Modern Age* (New York: Grove Press, 1978), pp. 131–192.

[85]Benhabib, The Rights of Others, 64.

[86]Benhabib, while recalling Arendt's understanding of genocide as the most specific "crime against humanity," says: "If, however, there are crimes which can be perpetrated against humanity itself, Arendt must consider the human being not only as a being worthy of moral respect but also as having a legal status that ought to be protected by international law. *The distinguishing feature of this legal status is that it would take precedence over all existing legal orders and it would bind them* (Correspondence, 419)." Seyla Benhabib, *Another Cosmopolitanism* (Oxford: Oxford University Press, 2006), p. 19 my italics. "*This legal status*" refers to "the right to have rights": it is both legal and moral, or rather represents the defining boundary that at the same time separates and connects the field of moral and legal rights, and it encompasses all the specific moral and legal systems. The text Benhabib refers to is Hannah Arendt-Karl Jaspers, *Correspondence:1926–1969*, ed. Lotte Kohler and Hans Saner, trans. Robert and Rita Kimber (New York: Harcourt Brace Jovanovich, 1992). My view on the problem is that, considered the relations that are developing between single nation-states and international institutions, we should aim at a *meta-democracy*, where local loyalties are not rejected but limited by the universal allegiance to the dignity and the interest of humankind. Humankind itself, though, should be entitled to political institutions that correspond appropriately to the national participatory practices. See chapter 3.

[87]See note 76 on the distinction humanity-humanness.

that, it is set at a very different level than the murder of an innocent within a state.[88] This latter is to be judged according to the state's laws. But the universal relevance of genocide elevates it to a global arena: states must be coherent with the concept and comprehended in the physical extension of humanity, therefore humanity embraces and surpasses all and each political community. By attacking the entire Jewish people, Eichmann exceeded the jurisdiction of the German state, and as a consequence was legitimately judged on very different bases than those regulating its national context only.[89] Eichmann's trial is an example of a trial in which humanity faced an individual who violated the "right to have rights": in other words, a trial where humanity confronted an individual who denied it.[90]

2.2.3 Humanity as an Agency

The problem posed by the recognition of a "right to have rights" (or the identification, creation, and distribution of a basic status to which rights apply) is not the same as a violation of an individual right.[91] When a person is not treated as such, despite being apparently given all the consideration that is due

---

[88] A community regardless of how this is defined: what is important here is the scale of the crime (or, more generally, of the moral-legal relation). If Eichmann had been accused of the extermination of the Berliners because of their being Berliners, this would not have changed much the substance of the trial. These mass crimes perpetrated against states, communities, groups, tribes, ethnicities and so on reveal that the relevant moral-legal relation is not *internal* to the groups themselves but is both collective and universal. See the following note.

[89] The fact that this very state was at that time accomplice does not alter the issue, but escalates it to an upper level. Individuals are subject to their states, but states *and* individuals are subject to humanity. The fact that the Jewish people was spread beyond German boundaries is also inessential: a genocide can be accomplished against a less populous ethnic group, and also against a group confined in one state, and still be a crime against humanity. It is still a crime based upon an ascribed status: it would be no different from persecute a person *because she is a person.*

[90] It is crucial not to depersonalize humanity, as it were an abstraction. Humanity means: what is inherent to every person and makes her a person. In this way Eichmann was different than a pirate, whose crime is to be judged even in the absence of a territorially competent court because of mere practical reasons. The universality of Eichmann's fault is conceptual: "he is the enemy of all, and hence can be judged by all." Hannah Arendt, *Eichmann in Jerusalem: A Report on the Banality of Evil*, rev. and enl. ed. (New York: Penguin Books, 1994), p. 261.

[91] "To have a status, as Hegel remarks, is to be someone; to lack it is to be nobody, the existence of which is not even to be counted. Accordingly, the formal rule of law may not fail to provide adequate protection from powerful private and public actors; but it can fail more deeply and sometimes catastrophically when people lack even the most basic legal status," Bohman, *Living Without Freedom*, p. 541. Compare with Arendt, *The Origin of Totalitarianism*, pp. 296–297 "Their plight [that of stateless people] is not that they are not equal before the law, but that no law exist for them."

to a human being, her rights are seen as the benevolent and dangerously contingent concession by a domineer. Thanks to the creation of the international human rights regime, this issue has become a practical question rather than a philosophical one. Still, the international rights regime does not specify agencies and means sufficient to enforce human rights, and the identification of these instruments is an urgent matter of philosophical, moral, and political reflection.[92] Collective actions and even an evolution of present institutions are needed to answer Arendt's plea for humanity to care for and decide on what affects humanity.

The otherwise legitimate distinction between citizens' and non-citizens' rights does not apply to human rights, as acknowledged even by those who argue for distinguishing such rights when it comes to distributive justice: I think here of Thomas Nagel, Andrea Sangiovanni, and Michael Blake.[93] One of the problems with these accounts is that they do not emphasize the continuity between human rights and the socio-economic dimension. In any case, a "citizenship gap" is affecting the stateless and displaced together with the citizens who, without a sufficiently harmonic cooperation of states and a more relevant international authority, are affected by the effects of globalization.[94]

2.2.4 Coercion and the Requirements of Reciprocity

Coercion, reciprocity, and participation in processes of autonomous deliberations generally make the bonds between citizens much tighter. This has been mentioned in arguments to justify international economic inequalities, as well as other such as cultural and the like. The question posed by Arendt, however, regards the justification of citizenship *as a guarantee of human rights*, its limits, and its compatibility with global duties.[95] It evokes, if not invokes, the possibility of a

---

[92]"[M]ost constitutional democracies already have these republican and cosmopolitan features, with respect to the right of persons... [T]here must be a set of overlapping and intersecting institutions, each with their own distinctive powers and capabilities" Bohman, p. 558.

[93]The articles I refer to here in particular are Michael Blake. (2001). "Distributive Justice, State Coercion, and Autonomy." *Philosophy and Public Affairs*, 30(3), 257–296; Thomas Nagel. (2005). "The Problem of Global Justice." *Philosophy and Public Affairs*, 33(3), 113–147; Andrea Sangiovanni. (2007). "Global Justice, Reciprocity, and the State." *Philosophy and Public Affairs*, 35(1), 3–39. Note that they do not justify *all* discrimination between citizens and foreigners, even in the restricted domain of distributive justice: "This [the argument about the legitimacy of two different degrees of reciprocity, that one could call a "strict" and a "loose" criterion] *does not imply that we have no obligations of distributive justice at the global level*, only that these are different in both form and content from those we have at the domestic." Sangiovanni, p. 4.

[94]*Globalization and Human Rights,* edited by Alison Brysk (Berkeley: University of California Press, 2002).

[95]"The European nation-state is the largest container of democracy and solidarity that has historically become possible... one needs to be skeptical about the likelihood that history

global polity, that emerged from the intertwining of human destinies made visible by the last centuries' historical developments and catastrophes. And, coupling this to the "right to have rights," it implies some form of global citizenship. A number of critical points should help reassessing this set of issues.

First, the *acceptance of a minimal respect for human rights* is taken as a given.[96] The enforcement of the human rights regime is considered a practical difficulty. Yet usually, theorists do not even list human rights in detail, which would already be

---

could go beyond that achievement" (Claus Offe. (1998). "Homogeneity and Constitutional Democracy: Coping with Identity Conflicts through Group Rights." *Journal of Political Philosophy*, 6(2), 113–141). While this exaltation of the Western nation-state should be qualified and relativized, one can agree on the historical importance and on the merits of the nation-state. I also doubt it would be either necessary or helpful to dismantle it. Still, there is no reason to consider it a definitive and insurpassable achievement, especially considering its internal evolution and that of the international institutions that flank it. I wonder whether the nation-state, which aggregated and surpassed parochial and tribal allegiances often without abolishing them completely, would not be a suitable model for the creation of an international regime compatible with its survival. According to Nagel "A subtle version of such a system has been outlined by Janos Kis in "The Unity of Mankind and the Plurality of States" (unpublished manuscript). He calls it a supranation-state regime: separate states would retain primary responsibility for just governance, but share sovereign power with international institutions with special authority defined functionally and not territorially, with respect to trade, the environment, human rights, and so forth." "The Problem of Global Justice", p. 119. I believe there are better and alternative models to this "vertical" conception for instance, in the age of multipolarity, a "horizontal" model with a community of states aided by common values and principles and supported by international institutions could work better at integrating individual, sovereign nation-states into a meaningful community to grant "global citizenship."

[96]Blake, p. 272 "The principle I defend, therefore, mandates the following: that all individuals, regardless of institutional context, ought to have access to those goods and circumstances under which they are able to live as rationally autonomous agents, capable of selecting and pursuing plans of life in accordance with individual conceptions of the good. There are, I think, several methods by which people might be denied the circumstances of autonomy; famine, extreme poverty, crippling social norms such as caste hierarchies-all of these structures seem comprehensible as violations of a liberal principle devoted to the defense of the circumstances of autonomy, although I cannot here defend these claims in detail. It is enough in the present context to notice that a consistent liberal must be as concerned with poverty abroad as that at home, since borders provide no insulation from the demands of a morality based upon the worth of all autonomous human beings."; Nagel, p. 118 "I assume there is some minimal concern we owe to fellow human beings threatened with starvation or severe malnutrition and early death from easily preventable diseases, as all these people in dire poverty are. Although there is plenty of room for disagreement about the most effective methods, some form of humane assistance from the well-off to those in extremis is clearly called for quite apart from any demand of justice, if we are not simply ethical egoists."; Sangiovanni, p. 5 "I will assume that all plausible criteria of distributive justice, whether national, international, or global, must at least require raising all human beings to a minimal threshold defined in terms of access to basic goods, including clothing, shelter, food, and sanitation. Although I cannot defend this stipulation in any detail here, all of the major forms of 'internationalism'[. . .] accept it as a starting point."

somewhat controversial.[97] There is disagreement over the precision and legitimacy of many Articles of the UD already, such as those regarding socioeconomic rights. How could the present world order be sufficient to the enforcement of human rights, if there is no clarity about what counts as a human right? And since there is neither a hierarchy of rights nor a definition or quantification of human rights violations that are "tolerable," these theories potentially expose every state to punishment if not outright aggression. Also, who should prevail between sovereign states and organizations like the UN and a single sovereign state? The "global justice theorists" have not fully spelled out their take on this respect. A coherent theory of combined (or clashing) sovereignties is, at least at present, missing, and it has been substituted by anarchical and chaotic practices.[98] *De facto,* the "burden" of defending human rights weighs principally on the nation-state. As long as the cooperation of the international community is dysfunctional, and its legitimacy is open to question, we will lack a workable philosophical and theoretical understanding of how human rights are to be understood, interpreted, assessed, measured, and enforced.[99,100]

Second, and relatedly, *political institutions* are also taken as a given.[101] This approach appears less naive than a utopian philosophy, which freely dreams

---

[97]"Those rights, *if they exist*, set universal and prepolitical limits to the legitimate use of power, independent of special forms of association. It is wrong for any individual or group to deny such rights to any other individual or group, and we do not give them up as a condition of membership in a political society, even though their precise boundaries and methods of protection through law will have to be determined politically in light of each society's particular circumstances." Nagel, p. 127, my italics. I agree with Nagel to the point that I also hold rights to be played out in accordance to particular circumstances, but without a more substantial world order based on non-domination I think it is hardly conceivable of a way to determine these rights' "precise boundaries" without letting powerful private and public agents abuse them and twist them according to their interests.

[98]I think it is interesting to report that while a Google search gives almost 200 million entries for the word "sovereignty," it yields less than a million when one search for the plural "sovereignties." Sovereignty has historically presented itself as absolute, and dictionaries reflect the difficulty of reappraising it. See next section on the "inclusive exception" as a paradigm of sovereignty.

[99]As evidenced by the current polarization and paralysis in many multilateral bodies in the context of the Collective West-China/Russia confrontation, and the outdated structure of international institutions, in particular with a view to equal and democratic participation.

[100]As Nagel (p. 126) says "If the conditions of even the poorest societies should come to meet a livable minimum, the political conception might not even see a general humanitarian claim for redistribution." The question is on who has the authority to define that minimum. I think non-domination requires that this is not settled arbitrarily, but that all those over whom this minimum is imposed have a say about it. There is no way to discuss these matters until even the poorest states are heeded globally as respectfully as minorities are within democratic, egalitarian nation-states. It is not because of the problem of "relative deprivation," but in order to enable everyone to reach a "livable minimum," which Nagel's analysis presupposes, that we have to challenge the present international order. By saying "international order," I refer also to issues like asylum, migrants' rights, and criteria for citizenship which arise within the national borders.

[101]E.g. in Nagel's "political approach" and Blake's "institutional theory." "Another sort of attitude would prompt one to ask not what institutions we ought to have, but what the institutions we currently have would have to do to be justified. This sort of theory – which I

about global polities as if nation-states had disappeared. "Global justice theorists" would rather accept the present world order, even when they advance requests for significant changes. This realism is to be welcomed. Consistently with it, one can notice that some important institutions defy the polar opposition "global-local (national)."[102] The EU is obviously the first example that comes to mind, but one can wonder whether federal states are not already situated beyond the protomodern, monolithic concept of sovereignty. Even strongly unitary states sometimes defy dualism between the national and international: for example, China's "Special Economic" and "Free Trade" zones.[103] States change and adapt seamlessly: it has always been so in history, and there is no reason to think that in the era of globalization, they will cease to do so. Rather, the relationships with outsiders and between states will adapt accordingly.

However, and as a third point, the most blatant examples of "blurring" between national and international are to be found at the individual, rather than institutional, levels. Migrants live more or less stably in between countries and this affects both the respect of their human rights and their equal status, whether based on their contributions as quasi-citizens or not.[104] They take part in the

---

call institutional theory – would take much more of the world as a pretheoretical given for purposes of analysis." Blake, p. 262. "Unlike cosmopolitanism, the second conception of justice does not have a standard name, but let me call it the political conception, since it is exemplified by Rawls's view that justice should be understood as a specifically political value, rather than being derived from a comprehensive moral system, so that it is essentially a virtue – the first virtue – of social institutions. On the political conception, sovereign states are not merely instruments for realizing the preinstitutional value of justice among human beings. Instead, their existence is precisely what gives the value of justice its application, by putting the fellow citizens of a sovereign state into a relation that they do not have with the rest of humanity, an institutional relation which must then be evaluated by the special standards of fairness and equality that fill out the content of justice." Nagel, p. 120. I find this neutralization of the critical potential of moral theory – as opposed to "institutional" political theory – to be a problematic radicalization of positivism.

[102] Nagel foresaw this remark about "an unrealistically sharp dichotomy between sovereign states and existing global institutions." For the details of his dealing with this objection and with the idea of "a sliding standard of obligation" (which he deems implausible) see "The Problem of Global Justice," pp. 141; 143.

[103] Ahiwa Ong, *Neoliberalism as Exception: Mutations in Citizenship and Sovereignty,* (Durham and London: Duke University Press, 2006), see especially chap. 4.

[104] Migration is considered specifically problematic within discourses on global justice: "J. Donald Moon and others have pressed on me the objection that the entire international system might be based upon coercion, seen, for instance, in the coercive exclusion of would-be immigrants at the border. This may be correct, but it is important to remember that each distinct form of coercion requires a distinct form of justification. The refusal of entry to a would-be member may or may not be justifiable; *the form such justification would take, however, would be significantly different from that offered to a present member* for the web of legal coercion within which she currently lives." M. Blake, "State, Autonomy and Coercion", note 30, my italics. See also Nagel, pp. 129–130.

hosting state's social and economic life, and they are exposed to state coercion, but often, their status is not proportionally enhanced. Citizens of a collapsed or failed state are in a much worse situation since they can be deprived for a long time of objective-institutional counterparts to subjective citizenship, namely without any appointee to the defense of their rights apart from the feeble and often *de jure* guarantees from the international community. This is also the case in most extreme cases: minorities who are persecuted to the point of being dehumanized, the state of war, the concentration camp.[105] And even such cases are not after all really "marginal," as exceptions may become the norm, wars are prolonged, and refugee and segregation crises affecting millions are protracted over decades.

The fourth and last point regards the definition of coercion presupposed by the "global justice theorists."[106] Establishing a cut-off point to determine whether people are coerced by a state or institution or not is not at all simple in theory and is bound to be contested and controversial in practice.[107] Partly, this is a matter of economics: decisions by one state, or even by private institutions, can plunge entire populations into poverty: and it is hard to find anything more coercive than the threat of starvation.[108] Also, paradoxically, within or without international institutions, nation-states have been able to inflict *more* coercion – through military intervention – on foreigners than on residents. These are ordinarily presented as reactions to threats from foreign countries, such as terrorism, diseases, and massive

---

[105]Famously, Giorgio Agamben has criticized the concentration camp as a paradigm of modern politics: *Homo Sacer. Il potere sovrano e la nuda vita* (Torino: Einaudi, 1995), pp. 185–201 "Il campo come nómos del moderno."

[106]"To insiders, the state says: Yes, we coerce you, but we do so in accordance with principles you could not reasonably reject. To outsiders, it says: We do not coerce you, and therefore do not apply our principles of liberal justice to you - although you do have an entitlement to the preconditions of autonomous functioning, and we will ensure that these are provided to you if you do not have them now." Blake, "Distributive justice", p. 287.

[107]"This is a powerful line of argument, and I believe that my analysis of the voluntary/ nonvoluntary distinction strengthens it: noncompliance or exit from most major international organizations, let alone the global institutional order as a whole, carries significant costs for states subject to them, especially smaller and less powerful ones. It stretches credibility to argue that these costs are small enough to make membership voluntary in the relevant sense, and hence to suspend a concern with distributive justice. Belonging to the WTO, UN, IMF, EU, and so on, is not like belonging to the local tennis club." Sangiovanni, "Global Justice, Reciprocity." p. 19. The coercive power of international institutions on a developing country like Jamaica is documented emblematically in *Life and Debt*, a film by Stephanie Black. Confront also with what Joshua Cohen and Charles Sabel say in their answer to Nagel in "Extra Rempublicam Nulla Justitia", issue 34 (2006) pp. 147–175.

[108]The market capitalization of Wall Street's "Magnificent Seven" (Microsoft (MSFT), Apple (AAPL), Alphabet (GOOGL) (GOOG), Amazon.com (AMZN), Nvidia (NVDA) and Tesla (TSLA)) seem to be around three times the GDP of Germany.

migrations.[109] Be it as it may, there is certainly no way by which "foreign subjects" can hold their dominators accountable. Therefore, the reciprocity-coercion argument should be played the other way around: in the cases in which we clearly detect international coercion, we should demand a proportionate transnational system of enfranchisement and participation also.[110] The contradiction between universal claims of equal concern and the exclusion of outsiders is thus far from completely settled, despite the arguments of the "global justice theorists," and the "outsiders" who live within state borders can constitute a constant reminder of pressing inequalities.[111] This is why Bohman consistently speaks of "Cosmopolitanism at home": the justice of the whole system is diminished if this proves ineffective in addressing anyone's legitimate claims for freedom.

It follows that justice cannot be reduced to the setting of "sufficiently fair" standards of (re)distribution in the local, even less, in the global arena.[112] Justice implies also an imperative demanding the expansion and implementation of just institutions (as well as practices and procedures) operating in all the relevant fields. Rawls argued that justice compels us to abide by just laws on the one hand and to reform them and establish new ones on the other.[113] Since consent plays an important role in

---

[109]But these could also be seen as opposite coercive phenomena: a state coerces another to dismantle terrorist activities, but the latter was already coercing the former when not impeding terrorists from planning attacks abroad. So even if these interventions were all genuinely justified, the problem of the fact of international coercion would remain. The question is merely who is the victim of the coercion, and who is the culprit.

[110]Compare with Nagel's conclusive "speculation": "The Problem[. . .]" pp. 146–147.

[111]Bohman, "Living Without Freedom", pp. 545–547.

[112]The establishment of such standards of course *is* a question of justice, and a very important one. In what follows I will rely on Jeremy Waldron's argument for natural duties to cast light on the other side of the demands of justice. Nagel's specific defense of a two-tier distributive criterion seems relatively compatible with Waldron's analysis of the natural justification of political institutions. According to Waldron: "Once again, this [the existence of a natural duty holding between an individual and her own national institutions] is not incompatible with theories of consent or fair play [see the role played by reciprocity in Nagel's argument]. *Maybe there are many layers to the moral issue of what one owes to the state.*" Jeremy Waldron, "Special Ties and Natural Duties", in Thomas Pogge and Darrel Moellendorf (eds.) *Global Justice: Seminal Essays* (Saint Paul: Paragon House, 2008), p. 398 (my italics). What Waldron says in this article applies only in part to the case of supranational institutions: but Waldron's view seems also not to be explicitly *against* such an extended application to these political problems. Moreover, Waldron's argument is intrinsically transnational.

[113]True, Rawsl's theory is famously "a reasonable conception of justice for the basic structure of society conceived for the time being as a closed system isolated from other societies" (*A Theory of Justice*, p. 8). But Waldron remarks that "the assumption that justice may be confined within the borders of a single society is unsatisfactory" ("Special Ties", p. 400). He put forward two examples as evidence of this: the outrageous disparities between, say, New Zealand and Bangladesh, and the power of influence and even of killing that a sovereign state exercised within the territory of another in the Rainbow Warrior Affair. This latter is also a graphic example of what I meant by questioning the assumption that coercion is exercised only inside national territory by the legitimate authority. But by leaving aside these topics, Rawls himself

legitimating an institution, the "institutional-political" implication of "global justice theorists" could have conservative implications.[114] The legitimization of an institution, in fact, is not contingent if it is predicated on its commitment to justice: the alternative to a recognizably legitimate international order is a Hobbesian-like state of war.[115,116] In my interpretation, the impulse to enhance global institutions together with ties between individuals and the national institutions they belong to, and also to favor the recognition of humanity "at home," is continuous and consistent with the primitive inclinations toward social and political life. The fact that we are already distributed in communities, does not eliminate the need for harmonization: a dispute between states over the control of some resources is not different from two individuals fighting but causing greater destruction.[117] In this limited sense, the "domestic analogy" between individuals and nation-states holds: states do not recognize any vertically superior power, nor do they behave like individual citizens, but conflicts between them cannot be abandoned to a Darwinian/Hobbesian fight for the dominance and survival of the fittest.[118] Poverty, attempts at genocide, crises in international relations, massive migrations, pollution, climate change, terrorism: all these can be addressed properly only *beyond* Westphalian sovereignty. Many accomplishments are already possible only through transnational alliances and cooperation at all levels. These need to be recognized, supported, and sustained by a cultural, social, and psychological effort for understanding, respecting, and harmonizing different civilizations and national communities. From poetry to science, to arts and sports, the achievements of our age exceed boundaries. Identities and meritorious traditions can be preserved and thrive, even more in the context of a harmonious global community. Benefits for individuals, from refugees and migrants to residents and citizens, are also

---

left the door open for the reassessment of the obligations of justice in writing that "[The duty of justice] also constrains us to further just arrangements *not yet established*, at least when this can be done without too much cost to ourselves" (*A Theory of Justice*, p. 115; confront with Waldron, pp. 392–393). The compliance to just institutions is to be flanked by the strive for bringing about those still lacking. See the duties I resumed in the previous paragraph, and the corresponding articles in the Universal Declaration.

[114]This issue is the main focus of Waldron's article: see for example "Special Ties", pp. 409–410.

[115]Against the objection pointing to the contingency of particular ties in a theory of natural duties see ibidem, p. 404.

[116]Despite his much more optimistic idea of human nature, Kant was equally persuaded that even "good nature and righteous" persons living without "a public lawful state" would not be able to avoid "fighting" and "wild violence." Immanuel Kant, *The Metaphysical Elements of Justice*, trans. John Ladd (Indianapolis: Bobbs-Merrill, 1965) section 42, p. 71, 76. See the discussion in Waldron, pp. 400–401, and also the first chapter in Benhabib, *The Rights of Others,* providing an accurate analysis of Kant's cosmopolitanism.

[117]As Waldron puts it: "If anything, such violence will be worse than that of the Hobbesian "war of all against all" because the battles will be better organized. The moral interest in reducing such fighting provides a reason for all of us to join and support the same organization[. . .]" "Special Ties", p. 407.

[118]The "domestic analogy" has been criticized by realists, to my view correctly, as a misleading perspective on international politics.

enormous, and the risks of an unsafe and dysregulated international environment are too grave to be dismissed. Originally, it was impossible for human societies to survive without a common organization: this led to the setting of principles of limited range. Yet these implied, e.g., a spatially unlimited principle of non-interference.[119] Now circumstances of justice have changed and require the integration of each state in a system of "global citizenship," as well as the reconsideration of non-citizens within the state's boundaries, of "marginal cases" and "states of exception." And these not for reasons opposite or additional to those which led to state formation, but rather as the natural continuation of those latter.[120] Just as entrance into society was indispensable for the communal enjoyment of rights, some form of *global* society is now needed to cope with global and local problems coherently: as a consequence, we have a natural duty to promote it actively, a duty that cannot be misrepresented as a matter of supererogatory generosity.[121,122]

2.3 Rightlessness as a Path Toward the Extension of Status

[T]he path from anarchy to justice must go through injustice.
Thomas Nagel.[123]

---

[119]The example is again drawn from Waldron, "Special Ties."

[120]"Certainly such resolutions are provisional. As the sphere of human interaction expands, further conflicts may arise, and the scope of the legal framework must be extended and if necessary rethought, according to the same Kantian principle." (Waldron, "Special Ties", p. 401). The principle may be "Kantian" or otherwise: what matters is that institutions concerned with global justice are not to be opposed to local cooperation, which they may even boost.

[121]"It is morally imperative that the demands of justice be pursued *period*. If institutions are necessary for their pursuit, then it is morally imperative that such institutions be established." Ibidem, p. 412.

[122]This is true if Waldron's arguments for natural duties are correct *and* if there is no alternative capable of providing the same benefit to the strengthening of the international polity, due to the twofold characteristics of justice which apply to an institution: namely that (1) it must be just in the way it operates (one could call this a "formal requirement") and (2) that it must be doing something that justice requires (one could call this other a "substantive requirement." See Waldron, "Special Ties[...]" pp. 413–414). The latter characteristic involves an empirical evaluation over the possibility of achieving the same outcomes within a system of independent states, but I believe this idea has been implicitly abandoned by independent states themselves from the creation of the League of the Nations on. See next section. The requirements of (1) are already demanding, for it seems to me that if we are to take seriously the justifications of democratic sovereignty, something more akin to it should be pursued in the international arena as regards especially direct participation, the separation of powers, equality of voice, and an effective power of coercion which, as in the case of sovereign states, is not to be confounded with violence: it has rather to do with the relevance, reliability and fairness of the sanctions and incentives.

[123]Thomas Nagel. (2005). "The Problem of Global Justice." *Philosophy and Public Affairs*, 33(3), 113–147.

As mentioned previously, history and globalization have brought the world to a condition of unprecedented connection. This factual condition, which one could call "cosmopolitism," precedes and integrates "cosmopolitanism," in the sense that the possibility of a global polity (*polis*) is a prerequisite for the existence of its citizens (*polites*). Nagel seems to believe that a coercive authority of sorts is likely to come into existence before the establishment of perfectly just power relations necessary to manage it. This resonates with Waldron's view that the suited institutions arise as a way to prevent injustice and as a reaction to it.[124] These institutions may be unjust to some extent too: their legitimacy depends also on their effectiveness, on popular support, and on their relative advantage over anarchy.[125] The "cunning of history" would be directing the formation of a global polity through global states of nature in which, with many accidental constraints, power legitimates itself. Irrespective of whether this is reflects the spirit of Nagel's own argument or not, I do not believe that this process should be deterministic and ideological.[126] This "dialectic" view of global development should not serve as a justificatory tale to excuse injustices. Rather, I believe the path *through* injustices can only be established if and when one *reacts* effectively to injustice.

2.3.1 Power Through Exclusion: The Paradox of Sovereignty

This lends the occasion to introduce a theoretical device both to understand that process, and to grasp better the ambiguity of the "right to have rights": the idea of "inclusive exclusion." According to Giorgio Agamben's theory, the space in which

---

[124]As I said above, Waldron's description of the "state of nature" is the classic one we find in the Hobbesian tradition.

[125]See Waldron, "Special Ties", p. 409: "In most cases, the fact that there *is* a state and that it is, for all practical purposes, dominant and unchallenged in a territory will be sufficient. This is the organization that deserves our support in the enterprise of doing justice if any organization does." The fact that the organization has just ends is not in itself sufficient to grant allegiance to it (ibid., p. 406) because effectiveness matters and no one is bound to "lost causes" (ibid., p. 405). This explains enduring loyalty to a country that is partly corrupt and unjust. It seems reasonable that there must be a considerable amount of injustice before a revolution becomes preferable. And the fact that there is such a red line witnesses to the reasonableness of overthrowing tyranny once that this limit has been surpassed. What is of moral relevance here is not only the quantity or the gravity of the state's flaws, but also the preconditions upon which an alternative might be established.

[126]"Unjust and illegitimate regimes are the necessary precursors of the progress toward legitimacy and democracy, because they create the centralized power that can then be contested, and perhaps turned in other directions without being destroyed[. . .] The global scope of justice will expand only through developments that first increase the injustice of the world by introducing effective but illegitimate institutions to which the standards of justice apply, standards by which we may hope they will eventually be transformed." Nagel, "The Problem", pp. 146–147. The question, once again, is what amount of coercive and unjust power we are to put up with before its sources are made accountable to the democratic process.

political power first arose is where law detaches itself from nature.[127] Since humans are naturally "political," that is, born in an organized society and acting according to judgments instead of mere instinct, the way in which sovereignty is originally exercised is by sanctioning or lifting the "banishment." "Banishing" consists of "abandoning" someone to the state of nature, therefore excluding the subject from the reign of law and by doing so showing her total dependence on the sovereign itself. It is through this exclusion that the inclusion in the state of subjection is made possible as a power exercised against all, a power whose limits are not visible because the subject lives within them, and trespassing them would cause death. An original "biological" world, a pre-legal state of liberty, is in modern politics unthinkable.[128] Freedom, in other words, a proper human life, comes to existence only through the polity: *libertas est civitas*.[129,130] And slavery, as Aristotle famously argued, is a condition less than humane, and is only pre-political life: outside of the city no human is found, but only gods, beasts, and "talking tools" (slaves). Still, even within the boundaries of the political life was something one could arbitrarily dispose of on some occasions, as with the Roman *vitae necisque potestas*.[131] Therefore the definition of the sovereign as the one "who decides on the state of exception" is consistent with Arendt's idea of a "right to have rights": the fullness of sovereignty is not in the decision on this or that particular right, but in the definition of who is entitled to bear rights *tout court*.[132] Sovereignty is traditionally unquestionable because all the political questions can be posed only within its framework, on its supporting basis. It is the condition of the possibility of politics, and, since human life is essentially political, it is also the condition required for living and respecting humanity. The outsiders, beings that barely exist, were correspondingly considered almost incapable of questioning anything, all the more the sovereign power. The "political view," which takes *present* institutions as a given, is therefore at a loss in considering how to opt in new members. Rather, already existing nation-states need, on this view, merely to justify their coercion, a requirement that is implemented only by the (recently acquired) democratic political agency of the people. But since such institutions, as Nagel clearly concedes, were not created for that purpose, tensions and discrepancies were to be expected from the very beginning.[133] A theory of rational sovereignty, and especially a theory of the rational

---

[127]"Phusis" and "Nomos" in the vocabulary of the Sophists: according to Agamben Hobbes's state of nature is not to be interpreted as an existing historical step, but as an internal condition of the sovereign power that was only more apparent in a time of civil wars. See Giorgio Agamben, *"Homo Sacer"*, pp. 40–42.

[128]Agamben thinks that two different concepts of "life," which the Greeks called *bios* and *zoe*, are now conflated into the all-embracing sphere of politics. See *Homo Sacer*, Introduction.

[129]For a more specific discussion on freedom see chapter 3, and the bibliography mentioned there.

[130]A statement that could be translated as "freedom is citizenship," or also "freedom is (in) civilization." Cicero, *Pro Balbo*, 9.24.

[131]*Homo Sacer*, pp. 97–101.

[132]Carl Schmitt, *Politic Theology: Four Chapters on the Concept of Sovereignty,* trans. By G. Schwab (Chicago: University of Chicago Press, 2005), p. 5.

[133]"Yet in thinking about the future, we should keep in mind that political power is rarely created as a result of demands for legitimacy, and that there is little reason to think that

evolution of sovereignty, is still needed. From this open question originates the problems of the "citizenship gap": the global extension of rights, which is not the mere enforceability or overreaching of sovereignties.[134] Contingent political institutions, for a number of reasons, disguise themselves as "natural," and by doing so they not only avoid the re-definition of the "social contract," but also confirm the dangerous confusion between law and nature, illegality and non-existence.[135,136]

If Agamben is right, in fact, something more relevant is at stake. If the "sovereign ban" is the original definition of who is included and who is excluded, a definition that by itself extends to both categories by implying that the excluded are, whether they like it or not, cut off from entitlements provided by that society (which, in practice, could mean excluded from society or life altogether), a global polity would be a very dangerous, totalitarian, and inescapable global subjection.[137] Is the idea of global governance, however imagined, to be coupled with the frightening possibility of a global state of exception, namely of the global suspension of *human* rights? Are we to face the difficult choice between (pre-political) non-disposable rights which are not enforceable and (political) enforceable rights which are necessarily disposable?[138] If so, it comes as no surprise that even some of the staunchest cosmopolitans are wary of the characteristics global institutions could assume. But otherwise, are rights always to be defined and restricted by a limited community, as Burke's "rights of Englishmen" illustrate? And which "third way" could be found out of this dilemma, if

---

things will be different in this case. If we look at the historical development of conceptions of justice and legitimacy for the nation-state, it appears that sovereignty usually precedes legitimacy." See "The Problem of Global Justice", p. 145.

[134]In Schmitt's conception of sovereignty, we can have even a *private* sovereign, a private force which is capable of dehumanizing persons by abandoning them, like in the cases of places ruled by tribes, terrorism, or *Heart of Darkness*-like exploitation.

[135]By "natural" I mean here that some political regimes tend to suggest that the way they receive and exercise power does not require any justification: it is presented as a mere fact, and an unalterable one. Sovereignty, not only in general but as wielded by this or that particular sovereign, is presented as a requirement of human nature, or of nature itself. This is most blatantly the case with monarchs "of divine right," and the like.

[136]I use this word in the broad sense of a general, constitutional agreement on who protects, who is protected, and at what conditions.

[137]Waldron brilliantly argues for the universality not only of natural duties, but also of special ties, since the latter obviously involve a universal request to refrain from interference (see note 93). This, in my opinion, explains many difficulties arising in cases of "humanitarian interventions": not only sovereignty requires delimiting, but delimiting (to some extent) is intrinsically a "sovereign" act.

[138]To temper this dilemma, one could consider theories of rights as a "common concern" – Charles Beitz. (2001). "Human Rights as a Common Concern." *American Political Science Review*, 95(2), 269–282 – they can be rights in a "manifesto sense" – Joel Feinberg, *Social Philosophy* (Englewood Cliffs: Prentice Hall, 1973), and as such different from prohibitions. A global regime of human rights, in this case, would imply something much thinner than a global governance. But the possibility, or rather, the fact of international coercion would remain unresolved and problematic.

traditional sovereignty posited itself as monist and unprincipled, a mere fact to be questioned and justified only after its establishment and acceptance?[139]

Nagel's realistic insight on this suggests that we can expect a regime of global injustice to consolidate before global justice becomes possible. But since this is no self-unfolding cosmological principle, and we are not assured of the extent of this injustice, nor of our own survival, it is reasonable to elicit as much resistance as possible as soon as we notice its symptoms. Political regimes often present themselves as natural and, if some form of the theory of natural duty is correct, we can take their point: even if no individual political institution is really so indispensable, the existence of *some* institution is necessary and required by the universal "right to have rights," namely by humanity itself.[140] But as the birth, the evolution, and even the dissolution of nation-states have revealed historically, a possibility of directing the process according to some requirements and ideals coexists with this necessity. The shape cosmopolitans give to their global polity is very indistinct, but so were other ideas advanced in the past while debating the constitutions of the states we see at present. In single, situated cases of rights violation, we can discern some paths toward the evolution of citizenship. There is no reason why one should wait until injustice has ripened to establish a more just global community. We do not need *total* injustice to move from anarchy to justice. We can proceed through facing limited problems, and then try to harmonize the institutions needed for their resolution. The characteristics of global justice are to be worked out as an answer to specific, contextual violations of justice and undue coercive oppressions. There is no assurance that, even in this way, necessarily just institutions will be the outcome. The sum of single improvements, each of which is positive in itself, could turn dangerous if unforeseen and difficult to control, and it could also be twisted to pursue ends that were not inherent in the process of its genesis. As it happened with the dissolution of feudal loyalties, the result can be a well-ordered, unified political entity, absolutism, or both at different times. But the perspective risks of the future do not excuse complacency with the injustices of the present – and the past. In fact, both the violation of minimal redistributive justice meant to redress dramatic deprivation *and* that of basic human rights undermine the credibility of institutions responsible for them. No individual, and certainly no state, should turn a blind eye toward such violations against any human being, and the discrimination of non-citizens in this respect turns out to be a challenge to state's legitimacy even in the citizens' eyes.[141] Yet, nothing in principle guarantees that a more substantial international order will promote these rights instead of greater domination, as nothing guarantees the same to the founders of any given country.

---

[139]Admittedly, this is not the case with all the instances of sovereignty. Sovereignty did in fact employ a variety of legitimizing strategies in human history and across geography.

[140]I refer here again to a theory such as Waldron's. It must be stressed that according to his theory the existence of *a* sovereign of some sort is justified, while the legitimacy of this or that individual regime is always opened to challenge.

[141]This seems to me the crux of the argument advanced by Bohman, "Living Without Freedom."

2.3.2 The Foundational Role of Outsiders

In many myths and national stories, the nation is re-founded by a foreigner who is capable of making the polity anew with his/her double nature of a revolutionary, threatening to destroy the establishment, and of a brave migrant bringing in new energies. Bonnie Honig has argued that the strangers, marginalized, and excluded bear the philosophical and political re-founding of the legitimacy of national institutions.[142] Democracy requires that all its power is grounded in the defense of people's authentic interests and freedoms, and this assumption is both challenged and verified through processes of inclusion. "Marginal" cases provide the nation-state with a test of embodied universalization: it is only through them that political principles of equality, fairness, fraternity, and universality are coherently embedded in practices.[143] In the era of globalization, non-citizens also work as tests for the nation-state to show that it is still able to perform its original instrumental function: protecting subjects from violence and injustice and coping with an environment that would prove dramatically too complex and hostile to individuals. Honig's idea of democratic cosmopolitanism does not determine a specific institutional arrangement, and she denies that either global citizenship or world government is implied by it. Since this idea relies on the particular and unpredictable demands of each practice of integration, the outcome of these trade-offs between in and outsiders will be understandable and explainable only retrospectively.[144,145] Yet independence or even opposition between laws and practices should not be exaggerated to the detriment of both. Laws and practices may sustain each other, and if one of the two poles becomes predominant, either fluidity is transformed into evanescence or solidity into rigidity.[146] Moreover, practices and laws must be in line with each other. The task of advancing both cannot be left on the shoulders of the oppressed, of those who most suffer for their defects: therefore, their expected roles should not be conveniently – and ideologically – exaggerated. It is, instead, a task human beings have in common by virtue of their nature and dignity.

---

[142]Bonnie Honig, *Democracy and the Foreigner* (Princeton: Princeton University Press, 2001).

[143]Honig suggests to transform citizenship from a status administered by the central institution to "a *practice* in which denizens, migrants, and their allies hold states accountable for their definitions and distribution of goods, powers, rights, freedoms, privileges, and justice," ibid., p. 104.

[144]By this term I do not refer only to the integration of foreigners into their hosting citizenry, but also to the integration of states into a sufficiently harmonic global community and world-order.

[145]This seems to be the meaning of the quote by Kierkegaard that opens Dora Kostakopoulou's work on citizenship: "The irony of life is that it is lived forward, but understood backward." Dora Kostakopoulou, *The Future Governance of Citizenship* (Cambridge: Cambridge University Press, 2008), p. 1. Confronts also with her definition of (national) culture as a "3P-Plex": Practice, Process, and Project (ibid., p. 64).

[146]I think the very existence of common, or precedent, law suggests that it would be more appropriate to focus on how practices generate laws, and laws stabilize practices (but the relation, on some occasion, could work the other way round) than opposing the two as though the concepts were independent.

2.3.3 Abject Cosmopolitanism: The Refugee/Stateless as the Essential Citizen

Peter Nyers' article on "abject cosmopolitanism" provides a case study and a restatement of such cases: it is however the very concept of "abject cosmopolitanism" that I find of theoretical interest.[147]

The situation of refugees is, more generally speaking, rich in insights into the essence of citizenship for many reasons. The most obvious and not negligible, despite not being central to the argument here, is that refugees make up a great proportion of displaced, stateless people, and constitute an urgent political problem playing a significant role in international politics and diplomacy.[148] Its dimensions and dramatic intensity make it impossible to ignore. This introduces the second, and philosophically more relevant, point: refugees embody the clash of sovereignties I referred to as an issue of (meta)political legitimization.[149] They are members of a community not *although* but rather *because* they are rejected by another.[150] And therefore, as a third and crucial point, they already embody the sense and the provisions of global (or fundamental-essential) citizenship and, in my view, also of citizenship itself.[151] In its deepest meaning, the meaning that probably came historically and conceptually first, citizenship is primarily the entitlement to human rights that fades if those rights are violated, and that must be conceded by any legitimate community capable of doing so, under penalty of losing legitimacy before its members' eyes, and before outsiders. The community itself might work as a local instantiation of humanity (*in loco civitatis*: in the place of humanity, as David Owen has it) corresponding to universal standards of

---

[147]Peter Nyers. (2003). "Abject Cosmopolitanism. The Politics of Protection in the Anti-Deportation Movement." *Third World Quarterly*, 24(6), 1069–1093.

[148]I owe this awareness also to a remark by professor Gershon Shafir.

[149]"Meta" politics is an ambiguous term: I am referring to political authorities which go beyond the traditional ones, namely national sovereigns. One could say that this is just the most recent evolution of politics itself.

[150]In this way, every refugee literally realizes the oxymoron employed by Nyers (see ibid., pp. 1072–1075), especially if seen from the standpoint of international law: they are citizens of the world because they are momentarily citizens of nowhere, they are cosmopolitan inasmuch as they are "abject" (in the literal sense of the word, which according to the Oxford Dictionary originated from "late Middle English (in the sense 'rejected'): from Latin abjectus, past participle of *abicere* 'reject', from *ab-* 'away' +*jacere* 'to throw'." The term is in this acceptation synonymous to "uprooted."

[151]*Historically*, because if Agamben is correct the sovereign has presented itself as the dominator over "states of exceptions", the arbitrator over exclusion and inclusion. So before humanity reached an awareness of universal human rights, sovereignty, and the citizenship status that only the sovereign could concede and secure, was first and foremost a *right to exist*, a set of human rights. But this is also *conceptually* true if Hobbes is right in holding that the sovereign always gets its legitimation by avoiding that subjects fall (again) in the state of nature. If so, Waldron's idea of natural duties is, as it presents itself, an explanation of the core justification of citizenship and "special ties" as purveyors of human rights. I leave aside for the moment additional particularities and sentimental allegiances pertaining to the field of nationalism: they will be given some space in the next two chapters.

morality and rationality.[152] Refugees lack human rights (legally), they deserve human rights; they lack citizenship, they deserve citizenship. Conversely, a community provides its members with human rights, and if it does not, it is not a legitimate, "decent" community anymore: depending on the scale of these violations, it can even be considered a tyranny to be overthrown. Ordinarily, however, the right to decide whether this threshold of injustice has been crossed or not lies with a country's own people, and with them exclusively. Otherwise, it is regulated by articles 24, 25, and 51 of the Charter of the United Nations, and implemented through the general provisions of Chapter VII of the same, so that armed interventions are restricted to actions authorized by the Security Council to preserve international peace and security, while states keep their right to self-defense. More recently, in 2005, (A/RES/60/1) "Heads of State and Government affirmed their responsibility to protect their own populations from genocide, war crimes, ethnic cleansing and crimes against humanity."

The right of asylum is, just like these international obligations and Francis Deng's innovative conception of "sovereignty as responsibility," a constitutive part necessary to global citizenship: but if we have, as I think we have, *collective duties to ensure that every human being enjoys rights proportionate to his/her dignity,* much more is required.[153] It may be necessary that states constitute a supranational community capable of dealing with problems of this sort.[154] And also through this means, states should study and realize policies for the betterment of the human rights regime worldwide: this would be properly a matter of foreign policy, that does not necessarily imply abuses of military interventions, even in case crises loom. Rather, international cooperation to enhance human rights worldwide is both compatible with national sovereignty and reinforces it.

Finally, there is a conception of "abject cosmopolitanism" that goes beyond the meaning initially attributed to the phrase by Nyers: "abject cosmopolitanism" is realized whenever states, peoples, and communities that have been forced at the bottom of the global hierarchy struggle to realize a freer, equal, just international order. In this line, countries and peoples who strive against colonialism and discrimination have all provided examples of "cosmopolitanism from below."

---

[152]See David Owen, "In Loco Civitatis: On the Normative Basis of the Institution of Refugeehood and Responsibilities for Refugees", in Sarah Fine and Lea Ypi (eds.) *Migration in Political Theory: The Ethics of Movement and Membership* (Oxford, 2016; online edn., Oxford Academic, March 24, 2016), https://doi.org/10.1093/acprof:oso/9780199676606.003.0013. Accessed February 5, 2024.

[153]I hold that not only Waldron, but also Rawls thinks that we have such a duty, and that it constitutes, we could say, about "half" of the requirements of justice. But note that the other "half," as Nagel acknowledges, namely distributive justice avoiding relative deprivation, *presupposes the creation of just institutions.* Therefore, the duty to bring about just institutions for everyone is morally necessary, but not sufficient, and the "two sides of justice," so to speak, are intertwined.

[154]Nyers, "Abject Cosmopolitanism", p. 1081.

2.3.4 Peace and the Teleology of Citizenship

On the very contrary, in Europe, where centuries of history disproved the illusion of fixing diplomatic issues through aggression, the human rights of citizens grew both within and without member nation-states thanks to the increase of economic, cultural, and personal ties, the improvement of mobility, the porosity of borders, disarmament, dismantling of colonial empires, and protection of a large number of citizens of any ethnicity and orientation through modern welfare-states.[155,156] These and many other technical-material improvements were coupled with a number of cultural and educational achievements, which are not as easy to list, but were no less effective in securing human rights at home and abroad: for example, the dismissal of racial and social-Darwinist discourses, and the cultural openness toward the "foreign" that increased over decades. Sure, progress is still required, and all these achievements might end up in peril at one point or another. But three aspects of the development of the EU are here interesting to focus on.[157]

The first is its past: the way through which the idea of a commonwealth of European nation-states emerged is exactly the one theorized by Nagel. Wars, oppressive and unfair treaties, and even the threat of a unified imperial tyranny helped recognize the mutual responsibilities, the strict bonds, and the possibilities of convergence between old enemies and disloyal allies. The second is its present shape: a supranational regime that, despite many, undeniable shortcomings, has persuaded members to agree on common standards and destiny with regard to fundamental matters. And this, without abolishing, perhaps even without diminishing national identities. The most relevant, though, is its possible future development: the *telos* of the EU was peace, that is to say, the free enjoyment of rights, and the strengthening of friendship among peoples who are different yet capable of being united. It is in opposition to the catastrophic effects of war that the process of European interaction started, and solely in the perspective of the attainment of peace, not only for its members but for the whole world, it could remain a relevant experiment and a model for international institutions. In Immanuel Kant's international political theory, a "Federation of Free States," and "Universal Hospitality" were joined together with "Perpetual Peace."[158] A century and a half, and many disasters later, European politicians started thinking

---

[155]Perspective Eurocentrism is here accidental and should not be misunderstood for some form of exceptionalism. I believe other supranational or federated states would give us as many suggestions as this case.

[156]Empires which destabilized democratic institutions at home (as in the case of the Algerian war) or fueled non-democratic regimes (like Spain's and Portugal's).

[157]For a classic account of the historical-ideological roots of Europe, see Federico Chabod, *Storia dell'idea d'Europa* (Roma: Laterza, 1965).

[158]Immanuel Kant, *Perpetual Peace*, ed. Lewis White Beck (Indianapolis: Bobbs-Merrill 1997); Jürgen Habermas, "Kant's Idea of a Perpetual Peace, with the Benefit of Two Hundred Year's Hindsight", in *Perpetual Peace: Essays on Kant's Cosmopolitan Ideal* (Cambridge: MIT Press, 1997), pp. 113–153.

that obtaining peace without shared institutions and hospitality would have remained impossible.[159] But before I consider national and international *peace* more thoroughly as the end toward which the instrument of *citizenship* could be oriented and the idea against which each local citizenship has to be measured, I have to turn to consider, in general, the flexible functions and the essence of citizenship itself.[160,161]

---

[159]See for example Monnet's speech delivered in Algeri on August 5, 1943 "There will be no peace in Europe, if the states are reconstituted on the basis of national sovereignty... The countries of Europe are too small to guarantee their peoples the necessary prosperity and social development. The European states must constitute themselves into a federation..." European States being "too small" is in my eyes an issue that can be applied to any nation-state now that globalization has developed. Every country is "too small" to "do it alone," when confronted with the immense potential for individual and collective development.
[160]This will be the aim of the fourth chapter.
[161]This is the main theme of the third chapter.

Chapter 3

Citizenship or the Right to Be Equal

If we look to the laws, they afford equal justice to all in their private differences. –Pericles[1]

What joy, for fatherland to die! –Horace[2]

I love my family more than myself; more than my family, my fatherland; more than my fatherland, humankind. –François Fénelon[3]

[N]one is born loving his country; such love is not natural, but has to be somehow taught, or acquired. –Walter Berns[4]

3.1 The Models of Citizenship

The political forms citizenship took over time are so strictly interwoven with the evolution of Western history that I deem it useful to add a summary here. I will focus only, or mainly, on concepts that will play a role in the next section of this very chapter, when I will criticize the concept of citizenship in such a way as to

---

[1]Thucydides, *Historiae in Two Volumes*. Edited by H. Stuart Jones and J. E. Powell (Oxford: Oxford University Press, 1942).

[2]Horace, *The Odes and Carmen Saeculare of Horace*. trans. John Conington (London: George Bell and Sons. 1882. III, 2, 13).

[3]Fénelon, François de Salignac de La Mothe. *The Adventures of Telemachus, the Son of Ulysses* (Manchester, Johnson, 1847).

[4]Walter Berns. *On Patriotism*. (Washington: Bradley Lecture, American Enterprise Institute, September 16, 1996).

---

identify which of its elements require further development. Schematic that it might be, this section will nonetheless give some content to the otherwise abstract notions I will discuss later. It is intended to reflect some of the variations of citizenship assumed in the Western context, and regrettably, I lack the space and the competences to cover other, no less interesting institutions and civilizations.

3.1.1 Citizenship From the Archaic Period to Hellenism

The Classical (Greek-Roman) world is not the only source for Western citizenship and the relative moral–political–legal traditions and institutions. Among a great number of influences – including, for example, Germanic customs, which impacted the Romans and the post-Roman world especially – another unavoidable mention is that of the Jewish-biblical tradition. In the Bible, as well as in Jewish and Christian religious narratives and traditions, one finds a conception of a people that is based on blood ties (Abraham and David's descendants) and, crucially, on religious grounds.

Nonetheless, the term "citizenship" comes from the Latin *civitas:* it refers to a "city" in the sense of a political community, an association of individuals and parties, in opposition to *urbs* or *oppidum*, respectively the words that designate "city" as a space, and a "military fortress." The Greek equivalent is *polis* (πόλις), from which descends the term "politics": "(relative to) the businesses of the city." The very first entities endowed with sovereign power in Western and Middle Eastern history, indeed, were far less extended than present nation-states, and their citizens composed a community of people living together and frequently meeting each other in person.

While inquiring into the cultural roots of Western society, between the first documents we could consider there are myths and accounts from the Archaic period of Greece. Both the *Iliad* and the *Odyssey* are probably to be dated back to this age, as the first cornerstones of Western literature, and somehow a representative of a stage of culture we could consider as primeval. The Homeric world is divided between different city-states whose governors are connected through webs of blood ties and covenants: the war against Troy is the war of a league of cities against a super-power that itself dwells in a single city. In poems and history, the identity of a character is determined by the mention of ancestors and tribes. Achilles, the quintessential hero, is the son of Peleus, and the other soldiers fighting in the Trojan War are presented similarly. Life, at least life for aristocratic adult men, who are the protagonists of these narratives and the most powerful members of a military society, is short, violent, dangerous, a quest for honor whose coronation is to honorably breathe one's last on the battlefield.[5] An incidental detachment from the group of peers implies agony in an untamed wilderness while failing to live up to one's duty is equivalent to social death. Philoctetes, whose story was played by all the three major tragedians of Classic Athens (Aeschylus, Sophocles, and Euripides), is emblematic of the

---

[5]Homer's world, while poetically enchanting, is not much different from Hobbes's state of nature, especially for (1) the unceasing peril threatening those who try to have themselves recognized as authorities (2) the almost absolute subjection of the physically and socially weaker, such as women, children, and the poor.

unbearable doom of the outcast. Life is either social life or it is not: Hector prefers to actually die while hopelessly fighting Achilles than to "die of shame to face the men of Troy and the Trojan women trailing their long robes." Sociologists and classical scholars such as Ruth Benedict and Eric Dodds have stressed the difference between the "guilt cultures" typical of Western modernity and such classical "shame cultures" (which on some accounts would be closer to the collectivist cultures of Africa and Asia).[6,7] To quote Moses I. Finley, "The basic values of society were given, predetermined and so were a man's place in the society and the privileges and duties that followed from his status."[8] For our purposes, it is important to underline this feature: *humanity consisted of a social status*, and almost nothing more, but of a status that was very different from the modern concept of belonging to a national community. The actions that the Homeric hero is able to accomplish and that constitute all his glory and respectability are the legitimization of his being given determinate portions of the spoils of war: in a sense, his warrior virtues are his "dignity."[9] Whoever takes part in the values of civilization, however, is granted hospitality, as it happens to Ulysses on the island of the Phaecians. Refusing hospitality, as the cannibal Cyclopes do most savagely, is the same as belonging to the world of beasts. The flexible boundaries of mutual recognition are those of a scattered elite of warriors: little is told about the precise conditions of the poor and the marginalized. We just know that they were conceived as hanging on their chiefs' and lords' fate, as Hector's farewell speech to his wife and the episode of the swineherd Eumaeus welcoming his king show. The relevant community was that of male kings and fighters, whose "rights" went beyond geographical barriers and overlapped with the frontiers of civilization, of their undertakings, and of their fame and glory.[10] In that way they responded to the logic of honor, hospitality, transgression, war, and slavery that animates the Homeric poems and, presumably, at least the prominent part of this archetypal Western societies.

The classic era of Greek civilization and philosophy is deeply influenced by the Homeric period and is riddled with references to its imagination. Some authors trace the first origins of the concept of citizenship and its opposition to slavery and servitude in the Greek *poleis*.[11] As Max Weber has persuasively argued, the Athenian

---

[6]Ruth Benedict, *The Chrysanthemum and the Sword: Patterns of Japanese Culture* (Boston: Houghton Mifflin, 1989).

[7]Eric R. Dodds, *The Greeks and the Irrational* (Berkeley: University of California Press, 1951).

[8]Moses I. Finley, *The World of Odysseus* (New York: Viking Press, 1954), p. 134.

[9]In the primordial Greek mindset it was perhaps difficult to distinguish between these actions and the entitlements they give rise to. The Greek words for "destiny," ("moros" μόρος, "moira" μοῖρα) mean something close to "part," "lot," "desert": an individual's destiny and one's earthly and even after-death life were one with their "sharing" and actions.

[10]The term is here in brackets because, as recalled in the previous chapter, it is certainly anachronistic to make use of it for this age.

[11]Allison Brysk and Gershon Shafir, "Introduction", in Allison Brysk and Gershon Shafir (eds.) *People out of Place: Globalization, Human Rights, and the Citizenship Gap* (New York: Routledge, 2004), p. 12.

idea of "citizen" was also militarily connoted: citizens were free men, capable of defending themselves and their households, who deliberated autonomously, in contrast to the Persians.[12] These latter were considered "slave-like" for their subjection to an absolute monarch. Accordingly, the foundational myths of Greek identity are the narrations of the conflicts against the Persian multicultural empire. A citizen defined himself by the differences that divided him from barbarians, women, children, and slaves. This intertwining between military activity, political freedom, and social respectability is "one of the great Western definitions of what it is to be human" but at the same time very restrictive.[13] It prescribed that individuals deprived of the possibility of self-government as a matter of fact or, worse, of principle, are not full-fledged human beings. These included slaves, women, and strangers belonging to non-democratic communities.[14] The towering political works of this era, from Plato's *Republic* to Aristotle's *Politics,* clearly show that the requirements of citizenship were very dissimilar from the 18th and 19th centuries' ideals of a commonality of blood, language, and religion. Even if some of these elements played a role in the politics of classic Athens, districts and tribes were not considered insuperable boundaries for the political community.[15] Granted, Demosthenes' *Philippics* used ethnicity as an argument against the Macedonian king, and the same reason compelled Herodotus to recall, or perhaps to make up Alexander's participation in the Olympic Games. Also, xenophobic anxieties were institutionalized in law, even in democratic Athens: for instance, in 451 BC Pericles restricted naturalization to the children of two Athenian parents. Years later, all who had allegedly claimed citizenship fraudulently were expelled from the city. Citizenship was so determinant that few Athenians were eager to widen it, and blood ties remained an essential component together with geographic proximity.[16] However, the borders of the polity, not to mention the nation or the culture, were often blurred and flexible, as illustrated for example by the great expansion of Greek colonies. Nevertheless, some thinkers openly defended the idea of "Greekness" as a sharing in a cultural project, a form of membership accessible to all those who were ready to embrace the values of the Greek communities. Language and the ability to argue one's case were a paramount asset in a

---

[12]Max Weber, *General Economic History* (New Brunswick: Transaction, 1981).

[13]The quote is taken from John G.A. Pocock, "The Ideal of Citizenship Since Classical Times", in Beiner, R. (ed.) *Theorizing Citizenship* (Albany: State University of New York Press, 1995), pp. 29–52.

[14]See the most famous argument about "natural slavery" by Aristotle in *Politics*, books III–IV. Against the prevailing view, I have over time become persuaded that Aristotle was in fact a critic of slavery, and that his discussion of the subject might imply a condemnation of slavery. See Wayne Ambler. (1987). "Aristotle on Nature and Politics: The Case of Slavery". *Political Theory*, 15(3), 390–410. JSTOR. http://www.jstor.org/stable/191210. Accessed February 11, 2024; Nah Dove. (2018). "Aristotle as Realist Critic of Slavery". *History of Political Thought*, 39(3), 399–421(23).

[15]Aristotle, for instance, seems not to discriminate against non-Greeks: Thornton Lockwood. (2021). "Aristotle's Politics on Greeks and Non-Greeks". *The Review of Politics*, 83(4), 465–485. https://doi.org/10.1017/S0034670521000462.

[16]Thomas R. Martin, *Ancient Greek from Prehistoric to Hellenistic Time* (New Haven: Yale University Press, 1996).

democracy based on public deliberation.[17] According to this view, political ability and intellectual skills were sufficient to endow with powers and rights. It is therefore scarcely surprising that the works expressing such viewpoints, their translation, and interpretation have always been controversial, especially in times of resurgent ethno-nationalism.[18]

Such "cosmopolitan" statements prepared the blossoming of multiculturalism during the age of Hellenism and Hellenic empires. The institution of slavery, the discrimination of women, and the contempt for strangers and metics explain much of the Athenian citizens' jealousy of their exclusive status. But when the classic world became "globalized" thanks to Alexander's conquests and explorations, the strictest criteria of exclusion needed institutional and philosophical revision. Aristotle's well-known sentence that "he who is unable to live in society, or who has no need because he is sufficient for himself, must be either a beast or a god: he is no part of a state," recorded in the first book of *Politics,* was paradoxically both challenged and validated by Diogenes the Cynic. This latter, according to the biography by Diogenes Laertius, was among the first to define himself as a "citizen of the world," but the nickname "Cynic" means in fact "similar to a dog."[19] Yet even the philosophical schools opposing the Cynics and Epicureans often displayed cosmopolitan features. The Stoics defended them by an account of universal law, or *logos*, connecting the individual and the conscience to the universe, beyond the mediation of communities. It is this theory that influenced the Roman development of an institution of citizenship even less ethnically rooted and, in the imperial age, also less politically substantial than the traditional Athenian one.

---

[17]"And she [the city of Athens] knew, furthermore, that whether men have been liberally educated from their earliest years is not to be determined by their courage or their wealth or such advantages, but is made manifest most of all by their speech, and that this has proved itself to be the surest sign of culture in every one of us, and that those who are skilled in speech are not only men of power in their own cities but are also held in honor in other states. And so far has our city distanced the rest of mankind in thought and in speech that her pupils have become the teachers of the rest of the world; *and she has brought it about that the name Hellenes suggests no longer a race but an intelligence, and that the title Hellenes is applied rather to those who share our culture than to those who share a common blood.*" Isocrates, *Panegyricus* sections 49–50, from *Isocrates with an English Translation in Three Volumes*, by George Norlin (London: William Heinemann Ltd., 1980). My italics.

[18]See for example Werner Jaeger's view on the passage reported in the preceding note as "a higher justification for the new national imperialism, in that it identifies what is specifically Greek with what is universally human" (*Paideia: The Ideals of Greek Culture*, trans. Gilbert Highet, volume III, *The Conflict of Cultural Ideals in the Age of Plato* (Oxford: Oxford University Press, 1986), p. 80). By so commenting it Jaeger already made explicit what is now called the "Arendt's paradox." Arendt's critique has stressed the dangerous overlapping of national causes with universal ideals, from the French Revolution to the "principle of national self determination" that led to the redefinition of European borders between the two world wars. See *People Out of Place*, p. 23.

[19]Diogenes Laertius, *The Lives and Opinion of Eminent Philosophers.* Compare to the portrait of Diogenes as an icon and a model for contemporary cosmopolitanism humorously depicted by Nussbaum in *Patriotism or Cosmopolitanism.*

3.1.2 Citizenship in the Roman Empire

Respect for the laws dictated by reason was mirrored in the observance of a detailed list of duties, tailored to each citizen's social standing, as in Cicero's *De Officiis*.[20] Thus while on the one hand, Pocock defines Athenian citizenship as the right to rule and be ruled, that is, essentially, political freedom under the same law (*isonomia*), he also sees the Roman legalistic definition of citizen as its reverse, and he employs these two extremes as paradigmatic conceptions explaining much of the history of Western citizenship. According to Gaius, jurisprudence concerned persons, actions, and things: therefore, these latter gained an importance that Aristotle would hardly concede to them. Roman citizenship was indeed a *status* with property rights at its core.[21] Thus the Roman conception of citizenship emphasized civil and economic rights, especially in the postrepublican period. Perhaps, this was no less due to the immense extension of Roman dominions than to internal revolutions. The Roman Empire bounded together many ethnicities but also many political systems which it tried to preserve without putting its own core interests and legitimacy in jeopardy. Therefore, it was easier to provide a common standard on a nonpolitical basis. Roman citizenship was a multilayer, flexible institution, much exploitable as a tool to unify the empire: it was eventually widened so as to gain the loyalty of this or that tribe and nation who had been previously hostile. Roman citizenship was a privilege to be sought for, and it hardly needed the kind of dynamic exertion of Athenian citizenship. Another "modern" feature of Roman citizenship was its inclusiveness. Paul, like many other historical characters, was born far away from Rome, even out of Europe, lacked any blood ties with the Eternal City, was most likely not proficient in Latin, did not share the Romans' religious beliefs: yet not only was he a Roman citizen *de jure* but this status often proved effective and crucial in his voyages. Hence, the rationale of Roman citizenship is not to be searched for in geographical, genetic, cultural, or linguistic conditions. It is noticeable that this latter was nonetheless the most important requirement, and there seem to have been cases in which someone was denaturalized

---

[20]"Stoicism became the ideological backdrop of the Roman intelligentsia, and it influenced the flexible, yet solid, concept of citizenship employed during the different ages of Rome. As Cicero lately defined it, Roman citizenship was far different from Greek: it was a legal society (*iuris societas*) [Cicero, *On the Republic*, 1,32]. Roman citizens had far more civil privileges and far less political dignity, even if this second significantly varied in synchrony with the revolutions at the top of the government. *Ius connubii, ius commercium, ius suffragium* were some of the gains that someone was granted access to when he became a Roman citizen." Peter Riesenberg, *Citizenship in the Western Tradition: Plato to Rousseau* (Chapel Hill: University of North Carolina Press, 1992), p. 74.

[21]"A 'citizen' came to mean someone free to act by law, free to ask and expect the law's protection, a citizen of such and such a legal community [...] Citizenship has become a legal status, carrying with it rights to certain things – perhaps possessions, perhaps immunities, perhaps expectations – available in many kinds and degrees, available or unavailable to many kinds of persons for many kinds of reasons. There is still much about it that is ideal, but it has become part of the domain of contingent reality, a category of status in the world of persons, actions, and things." J. G. A. Pocock, "The Ideal of Citizenship Since Classical Times."

for the inability to speak Latin.[22] This reminds us of Isocrates' argument about the centrality of language to politics and identity. Still, and contrary to the conditions required by both *ius soli* and *ius sanguinis*, a new language can be acquired and is much less bluntly defined than a geographic area of birth or a familial relationship.

3.1.3 Medieval Feuds and Cities and Renaissance Republicanism

In general, the conception of citizenship during the early Middle Ages inherited from the Romans the disregard for political rights. In the age of kings and emperors, the major boundaries were those binding a person to another in the context of a hierarchy, a pyramidal structure based on mutual transactions of concessions and obedience. Leaving aside the "free cities" and *comuni*, the "burgs" who gave origin to the word "bourgeoisie" by endowing their residents with privileges and exemptions, in general, and as Dora Kostakopoulou notices, feudal ties brought about a link to territories as a consequence of customs and traditions.[23] Later, the requests for definitions of the nature and limits of powers contributed to the drafting of precocious schemes of citizenship as the *Magna Charta Libertatum.* Some Medieval thinkers, like Marsilius of Padua, Nicholas Cusanus, and William of Ockham, went even further by claiming the dependence of the power of the sovereign, at least to some extent, on the body of the people. So medieval "citizenship," or rather the ensemble of powers, claims, and duties originating from social relations, was nonterritorially, nonethnically, and nonculturally restricted, at least not rigidly.[24] Dante's *De Monarchia* bestows on the German emperor sovereignty over Italy, Europe, and the very universe, not only on Christians but, in the same fashion as the Roman multinational empire, also on Jews, Muslims, and Gentiles. The most relevant and paradoxically "modern" aspect is obviously the transmission of special privileges and duties through birthright: yet these were not rigidly defined, as shown by the possibility of entering the world of

---

[22]J. N. Adams explores the issue at length in his essay "Romanitas and the Latin Language", in *Classical Quarterly,* volume 53, issue 1 (2003) pp. 184–205. In the next paragraphs I will often return to the performative function of language to define and strengthen a community of citizens while noting its importance in processes of national unification. The diffusion of local idioms both mirrored and contributed to the decline of the universal ideals of medieval empires in the aftermath of the printing revolution and of the Westphalia treaty: see below, "Westphalian Citizenship."

[23]Kostakopoulou, *The Future Governance of Citizenship*, p. 17.

[24]Obviously all these three assertions are generalizations. Territories had a very important role in the laws of feuds, but feudal obligations were often not coextensive to them: they were more akin to a private pact. Culture was of course of immense importance, and the dreamed-of community of European people was usually referred to as "Christendom." Finally, tribal and above all familial relationships were between the most relevant if not sometimes the unique sources of status. But the sketch resumed here about the insufficiency of these elements to explain "medieval citizenship" (in itself a concept very hard to define) is to be understood in the light of the many changes which took place in a time span of approximately 1,000 years over an entire continent. Therefore what I am saying applies less to some cases and more to others, such as contexts like multicultural Spain before the completion of *Reconquista* and the expulsion of Jews in 1492.

nobility by taking part in military conquest or by climbing the hierarchy of the clergy. Birthright aristocracy endured until the beginning of modernity but was already challenged if not rejected by medieval intellectuals invoking a more substantial and universally accessible standard for social prestige.[25] After the development of the feudal order, social and political rights still depended on relationships between individuals and groups like trade guilds and leagues of craftsmen. In those associations, as well as in urban centers, a relative measure of equality was increasingly invoked. Citizenship, in these contexts, meant a share of obligations and advantages and was a pact renewed regularly in a public oath ceremony.[26] These institutions were sometimes able to achieve independence from authorities imposed from above, like in the case of the cities scattered throughout Northern Europe. Despite abhorrent discrimination, for example, the segregation of the Jews, some forms of citizenship consisted of statuses whose acquisition was open to outsiders. This was the case with both membership in the civil leagues, such as those mentioned above, and an entitlement to a large rank of honors and responsibilities. In general, medieval political communities were porous. In some periods, it was common even to appoint a foreign major (*podestà*), in Italy and elsewhere, to avoid power struggles among local families. In medieval universities, which were, as the name reveals, aiming at uniting all human knowledge beyond borders, "nations" referred merely to colleges or unions of students of a common origin.

The Renaissance greatly developed the partial forms of openness of the medieval period, even if in institutional and practical terms the progression of state and nation-building and centralization of power may have strengthened some geographic and legal borders. With the rise of humanism, classic culture, started playing a role in the identification and shaping of the political community. The rediscovery of Greek and Roman values, and of the associated conceptions of citizenship, had such a great impact that by the time of Erasmus of Rotterdam, the polity intellectuals most cared for was not a particular geographical or institutional framework but rather a "republic of philosophers" or "of literates." Erasmus's contemporary Niccolò Macchiavelli devoted much of his political thinking and unlucky undertakings to a reconstruction of virtuous republicanism and unification of Italy in a renovated "classic" citizenry. His passionate activity, though, is fully understandable only in the context of the revolutionary changes that were to consolidate modernity and its peculiar political ideals and institutions. In Machiavelli's view, religion was not merely an end, the establishment of which was to be pursued through civil struggles, but rather an *instrumentum regni* (a "means to rule") that should be criticized based on its conduciveness to civil and public virtue. On the other hand, the French and

---

[25]For example in the Italian predecessors of Dante's poetry, the "nobility of soul" or "of intellect" was already a virtue to be distinguished from both vulgarity and mere aristocratic descent. See especially the poet Guido Guinizzelli and the studies on the issue recently published by Paolo Borsa.

[26]*The Future Governance of Citizenship*, p. 18.

Germans were not seen as potential "sacred" emperors anymore, but as "barbarians" the Italian peninsula should be freed of.[27] The "two suns," toward which Dante's world was oriented, that is, universal authorities spiritual and secular, were setting, and a secular world of distinct nation-states was rising in their place.

3.1.4 Westphalian to Contemporary Models of Citizenship

The result of the diplomatic attempt to solve European religious wars contributed to producing what we now see as the Westphalian model of citizenship, a compromise that distinguished between state, supranational powers, and religion, allowing individuals to choose their private worship and at the same time attributed to the sovereigns the power to decide which cult they wanted to adopt publicly.[28] The Westphalia Treaty is a step toward the modern nation-state endowed with territorial sovereignty and capable of excluding foreign intrusions through the newly developed military, technological, and juridical devices (as well as increasing population density and the growing development of national languages and cultures).[29] In the following centuries, national identities were reinforced, for example, thanks to the invention of printing, and the individual rulers' expanded powers gave way to absolutism.

The French Revolution, which broke out in reaction to this, is key to understanding contemporary citizenship. Through the *Declaration of the Rights of Man*, the "fundamental paradox of modern citizenship" became explicit: the universality of

---

[27]See the final chapter of *The Prince*, the emphatic "Exhortation to Take Over Italy and to Liberate It from the Barbarians," but also, on Machiavelli's republicanism, the *Discourses on Livy*.

[28]Yet much of the "Westphalian conception" is *ex-post*, interpreted, and mythologized: see the works by Andreas Osiander (such as "Sovereignty, International Relations, and the Westphalian Myth." *International Organization*, 55(2), 2001, 251–287. JSTOR. http://www.jstor.org/stable/3078632).

[29]According to Richard Falk, this state of affairs was not unchallenged: rather than by medieval authorities and conceptions, its evolution was driven by secular statism, and this latter needed to exploit the ideological power of nationalism for its aims up to our days: "In the pre-1990s period the Westphalian model of world order based on a society of states prevailed to such an extent as to associate citizenship, as a meaningful dimension of political participation, quite totalistically with full membership in a sovereign state. The state, with the reinforcing support of international law, deliberately subordinated the idea and practice of nationality to statehood, thereby attempting to coopt divergent nationalist loyalties of its inhabitants. This effort was not consistently successful. As a result, periodic attempts were made by dissatisfied minorities to reconfigure the boundaries of state or to establish zones of autonomy within existing boundaries. The rise of 'nationalism' as the basis for community was itself a major dimension of the secularizing project that accompanied the rise of statism from the 17th century onward, and was complementary to the determined effort to exclude religious influence from the public sphere of governance. But it was always an ambiguous reality, conflating juridical ideas of membership and affiliation with a more spontaneous politics associated with identity and desire." *People Out of Place*, p. 177.

ideals was coupled with the locality of authority. When the Napoleonic wars secured the spread of one of the first modern empires, almost all the constitutive elements of modern citizenship were developed to completion, and distributed across European national communities - and beyond.[30] There was a conception of sovereignty over a territory and over nationals abroad, a secular moral-legal code of conduct, namely the "rights of the citizen," and their enforcement granted through the former. Social and economic rights now associated with membership were still defective or lacking altogether since they advanced only in the 19th and 20th centuries, but the emergence of a modern-contemporary conception of democracy had as its temporary byproduct the enforcement of feelings of nationality. Peoples finally shared in their sovereigns' political power but also in their bellicosity, as required by the introduction of mass conscription, again with the French Revolution. The sovereign was still able to define membership and to claim unquestionable authority: instead of kings by divine right, we had assemblies and sovereigns by *natural* right.[31] Foucault argues hereon that the modern subject is understandable only if framed within a conception of *human nature*.[32] Coherently with this idea of political sovereignty,[33] Western states tried to

---

[30]Ibidem, p. 23.

[31]This, at least, may hold in respect to radical democracy: consider for instance Rousseau's controversial "general will." According to Christopher Bertram, this idea influenced significantly Kant's moral system, as would appear from the so-called "formula of the kingdom of ends." Rousseau, it seems, rejected the very concept of a "general will" of humankind. Regardless of the (dis)similarities with Kant and Rousseau's specific positions, and between them, the modern state presents its sovereignty as *morally* and *universally* justified. And this, coupled with the dismissal of medieval theology, implies that modern politics is bound to the idea of natural -or human-rights. See Christopher Bertram, "Jean Jacques Rousseau", in Edward N. Zalta (ed.) *The Stanford Encyclopedia of Philosophy* (Winter 2012 Edition). http://plato.stanford.edu/archives/win2012/entries/rousseau/, and confront also with Robert Johnson's entry, "Kant's Moral Philosophy", in Edward N. Zalta (ed.) *The Stanford Encyclopedia of Philosophy* (Winter 2013 Edition). http:// plato.stanford.edu/archives/win2013/entries/kant-moral/, especially on "The Kingdom of Ends Formula."

[32]Michel Foucault, *The Foucault Reader*, Introduction.

[33]What I am saying here is just that sovereignty was justified by upholding human rights. My argument too is largely sympathetic to this idea, as should be apparent from the previous chapter. What I dispute is not that the state must derive its legitimacy from human rights, nor that the nation-state has been a much effective agency in eliciting their respect. Yet the limits of such institution have become apparent since at least World War I and II, when attempts at mitigating these were made through the Society of Nations and the UN. I do not believe that the solution is a Kantian "federation of states," in some substantial and (quasi)state-like sense of the word "federation." Rather we need at the very least an international community, organized around the same principles of liberty, equality, and solidarity that hold at the domestic level. Otherwise, we will suffer not only discrepancies between entitlement to rights (all human being) and entitlement to rights' enforcement (each individual citizenry). We will face also the mismatch between states committed to human rights and the international community: namely, a constant source of "war of civilization," in which some conception of human rights more or less pretentiously embodied by this or that state will instigate conflicts against another.

universalize in practice what was already recognized to be universal in principle. Each state identified itself with the mission of human progress and civilization, and the religious colonialism of the Middle Ages was substituted by a secular duty of carrying on the "White Man Burden" (Rudyard Kipling), *Zivilisation/Kultur* (Max Weber), *Civilisation* (Émile Durkheim), etc., all interpreted according to the national ideology.[34] The 18th century is therefore the origin of contemporary citizenship, with its components and problems: at least until its crisis and revision in the recent process of (de)globalization.

A critical regard can be cast on these historical and political processes. The English and French revolutions had vindicated different versions of self-government: much of the sought-after structure of "government" was explicitly debated, but the definition of "self" was sometimes strongly presupposed. But who were the people, this new sovereign, the protagonist of this progress?[35] All humanity, or a special race whose destiny was that of enlightening other nations, and maybe that of dominating them until their emancipation, or forever? Romanticism often shaped the identity of the democratic sovereign indirectly, mingling the rationality of the Enlightenment – and its neoclassic institutional ideals – with claims for culture, and tradition.[36,37] In the extreme, the

---

[34]Many modern states maintained the belief of accomplishing a religious mission. When, after World War I, such myths were almost completely abandoned, states conflated national interests and more up-to-date universal ideologies, as in the Cold War. Of course, interest and identities mattered as much as ideologies, or more.

[35]"On the surface [self-determination] seemed reasonable: let the people decide. It was in fact ridiculous because the people cannot decide until somebody decides who are the people." W. I. Jennings, *The Approach to Self-Government* (Cambridge: Cambridge University Press, 1956), p. 56; taken from C. R. Beitz, *Political Theory and International Relations* (1999), p. 106.

[36]It is not easy to distinguish the philosophical traditions which are co-responsible for the upsurge of 19th century's nationalism and ethnocentrism. Dora Kostakopoulou calls into question German Romanticism and refers to Herder (*The Future Governance*, p. 25) or to the "Herderian conception" (p. 60) while holding that "the democratic broadening of citizenship was accompanied by its progressive nationalisation." But according to Michael Forster (Michael Forster, "Johann Gottfried von Herder", in Edward N. Zalta (ed.) *The Stanford Encyclopedia of Philosophy* (Fall 2008 Edition). http://plato.stanford.edu/archives/fall2008/entries/herder/). Herder was a "committed cosmopolitan" whose cosmopolitan pluralism was much more genuine than Kant's(!). Forster suggests that the main "culprit" is instead Johann Gottlieb Fichte. This seems a convincing reading of Fiche's "Discourse to the German Nation." At any rate, what is uncontroversial is that (1) there were philosophers and ideologues committed to national supremacy of one people, one language etc. (2) they often used arguments drawn from linguistics, anthropology, geography, biology which to some degree infiltrated into the national institutions of the time (such as universities) (3) these claims were often connected to ideals such as democracy, or more frequently to self-determination (for example against the foreign power of France, as in Fichte's addresses).

[37]Eric Hobsbawm explored the tension between social and political democratization and colonialism in *The Age of Empire, 1875–1914* (New York: Pantheon Books, 1987) especially in chapter 3.

idealization of ethnicity and territory anticipated the duo "blood and soil."[38] The late 19th century's "scientific" racism could be seen as a rationalization of, or an addition to, this mishmash. Nationalistic myths and ethnocentric philosophies of history were used to back up the assumption that the cause of humanity coincided with the cause of some particular nation tasked with its "redemption."[39] The notion of citizen was ambiguous, subject to definition and redefinition by the political power and so was the idea of "human," doomed to be narrowed or denied by Darwinian, eugenicists, Nietzschean, and finally and most blatantly, Nazi theorists, and "scientists." From the very beginning, though, those who seized the power to itemize the rights of men were thereby enabled to suspend them if, according to the "general will," it would have been convenient. Agamben's theory is that the notions of "state of exception," "state of siege," and similar, which were created to deal with exceptional circumstances but soon engulfed the ordinary political process, are inherent to the shaping not only of the institution of citizenship but of modern politics altogether.[40] Foucault and Agamben's views partially converge on these points, but the former notices that for complicate reasons, among which there might be also the growth of the population and the development of modern technologies, the modern sovereign powers started dealing with matters of anthropology, race, and culture in a way much different from what was achievable before.[41] What happened as a consequence is that educational, military, and apparently neutral institutions and

---

[38] Agamben has argued that Rosenberg's usage of the couple *Blut und Bode* might be quite less original at first sight if it is understood as a reworking of the criteria which restricted the concession of citizenship from Roman law on. But this, on the other hand, could be even more concerning because it means that Nazism is not exceptional in its biopoliticization of "bare life" on the background of Western political history. See *Homo Sacer,* pp. 142–143.

[39] See for example Laura E. Gómez, *Manifest Destiny: The Making of the Mexican American Race* (New York: New York University Press, 2007).

[40] "The institution of the state of exception has its origin in the French Constituent Assembly's decree of July 8, 1791, which distinguished among *état de paix,* in which military authority and civil authority each acts in its own sphere; *état de guerre,* in which civil authority must act in concert with the military authority, and *état de siege,* in which 'all the functions entrusted to the civil authority for maintaining order and internal policing pass to the military commander, who exercises them under its exclusive responsibility'[…] The decree referred only to military strongholds and ports, but with the law of 19 Fructidor Year five, the Directory assimilated municipalities in the interior with the strongholds and, with the law of 18 Fructidor of the same year, granted itself the right to put a city in a state of siege. The subsequent history of the state of siege is the history of its gradual emancipation from the wartime situation to which it was originally bound in order to be used as an extraordinary police measure to cope with internal sedition and disorder, thus changing from a real, or military, state of siege to a fictitious or political one. In any case, it is important not to forget that the modern state of exception is a creation of the democratic-revolutionary tradition and not of the absolutist one." Giorgio Agamben, *State of Exception,* translated by Kevin Attell (Chicago: University of Chicago Press, 2005), p. 5.

[41] Michel Foucault, p. 264.

practices, like poetry, music, and literature, contributed to strengthening the modern citizens' perception of national belonging as a "second nature."

3.1.5 Nationalism and Performative Citizenship

Endowed with freedom from external interference and a unified national project as a catalyst for social cohesion, the modern state's consolidated institutions needed to instill enduring loyalty into its subjects: the result was the belief and sentiment that national membership is a firm and stable feature and one of the greatest relevance.[42] The "constitutional" power of the modern state does not concern merely the state itself: it molds and informs its citizens' lives. In its dramatic, demiurgic comprehensiveness and effectiveness, it can coexist and compete with other quintessential identities: humanity, cultures, and even familiar ties.

In the modern age, the fount of rights resides in the nation. "We, the People," was *subjectively* only the declarant of rights all persons were "endowed by their Creator," but *objectively* the legitimate sovereign entitled to their interpretation and enforcement.[43] Another presupposition is to be noted here. The backdrop of this supposedly universal and self-evident ideal of "people" included racial conceptions that often did not need even be spelled out.[44] In several contexts, these prejudices added to the most explicit restrictions imposed on those who were not "white male property owners" by the "democratic constitutions" of the time. The problem does not lie exclusively with the *content* of such discrimination, since the sphere of citizenship progressively expanded to include people of any income, women, ex-slaves, and so on. The most relevant difficulty is the tacit restriction imposed on this potentially universal demos, the *form* of exclusion that, once again, characterizes sovereignty. In other words, what most matters for this critical appraisal of nationality and citizenship are the decisions that precede democratic deliberations, and are presupposed by it. This should not belittle what was a very advanced, or maybe even the most advanced expansion of franchise achievable at the time. On the contrary, once that light is cast on the complex relations between its statement and enforcement, between principles and institutions, between depth and scope of values, it is possible to envisage a new

---

[42] See Kostakopoulou on "the essentialist conceptions of national identity", *The Future Governance*, p. 31.

[43] Agamben devotes an interesting note to the "semantic ambiguity" of the term "people," not only in the American and French Revolutions but in modern politics in general. He thinks that there is a sort of dialectic procedure through which the people is both the beginning and the end of the political process, the miserable masses and the merciful, philanthropic sovereign devoted to their emancipation. Therefore, by fighting for the emancipation of the people democracy fights against the "state of nature" that every community sees *in itself*. Compare with *Homo Sacer*, pp. 198–201.

[44] See, for example, Benjamin Franklin's worries about the increase of settlers of German ethnicities exposed in the *Observation Concerning the Increase of Mankind, Peopling of Countries Etc.*

direction which it is to take for a coherent development. According to Agamben, these political paradoxes are embodied in the historical process of the French Revolution: from the people fighting to free themselves from themselves, in the period of the Terror, to the long state of exception in which Napoleon took over, and in the end even established something very close to a new absolutism. Since in this era human rights were laid down "by the people for the people," but only by *one national or "civilized" people,* without any other limit to restrain them, or rationale to expand them, one could suggest that in addition to the definition of absolute monarchy, a system whose chronological limits are included approximately between the Westphalia treaty and the French Revolution, one could also speak of "absolute democracy" to characterize some of the institutions and conceptions that dominated the world, from then until at least the end of the Second World War.[45]

In the heyday of nationalism, even more striking contradictions took place. Consider two problematic cases: late unification and state-building that, in both cases, soon gave way to Nazi-Fascism.

The unification of Italy, like other national struggles of the time, was pursued from the perspective of vindicating political institutions in harmony with the authentic local culture and ethnicity of the country. This was, at least, the ideological justification for the role of liberator claimed by the House of Savoy. It is worth stressing that this nobility were natives of Chambéry (in the homonymous High-Savoy region), now in Southern France, and this place had remained their capital city for centuries. The Savoy were even used to speaking French within their courts and as an official language, and so did their Prime Minister the Count of Cavour when he wrote to Massimo d'Azeglio that the state of Italy had eventually been created.[46,47] To Cavour's correspondent is attributed in turn this

---

[45]This paradoxical expression refers to the fact that, since constitutions could be suspended, and no international legal-moral framework was available to serve as backup or safety net, modern democracies could "legitimately" transform themselves in totalitarian regime, as in the transitions between the French Revolution to the French Empire and the Weimar Republic surrendering its power to Nazism. These two contexts, which open and close the historical period of reference here, are cited as exemplary and analyzed at length by Agamben in *State of Exception.*

[46]"Quando i Savoia parlavano francese" ("When the Savoy Spoke French"), in *Corriere della Sera* (October 2, 1996), an interview by journalist Antonio Troiano with the historian Silvio Lanaro.

[47]"Dès ce jour, l'Italie affirme hautement en face du mond sa propre existence" ("Italy proudly affirms today in front of the world its own existence"). This famous letter is recalled and discussed by the linguist (and writer, and intellectual) Umberto Eco in a speech for the anniversary of Italian unification. Eco's lecture deals thoroughly with the role of a national language in shaping national identity. He argues that the lowest populace was Italianized only during the First World War. See *L'italiano di domani.* Accessed online May 6, 2013. http://www.quirinale.it/qrnw/statico/eventi/2011-02-lett/doc/Eco.pdf.

famous maxim: "Italy is made, now we have to make the Italians."[48] Institutional celebrations of these founding fathers have long taught Italians to see in such a statement an invitation to rise national sentiment and patriotism to match the their nation-state. But a more sobering philological and historical interpretation suggests that this expression implied that a sense of "Italianness" was in part to be invented, at least for the masses. And contrary to the usual rhetoric of "popular liberation," the process of creation worked actually from the top down. The ideological underpinning of the process of unification – natural unity of language and culture – was in fact a desired and partly artificial outcome. Even more complicated was the case with the third component of romantic national identity: religion. Catholicism was immediately adopted as a symbol by the new state, and established as the official creed, but many of the protagonists of state-building, including Cavour himself, were excommunicated for endorsing the military campaign against the Papal States. In a circular process of justification, 19th-century Italian nationalism, no less than others, shaped the cultural unity that it presupposed as its very reason for existence, while ironically, the unity "of language, of creed, of territory" was established by an excommunicated élites of French speakers.[49]

In Germany, the cause of *Einheit, Freiheit, und Macht* (unity, liberty, strength) was also pursued in the same years with a similar ambiguity. Sometimes "unification" came closer to "conquest," as in the 1866 war between Prussia and the Austrian Empire. The existence of Austria witnessed to the plurality of religions, customs, and institutions in the German world until the Nazi annexation, and so did the ancestors of the contemporary "free states" which are now part of the German Federal Republic. According to historian Geoffrey Barraclough, the public opinion in the German states and in Europe was, at the time of the Prussian campaigns, leaning toward Austria.[50] Even after the unification it was necessary to re-educate the subjects through what is now known as *Kulturkampf* ("culture struggle"). Once again, after the making of Germany, it was necessary to make Germans, and Bismarck knew this well.

Instances of the institutionalization of the modern idea of citizenship as the counterpart of national identities were not limited to the European scenario. European colonists exported their belief in a racial hierarchy in parts of the world where, for lack of centralization of power and sovereign independence of the Westphalian

---

[48]The history and also the paternity of this popular motto, which nonetheless summarizes the spirit of Italian unification, is a rather complicated question: see Carlo Formenti "Siamo una nazione ma chi ha fatto l'Italia?" ("We Are a Nation: But Who Made Italy?"), in *Corriere della Sera,* (July 17, 1993).

[49]Confront these historical cases with Kostakopoulou's rebuttal of "instrumental" nationalism "[P]erhaps, the most important weakness of the strategy of making a virtue out of the necessity of nations entails a circular reasoning whereby the fact and the reasons for it somehow converge" (*The Future Governance,* p. 51).

[50]Geoffrey Barraclough, *The Origins of Modern Germany* (Oxford: Blackwell, 1962).

kind, the existence of the very concept of "nation" was until then dubious.[51] Through contact with other civilizations, and sometimes by mimicking these, traditions were invented and strengthened, so to provide the bedrock for resisting the influence exerted by aliens. They also contributed to the integration of those who willingly welcomed the political power of the rulers. Daily practices were pervaded by the terms and tones of national identification, from flag-raising ceremonies at the workplace or school to the hymns that accompanied parades and festivals.[52] This way, citizenship was performed to such an extent that national customs were repeated as often as eating or sleeping, and as solemnly as religious rites: and these performances were soon turned into "traditions."[53] Hence the loop that connected, first, the individual sphere, (the inner, sentimental perception of belonging to a group); second, social practices like jubilees, independence days, and so on; and finally, the most essential institutions of a country (the armed forces, the police, but also the public assistance, on the wake of the modern, state-managed welfare state). The scheme appears similar to the following:

- National feelings of attachment.
- Social coordination and solidarity.
- Institutionalized performances.

This process works in both ways: from the individual persuasion of belonging to a nation stems the motivation to act in his or her group's interests and from these actions derive practices that can establish institutions. Conversely, the collective example of one's neighbors, led by state incentives,

---

[51] The most famous and most frequently discussed case is the effect of colonization on Rwanda's identity.

[52] Earlier, I mentioned in passing the importance of the Olympic games to solidify Greek national identity in the classic era. Modern sports played a similar role as well, as did arts and plays: "Existing customary traditional practices – folksong, physical contests, marksmanship – were modified, ritualized and institutionalized for the new national purposes. Traditional folksongs were supplemented by new songs in the same idiom, often composed by a schoolmaster, transferred to a choral repertoire whose content was patriotic-progressive [...] The statutes of the Federal Song Festival [...] declared its object to be 'the development and improvement of the people's singing, and the awakening of more elevated sentiments for God, Freedom and the Country, union and fraternization of the friends of Art and the Fatherland' (the word 'improvement' introduces the characteristic note of nineteenth-century progress)." *The Invention of Tradition,* edit. Eric J. Hobsbawm and Terence Rangers (New York: Cambridge University Press, 1983), p. 6.

[53] See Hobsbawm: "[Traditions] seem to belong to three overlapping types: a) those establishing or symbolizing social cohesion or the membership of groups, real or artificial communities b) those establishing or legitimizing institutions, status or relations of authority, and c) those whose main purpose was socialization, the inculcation of beliefs, value systems and conventions of behavior. [T]ype a) was prevalent, the other functions being regarded as implicit in or flowing from a sense of identification with a 'community' and/or the institutions representing, expressing or symbolizing it such as a 'nation'." Ibidem, p. 9.

eventually elicits one's conformity. With the help of arts and literature, what Benedict Anderson defines as "imagined communities" were powerfully reinforced, and they ceased to be mere imaginations from the legal and political – although not the sociological – perspective. The media also had an important role in this, as revealed by the use of national broadcasting institutions not only by dictators, even if outstandingly by them, but also by democratic programs sincerely committed to, say, alphabetization. Dictionaries and schools became another instrument for the consolidation of nationalism. National languages gradually replaced Latin, Arabic, or, in southern Asia, Sanskrit, and by this very process, they absorbed something of the religious sacredness of their predecessors.[54]

3.2 Local Communities and Universal Rights

> Thus, in reality, the claim of traditional nationalism has often been inverted – it is not the identity of a nation that has set the boundaries of the state but the existence of the state has created a sense of national identity. –Peter Jones[55]

Among the various instantiations of membership listed in the previous section, commonalities include some sets of rights and duties to be specifically characterized by the particular social and political context. Thus in ancient Athens, for instance, the right to speak in assembly was coupled with the duty to participate in the military, and the same duty to serve in war accompanied the medieval count's right to collect taxes and the revolutionary Frenchman's universal suffrage. Only for the most egalitarian of these forms of citizenships, one could argue that an equal – or balanced – set of rights and duties compensated for social divisions: this is perhaps a characteristic divide between modern and pre-modern citizenship. Yet in each case, both rights and duties are normative relations between human beings, and they presuppose the recognition of the humanity of the right or duty-bearer. This brings us back to the "citizenship gap" – between universal rights and local institutions – and to consider ways it could be filled by future models of citizenship. This gap has to do, essentially, with the relations between citizenship, human rights, and liberty: since *human* rights are defended mainly by *national* institutions, the equal protection of all under the law remains partly *subjective*.

---

[54]Benedict Anderson, *Imagined Communities: Reflections on the Origin and Spread of Nationalism* (New York: Verso, 1991), pp. 37–47.
[55]Peter Jones, *Rights* (London: Macmillan, 1994).

3.2.1 Subjective and Objective Citizenship: Main Distinctions

Subjective citizenship is the set of normative relations (rights and duties) that an individual possesses within the context of the individual's community.[56]

What is of central relevance here is the word "community." Consider the citizenship of a country. Thanks to, say, Danish citizenship, one has the right to vote (that is, among other rights, the power to enable some of one's fellow citizens to create, modify, and repeal national laws, therefore altering one's normative condition), the right and duty to pay taxes (a liberty right, coming with a claim right not to be asked to pay it twice, etc.), the right to cross some borders (e.g. within the EU) without a VISA (again, essentially a liberty right) and many others.[57] But one also has rights and duties with respect to fellow human beings, according to the Universal Declaration and many other written and unwritten moral and legal codes, both at the national and international level. In short, with the Universal Declaration's opening of the age of cosmopolitan norms, the community recognizing the *subjects* of rights enforcement switches from the nation-state to humanity as such.

Except for extraordinary circumstances, such as the fictional encounter between Robinson Crusoe and Friday, two apparently obvious reasons make the "citizenship gap" less visible in practice:

(1) The majority of human beings (except for some stateless and citizens of failed states) already belong to a state that is relatively capable of enforcing laws, that is, to realize rights and duties. This means that in many cases, subjective citizenship is almost completely realized *nationally,* and that universal subjective citizenship would simply be, in this fashion, a reinstantiation or abstraction of minimal national citizenship on a global scale.

---

[56]Confront with the definitions given in Dominique Leydet, "Citizenship", in Edward N. Zalta (ed.) *The Stanford Encyclopedia of Philosophy* (Fall 2011 Edition). http://plato.stanford.edu/archives/fall2011/entries/citizenship/: "A citizen is a member of a political community who enjoys the rights and assumes the duties of membership. This broad definition is discernible, with minor variations, in the works of contemporary authors as well as in the entry 'citoyen' in Diderot's and d'Alembert's *Encyclopédie* [1753][. . .] The concept of citizenship is composed of three main elements or dimensions[. . .] *The first is citizenship as legal status, defined by civil, political and social rights* (emphasis added)[. . .] The second considers citizens specifically as political agents, actively participating in a society's political institutions. The third refers to citizenship as membership in a political community that furnishes a distinct source of identity." As should appear from the last section, I consider these three dimensions to be closely intertwined, as Leydet himself does (see the discussion that follows the quoted excerpt in his entry).
[57]It has already been mentioned in Chapter 1 above that liberties are of consequence only when "embedded" in claim rights, at least of a negative kind ("I have the liberty to read" = I have the claim against someone interfering with my reading).

(2) When people de facto lack such citizenship, the perspective solution that is naturally considered is merely the adoption of a national citizenship (naturalization in the case of the stateless; state reform when it comes to failed states). So in the framework of the *already existing* cosmopolitan rights, rights that bind together directly individuals and international institutions, it is undeniable that one acts as a member of a community when one infringes rights or duties in regards to *any* individual.[58]

Objective citizenship is the set of laws, institutions, and organizations through which a community secures the enjoyment of the rights and the fulfillment of the duties possessed by its members.

Objective citizenship might also be presented as a symmetric counterpart of subjective citizenship: *the set of normative relations[. . .] of a community with respect to each of its members.* Of course, the matching between the two dimensions is a matter of perspectives, as well as of the material and practical realization of the normative relations that hold – morally, legally, politically, etc.– at the subjective level.[59] There is a reason, though, that suggested substituting "norms" with the objective realizations responsible for their enforcement. The mismatch between subjective and objective is in fact less apparent, even if just as substantial, with specular definitions. Again rephrasing, subjective citizenship is the endowment with rights (concretely, the citizen endowed with rights and duties), while objective citizenship consists of the appointee to rights enforcing (the community the subject belongs to in all its components). Examples of objective citizenship at work might be those of defense forces who must protect fellow citizens from an ongoing emergency, or the national healthcare that campaigns in a territory to prevent diseases, and the like. Subjective citizenship is the mere endowment, even in principle, with rights, such as through the Universal Declaration – a pillar of (subjective) global citizenship.

3.2.2 Subjective and Objective Citizenship: A Closer Inspection

The distinction just introduced is as important as it is open to misunderstandings. To clarify, consider the Hohfeldian incidents mentioned in Section 1.1.1. All those

---

[58]A relevant part of the issue discussed in this work has to do more with "cosmopolist" claims than with "cosmopolitan" claims. Deciding whether we are confronting a "global polity (polis)" or not is not only a matter of sociological and anthropological research: it depends on the conceptual definition of polity that we adopt. To this regard, I believe that Arendts's claim that we are already living in "one world" is today even sounder than when it was pronounced.

[59]Including because of the rather complex relations between rights and duties I mentioned in the first chapter. But this is not the focal problem here anymore.

listed hereunder are legal rights.[60] The example is meant to illustrate that, for what concerns national citizenship, rights are specified in detail and they are immediately and clearly linked to institutionalized realizations. International human rights are different: it is left unclear who is to provide, for example, a right to a shelter (Universal Declaration Art. 25), namely whether it is the state itself or the organizations and individuals in the country, whether the right is positive (one is entitled to be given a shelter) or negative (one is entitled *not* to have their shelter destroyed), etc.

Hohfeldian Incidents	Subjective Citizenship	Objective Citizenship
Liberty/ Privilege	I have the liberty to think whatever it pleases me	X
Claim	I have the right	That my country's public school system accepts my children
Power	I have the power	To sign a contract
Immunity	I have an immunity	From discrimination against me

It has therefore been argued that citizenship stands for a bundle of normative relations (between right holders and duty bearers, and everyone may hold both roles at once) whose most fundamental and original instantiation consists in human rights (and their correlative duties). Now, while we can see the subjective component of this condition widely realized, the objective component is far from established globally, as many individuals do not have their fundamental rights protected nor can they exercise them lacking an adequate institutional structure that enforces them. This lack of a realization is not only due to practical difficulties but also to the incompleteness of the global framework of rights and duties. All persons are endowed with rights such as those listed in the Universal Declaration, but the issues become more complex and contested when it comes to the complete analysis of these rights and their correlative duties in terms of their ascription to national and international institutions (and the individuals within them). The difficulty is first of all theoretical since we are not used to thinking *outside* the box of the nation-state. It must be stressed that this leap in thinking does not merely amount to *abandoning* the framework of the nation-state: *beyond* is not a synonym for *without*.

The distinction is therefore aimed at highlighting both the subjective and the intersubjective aspects of citizenship. These latter become more apparent when we consider the correlative duties that rights impose on other persons. From a strictly legal positivist perspective, it would be hard to disentangle the subjective existence of a right from its effective enforcement. In this way, the two components of citizenship

---

[60]I speak here of legal rights, but it is worth noticing that human rights – and therefore the right that I attribute to universal citizenship – have a complex relation with moral rights. For this issue, see Amartya Sen, "Elements of a Theory of Human Rights", in *Philosophy and Public Affairs* (Fall 2004), 32, 4, especially section III: "Ethics and Law."

would simply represent parts that cannot be disjointed. The distinction would thus collapse into something very close to the Hegelian couple "abstract right – *Sittlichkeit.*"[61]

A question thus naturally follows: are the duties of objective citizenship merely a complex aggregate of individuals' and institutions' duties? Or perhaps in this case as well the whole is more than the sum of the parts? This depends on whether we accept a form of moral/political emergentism or a moral/political reductionism, a problem that would need specific research to be properly addressed, and that verges on metaphysics. Here I use the word *community* to leave the door open to emergentism, but I will not rule out the possibility that problems of collective agencies are avoided simply by employing a complete analysis. Furthermore, the word *community* is of classic usage in similar contexts.[62]

The problem with the current world order – and I refer to its *de jure* condition, not merely to its rather concerning state *de facto* – is that much objective citizenship is missing. States are essentially, constitutively focused on the human rights and national rights of their subjects, sometimes confounding the two. While I will later elaborate on the merits and legitimacy of these national priorities, it is also true that the state derives its ultimate and most substantial legitimization from the prevention of human rights abuse against all. This is also implied by the theories of the state of exception, and of the natural ties arising from the state of nature, that have been recalled above. The many local and particular justifications, such as the origin of the state as a "family" of people with tight blood ties, can accompany and integrate but cannot substitute this central legitimization. When one reflects upon it, the very idea of the international recognition of sovereignty and the limitations to the state of war are both predicated on each state being recognized as an entity compatible with the freedom and rights of all and not merely with its citizens.

States are therefore legitimated by justice, in the twofold sense of the word that, as we have seen, Rawls attributed to it: (1) the establishment of just institutions and (2) the establishment of just distributions under them.[63] Noncitizens' human rights can appear as "subsidiary" rights, as it happened historically. But in reality, these rights are far from accidental. If individual A has a human right to X, state B has also a natural duty to enable A to enjoy X – either by acting or

---

[61]"Hegel passes from the abstract individualism of 'Abstract Right' to the social determinacies of 'Sittlichkeit' or 'Ethical Life' via considerations first of 'wrong' (the negation of right) and its punishment (the negation of wrong, and hence the 'negation of the negation' of the original right), and then of 'morality,' conceived more or less as an internalization of the external legal relations." See Paul Redding, "Georg Wilhelm Friedrich Hegel", in Edward N. Zalta (ed.) *The Stanford Encyclopedia of Philosophy* (Winter 2013 Edition). http://plato.stanford.edu/archives/win2013/entries/hegel/. I am indebted to Ian Carter for noticing this correspondence.

[62]"Kant's idea, conceived on the model of the physical principle of action and reaction, was structured by the category of '*community*' or reciprocal interaction[...]": Paul Redding, "Georg Wilhelm Friedrich Hegel", emphasis added.

[63]In section 1.2.4.

abstaining – no matter if (s)he is a national or not. If A is not a national of B, A might hold another state responsible, and therefore B's direct duty would be principally or exclusively a negative duty not to interfere. Probably, the state will have a much more restricted *possibility* to intervene in this latter case than if the right were to be claimed within its borders. Yet theoretically, this can imply only an inferior degree of liability: the relationship is not *qualitatively* different. The existence of a world order of independent nation-states disguises this state of things, since each state protects its members' rights, be they human rights or rights of a different sort. A more fundamental relationship between citizens and political authorities becomes visible in rare cases like migrations, collapsing states, and above all refugees. If the general cause of nation-states conflicted with human rights, there would be no doubt that the latter has precedence over it. Yet this needs not to be the case. What happened historically – for instance, with Nazi Fascism – is that this or that particular state made its existence incompatible with human rights for all. And it was the state that ultimately had to yield: as a matter of fact that aligns with a matter of principle.

3.2.3 Objective National Citizenship, Subjective International Citizenship, and Objective International Citizenship

It seems that at least two reasons back the assumption that we would require much stronger international institutions and possibly also a more workable distinction between the essence of any given nation-state and the essence of citizenship based on human rights. The first is that a great deal of coercion, the certainty of state's intervention, and well-defined legal rights are necessary before violations of human rights end. The largest national expenses are usually on healthcare, other essential services, and armed forces, rather than matters that would be so culturally determined to appear obscure to other countries. The state's gird is the defense of human rights, and its self-preservation – that is, sovereignty. And the interests manifested by the people, say in protests or voting, very often revolve around these very issues. There is little hope that tasks that the nation-states find arduous to solve can be settled without a great level of international integration. In short, *the domestic and international legitimacy of a nation-state is based on its respect for human rights more than anything else.* Yet the understanding of these human rights should be all-encompassing rather than a culturally determined cherry-picking based on a peculiar perspective. Also, this core legitimacy does not imply the existence of a more or less formal international tribunal tasked with assessing any given state's legitimacy.

The second reason has to do with procedures, it has to do with the way rights are discerned and enforced: without an international, impartial, and stable order, the sanctioning of justice will be exposed to the risks of arbitrariness and paternalism. We have seen that the right "to rule and be ruled" played a very important role in the history of citizenship. It is at least dubious that without some reciprocity in the relation between world citizens and world sovereigns both sides of citizenship, the subjective and the objective, would develop substantially. If world institutions are to hold any authority, they are to be ruled in turn. They need to be the genuine and equitable expression of the entire world's population, of humanity as such. And this is no mere practical challenge. It has to do with what Benhabib sees as the central feature of the "cosmopolitan right."[64] "International norms of justice" consist of direct normative relations according to which, as in the case of Eichmann, an international institution or a state acting as a proxy for it can act sovereignly over an individual.[65] This kind of norms superseded the previous model, that of international treaties understood as agreements among sovereign states only. But the counterpart to these "cosmopolitan norms" is still lacking. If there are new laws, it is not unreasonable to expect new forms of lawmaking and also new forms of control for law enforcement. An assembly of nations, such as the UN, despite its centrality in this new age, might not be enough for such a requirement: they would at least require radical reform.[66] World citizens still lack direct and equitable political relations with the international order. *In short, even the subjective parts of international citizenship need institutions and rules to be correctly administered.* Thus the *objective* element of citizenship needed to give rise to a substantial international, human rights-based citizenship is still partly missing too.

3.2.4 National and Universal Citizenship

In well-established nation-states, though, the objective citizenship that is lacking is, of course, not the same for all. A national relies on institutions enforcing all his or her rights and asking from him or her the fulfillment of his or her duties, be they "human" (universal) or merely national. Still, according to the definitions of citizenship I suggested, one is objectively a citizen in many senses, depending on the community considered. The international order endows one with rights and duties toward humanity, independently from one's belonging to one's own country or any country at all. In this sense, one has some clear normative

---

[64]As we have seen, she draws this very concept from Arendt and Kant.

[65]See above, section 1.2.2.

[66]A model that comes to mind here is the one pursued by Daniele Archibugi and David Held, who also inspired and collected similar proposals for reform (see for instance Daniele Archibugi and David Held (eds.) *Cosmopolitan Democracy: An Agenda for a New World Order* (Cambridge: Polity Press, 1995)). However, a number of considerations are in order to qualify their model of a strong, direct cosmopolitan democracy to override national sovereignty. First, in the current age – as opposed to 1995 and much of the past decades – such proposals are even less realistic due to the polarized, fragmented conditions of the international environment. Second, the centrality of sovereignty in any post-Westphalian system makes such a picture unrealistic even on a broader view and a longer run: and were it to be realized, it could be skewed by the framing given by the most powerful states. Third, the gap between global politics and life at the individual level is too large not to require filling by intermediary bodies. Democracy could not be exercised on such a scale, and there would rather emerge a risk of assembling an either ineffectively chaotic or powerfully dangerous Leviathan.

relations, even if these are mostly subjective and not immediately enforceable. If citizenship is a set of rights and duties, in reality, every human being is already a "citizen of the world."

Global citizenship: A is a global (minimal, non-national, essential[...]) citizen of B if and only if A has a "right to have rights" under B's sovereignty.[67]

In fact, if we accord rights to human beings only, one bearing rights implies that one is also endowed with *human* rights and that one is a member of the international community which in turn, according to "cosmopolitan norms of justice" is directly bound by international institutions, states, and states' assemblies at all levels.[68] What is more problematic, though, is the mention of *sovereignty*. Since it is not appropriate to speak of global sovereignty as though such a principle were already fully realized, I believe that, at any rate, for the moment a very thin form of global citizenship is generally enjoyable, for example by a tourist, only within the territory of some nation-states and depending on the bilateral relations between these.[69] Another and more restrictive formula can represent national citizenship:

National citizenship: A is a national (maximal, local, accidental) citizen of B if and only if A has a "right to (full) national rights" under B's sovereignty.

Some clarifications are in order. First, the second formula is merely a specific instantiation of the previous, since one must possess the right to have rights of any sort to be endowed with national rights.[70] In other words, national citizenship is a subset of global citizenship. There is nothing counter-intuitive in this specification. What sounds unnatural, and for someone perhaps wrong or absurd, is calling national citizenship "accidental." This adjective is not meant to suggest that national citizenship is "less relevant": to the contrary, I have claimed that objective citizenship – be it national or global – is currently realized by and large by national institutions. Let me voice for a moment possible reasoning by a "classic nationalist," according to which national differences are first of all *a fact*. There are many reasons to consider citizenship as inherently bound to at least one nation state. Some of these reasons are statistical or historical: almost all of us are national citizens by birth, and our states have been for millenniums the only appointees to rights enforcement.[71] One could respond to these that as a matter of

---

[67]That is equivalent to saying that A "possesses the status of a rights-bearer."

[68]This is obviously disputable: things and animals according to some scholarships are rights-bearer too. I do not want to dismiss nor to discuss such an issue, simply because my thesis focuses on human citizenship. In principle, I think those views might be compatible with my argument depending on how they are restated, expanded and precised.

[69]Not in the sense we usually attribute to the word sovereignty. Of course, if a theory of "spheres of sovereignties" is developed, speaking of an international sovereign would be suitable even without revolutionary changes in the objective international citizenship institutional framework. But as a matter of fact, it seems that we are still far from living within any such scenario. See *People Out of Place,* for example the conclusion.

[70]Again, or the "status of a statuses-recipient."

[71]Think of an orphan found aboard a raft in the mid Mediterranean Sea, or of children born on airplane.

fact there are also people who lack any national citizenship and then recall the normative requirements of the Universal Declaration which sanctions the existence of a right not only to have citizenship but to change citizenship, which is here more relevant.[72] Few that they may be – and they are not so few in reality – there are stateless and denaturalized people, refugees, and exilees. Citizenship in a particular country is neither innate nor impossible to loose: it is *accidental* also in the sense that some of the rights it specifically protects are additional to fundamental rights, while others are a *national* interpretation of the former.

3.2.5 National and International Rights

It would be hard to spell out every aspect of citizenship in Hohfeldian terms. National citizenship entails a large bundle of rights and duties, indeed *all* the legal rights and duties that were conceivable until a very recent time. The national sphere encompassed, especially in the past, another large share of the *moral* obligations one felt compelled to observe in one's life. The "right to have rights" involves liberties and claims, immunities, and powers since it affects the whole sphere of normative relations between citizens and the state.[73] Powers are among the most distinctive characteristics of national citizens, as they allow them to modify other norms (e.g. through voting). Nonetheless, the divide between the two cuts across the whole spectrum of normative incidents.

The "citizenship gap" is understandable not merely as a gap between subjective and objective citizenship but also as a gap between global and national rights, and in particular as a difference in terms of powers and immunities. The citizenship of the future might consist in the empowerment of noncitizens rather than a dismissal of the nation-state, and in a reappraisal of national rights as backed up by international, fundamental citizenship. The full accomplishment of decolonization, the reform of the UN, and the establishment of more equitable mutual relationships between all states are some of the central pillars among the desirable developments in objective global citizenship. As it happens, none of these threatens "national rights" per se.

3.2.6 The Requirements of Global Citizenship

How is it possible for the development of global citizenship to take place? As mentioned in Section 1.2.2, I believe that the safest and most appropriate way to deal with issues related to global citizenship is by contrasting injustices that arise systematically and

---

[72]The Universal Declaration's Article 15 reads of a right to *nationality*. Disentangling citizenship and nationality would be hard, and depend on the specific context. I use the two terms as synonymous here. A national is, according to the Oxford Dictionary, "a citizen of a country."

[73]I recall here for the last time the fact that in a legal system all rights are usually entrenched in a system of negative and positive claim rights, for example that of abstaining from interference, which refers to other individuals, and that of intervening in case of rights violation, that affects institutions especially.

progressively: "locally," so to speak, that is, one by one. This means that practices are needed in order to improve each party's ability to resolve inequalities and other problems through agreements rather than force or coercion of any kind. Possible examples are a renewal in international relations to encompass both multi and bilateral cooperation and institutions, activism, and information campaigns, but legal reform will necessarily accompany practices on many occasions.

No social class or nationality should be excluded: cosmopolitanism is actually both a fact and an urgency since according to IOM data, in 2020 there were about 281 million people living outside their country of birth, that is 3.6% of the global population.

Possible agencies for the improvement of global citizenship are easy to find: besides already existing international institutions and the activism of concerned citizens – or even more concerned stateless and displaced people – the push for progress should come from reasonable states. These latter would share with citizens the interest to lay the foundations for a harmonious, pluralistic, cooperative international community that every individual and every people can consider a home.

For the moment, I merely consider some of the features of the world order that would be consistent with such global citizenship, in particular with the objective international citizenship that I believe to be especially in need of development. There would also be very relevant practices and legal reforms to be realized at the national level to which Bohman's expression "cosmopolitanism at home" is particularly suited. Yet the variability of national contexts is too great to advance general considerations in this sphere. In the following Chapter 3, I will expound more on this duality and discuss to which extent it is substantial rather than apparent. Another specification is needed: consistently with the method I delineated already, I do not need, in Marx's words, to write "recipes for the cookshops of the future": that is, to spell out a complete global structure.[74] It should suffice to specify that the model I have in mind differs from a global state and also from a federation. This is why I generally talked of institutions or world-order or similarly general terms thus far.

The first problem to consider is *coercion*. As I recalled before, Blake suggests this feature as the distinguishing characteristic that allows for a stricter distributive standard. It is not necessary to reject such a claim. It suffices to remark that, in the actual world order, states sometimes possess even larger coercive powers against nonnationals than against nationals. For the moment, states have only a few direct commitments to the improvement of the most basic human rights in a foreign country but for a matter of "charity."[75] States, therefore, take part more or less at their discretion in assistance programs, and ordinary diplomatic and economic relations, which affect the quality of human-rights observance in other countries, even without considering distributions concerned with relative deprivation. Through

---

[74]Given the unpredictability of history and politics, and the enormous disparity between an individual's field of vision and the global scale, such an attempt would be at risk of being useless even if it were the unique focus: and as explained in the Introduction, this is not the case here.

[75]Interestingly, Blake has recently shifted his focus to issues of "mercy": Michael Blake, *Justice, Migration, and Mercy* (Oxford: Oxford University Press, 2020).

these means, a state influences another in ways that are hard to measure but virtually unconstrained. Suppose state A is a powerful and affluent country that established with B, a very poor and under-developed country, close ties of cooperation. B is dependent on A's monetary aid, especially as regards vaccine campaigns to eradicate mortal diseases. At one point, the two states come into conflict over a completely independent matter, say B's reform of the education system. By threatening to stop financing B's health system, A coerces it to adopt its favorite policies instead of what B's citizens and authorities prefer. Such a threat, through skilled diplomacy, need not be explicitly formulated. If B does not comply with A's requests, many citizens will be abandoned to death. And therefore a foreign government influences sovereign decisions to an extent that would be impossible domestically, as a government cannot threaten the withdrawal of life-saving measures in order to be re-elected. Such international blackmails, which define the two-tier model of domestic and international justice elaborated by "global justice theorists," would also be technically legal.[76] Redirecting millions originally destined for humanitarian aid can be as coercive as punishing a crime, and yet this is something sovereign states can do freely. A perhaps greater source of coercion is to be seen in military power. Historical reasons, including colonialism, have provoked an enormous gap between countries in such matters. About one-tenth of the world population contributes for more than half of the military expenditures.[77] And the countries with the largest armed forces are those very ones that are members of the UN Security Council. With the liberty that nation-states actually enjoy about military expenditures, there is no way to avoid coercion – both perceived and exerted – stronger than that applied to the country's nationals: against these latter, at least, waging war is not possible. Outright violence explodes only in rare circumstances. But obviously, *potential* coercion is in politics *effective* coercion. Finally, besides the economic, diplomatic, and military imbalances that have been recalled, one should not forget other means, ranging from mediatic influence to intelligence agencies. Unless the coercive power is distributed and more safely controlled than at present, and possibly also globally diminished, there is no hope of obtaining equal global citizenship in the near future.

A similar argument applies to the *distribution of goods and resources*. Again, I am not rejecting Nagel's distinction between two different standards, domestic and global, for distributive justice. However, one of the assumptions of Nagel's argument itself is that the issue of absolute deprivation should be tackled independently. As with military power, economic influence can make one country's sovereignty fade together with its citizens' autonomy. If the means to achieve a standard of mere subsistence are controlled by foreign powers over which one lacks any direct influence, nondomination becomes impossible to achieve. As Sangiovanni writes, the fact that we have two legitimate and different rationales for distribution does not mean that there is *no* global distribution required by

---

[76]See chapter 1 section 1.2.4.

[77]Figures are available on the website of the Stockholm International Peace Research Institute.

justice.[78] This leaves the door open to a distribution that makes economic resources sufficient for the establishment and the protection of human rights regimes worldwide and maybe even more just than that bare minimum.

Another issue I would signal briefly is the problem of *political representation* that I mentioned before. In the actual conditions, persons are represented in international institutions almost exclusively through their nation-states' mediation. This creates blatant democratic imbalances, with states whose population exceeds one billion people having one vote only, just like a tiny island state. Thus, internal lacks of democracy are also magnified by international institutions. An oligarchy representing the interests of a minority can therefore use the international system as a platform to extend its domination to other countries, instead of being pushed by it to give it up. As I mentioned in a previous note, I do not believe that Daniele Archibugi and David Held's proposals for cosmopolitan direct representation independent of nationality would be the solution.

The main perspective to solve such problems is rather a reform of global institutions based on the sovereign equalities of peoples and states, as well as on democratic principles granting global masses a corresponding voice. It is not concessions, "charity," or "mercy" that are needed. What is called for is the dissolution of colonial ties and of the imbalances that put poorer and less technologically developed countries on an uneven playing field.

Two last directions for the evolution of global citizenship are in my opinion worth stressing. As proved by the history of nation-states, *culture,* and *social ties* are indispensable means to create and maintain cohesion. If we are left without common languages for communication, and secure contexts for strengthening the "global civil society," institutions will appear distant, void, and ineffective. The lack of a global *demos* is not only a matter of fact: it is also a considerable obstacle on the way of addressing issues of global injustices *already* present.[79] National media and information are in some cases too limited to encompass all the relevant effects of actions and inactions. Direct access to independent sources, alternative points of view, and personal exchanges would facilitate the removal of prejudices and undermine the ability of national agencies to reshape reality according to restricted horizons. We need a cosmopolitan education centered on equality and diversity: of languages, experiences, and, to some extent, even values. Only by unleashing the energies of humanity by removing any reins of unilateral domination can global understanding and ultimately, global citizenship flourish.

These listed are just some possible directions along which world citizenship could evolve. They are all compatible with the survival of the nation-state – they actually *require* it to play a reasonable, balanced, and healthy role, to some extent – but they would integrate its intact sovereignty within the framework of a harmonic global community that dares realize substantially the promise of global citizenship.

---

[78]See Sangiovanni, "Global Justice," p. 4.
[79]See Nagel, "The Problem," p. 143.

3.2.7 Negative and Limited Rights

The rights of universal citizenship might not be always distinguishable from national rights since the state has been and to some extent still remains the source of both. Two features of universal rights may be stressed, despite their not being enough for a full account.[80]

First, a significant range of universal rights consists of negative rights. Sometimes, refraining from interference – or protecting from interference – is all that is due to nationals and human beings in general. This is evidently true if we consider again the natural and implicit ties that, according to Waldron, bind each human being to just institutions. If a foreign state is effectively safeguarding its nationals' rights, one is not allowed to reject the state's authority. This does not rule out human rights violations in foreign countries only but also nationalistic dismissals of a foreign state's dignity. As to noncitizen momentarily or permanently living outside of their countries, their negative rights may include them not being deported if unnecessary, their being exempted from observance of some national customs if avoidable and so on. Nonnational citizenship is composed, of course, mainly of essential rights like liberty rights which are considered human rights, and the associated claims have as correlatives negative duties of non-intervention by the state. In some cases, however – say assistance to shipwrecked foreigners – duties and rights are of a positive nature, even when it comes to non-citizens.

Second, thanks to the international order it presupposes, international citizenship implies also indirect and limited rights, with some exceptions (like in the extreme case of refugees). If a foreigner falls ill and is in need of immediate assistance, (s)he can be given it and then be returned to his or her motherland as soon as possible, instead of receiving the follow-ups that would be dedicated to nationals. In many particular cases, it would prove convenient for the state itself to provide additional help, but in the theoretical scheme of global citizenship, I think there could be a place for continuing to reserve services and resources to nationals only. The very same holds with regard to welfare, healthcare, and so on. Since international citizenship is conceptually paired with international institutions, many positive rights it requires could be met through indirect interventions by the nation-states, through conventions and treaties between states or through direct intervention backed up by international assistance. In general, my point is that global rights often consist of negative and limited rights; therefore, the realization of objective global citizenship is not necessarily onerous.

3.2.8 The Problem of Enforcement

What happens when human rights – and objective global citizenship – are violated by a state?

Some cases are and will remain controversial. An example could be the toleration of polygamy: according to a majority, this institution violates a human right to equality between the sexes, but according to many others it does not. In a context

---

[80]It is important to remark that I do not hold either to be necessary or sufficient to distinguish fundamental and national rights: but they can be both useful.

where the right (not) to marry freely is beyond dispute and emigration is always an option – and notice that both are granted by the Universal Declaration already – the issue will spark controversies and elicit legal, political, cultural, philosophical and anthropological reflections, but would not amount to a massive violation that demands intervention.

Other cases are more problematic: for instance, Female Genital Mutilation (FGM). Here we consider a grave violation of bodily integrity. Yet by no coincidence, there is no state in the world where the practice is explicitly legalized. Therefore, the responsibility does not lie entirely on states' institutions, and intervening in them would often be off the mark. A different case is represented by the death penalty, especially when carried out relatively often and with cruel and degrading means. Yet once again, opinions on the subject vary widely: many would argue that capital punishment is *not* incompatible with human rights, and even those who are of the opposite persuasion would believe that direct, coercive intervention would be illegitimate and/or counterproductive. For all these three examples, intercultural dialogs, research, and sensitization campaigns seem more appropriate.

Finally, there are exceptional, rare, and dramatic circumstances where state institutions are responsible for massive, grave violations of human rights. I am thinking of the clearest example of genocidal actions carried out against one's own people or against foreigners. In such cases, when the dozens, the hundreds, and the millions are threatened with loss of limbs and life, intervention can be a proportionate response. Sometimes armed intervention is possible and appropriate. Other times, coercion through international pressure, sanctions, embargoes, and other means will suffice. In any case, the ethical principle of nonmaleficence[81] – and a strict proportionality – you cannot kill a million innocents to save a 100,000 – should be strictly adhered to. Calculations on these matters should be comprehensive and include consequences in the long run: when in doubt, prudence and caution should prevail over the impulse to interfere.

In a subset of cases – the exceptions within the exceptions – it will be within the remit and duties of one state to act rapidly. But in most cases, it will be the international community as a whole that decides democratically through its established mechanisms. No state should arrogate the monopoly of "humanity" to pursue its unilateral goals and agendas at the expense of global justice and peace.

What I am sketching is of course no new theory: rather I hope to offer a balanced interpretation of the principles already enshrined in the Charter of the UN and in the more recent reflection on the Responsibility to Protect as detailed in the Outcome Document of the 2005 World Summit.

3.2.9 Globalizing Marshall

Thomas H. Marshall famously argued that citizenship rights widened gradually in the last two to three centuries, from *civil* rights in the era of revolutions to *political* rights between the 19th to mid-20th centuries to full *socioeconomic* rights in the contemporary age. It is not clear whether something similar is likely to happen globally since the

---

[81] *Primum non nocere*: "first, do no harm."

Declaration and the following documents issued by the UN and international institutions cover a broad range of diverse rights. It is also true that the very analysis by Marshall is somewhat at tension with the mutual support these rights give one another: the right to vote facilitates the introduction of welfare measures, and the welfare enables people to cultivate their political conscience, for instance. As mentioned, the key lack in objective global citizenship is in political rights, but of course, world hunger plays a fundamental role in diminishing the influence of poor countries, so once again we witness a vicious cycle. What seems to be crucial here, though, is not the particularity of each set of rights described by Marshall, as much as the insight he had on the function socioeconomic rights performed in establishing a standard of equality that allowed other inequalities to take place. Through socioeconomic rights, the nation-state was able to secure social peace and loyalty by providing even the worse off with a platform of fairness and a source of gratitude.[82] I think this model should be applicable to matters of global justice. What matters is not, as Nagel has shown, the illegitimate claim for the abolition of relative inequalities. It is rather that a minimal standard is met, so as to allow less vital inequalities – or rather, differences – to take place. This "globalization" of Marshall's argument has two dimensions. One concerns material equality: all human beings must be helped reach a threshold of decent life.[83] Otherwise, discussing international justice would always be as dramatic as dealing with war. The other dimension of the "globalization of Marshall" is the cultural dimension I already stressed when emphasizing the role of education for global citizenship. After that a universal, humane standard is met, national differences are not only welcomed, but cherished. The problem is not the prevailing of this culture over the other, but that of identifying and defending a common measure of humanity that all cultures, all nation-states, can embody. For example, patriotic beliefs should be tolerated and encouraged, as long as they shun racism and discriminatory practices. So the two "floors" of equality on which inequalities could legitimately stand are (1) providing the necessary for subsistence in a very literal sense and (2) the basic acceptance of human rights and the inherent dignity of all persons, after which cultural disagreements and peculiar practices find their proper place.

3.2.10 Latitudinal Citizenship

Marshall pays almost no attention to transnational diversity. He sets forth an explanatory model that can be successfully applied to many European and non-European nation-states, even if it naturally assumes an Anglo-centric perspective.[84] In fact, the dawn of modern citizenship coincides with universal

---

[82] I use social to point to refer peace achieved by tackling social inequalities.

[83] This is a rather literal reading of Marshall, but applied to a context which differs from the nation-state he was theorizing about: a common standard of socioeconomic equality would grant "a general enrichment of the concrete substance of civilized life, the general reduction of risk and insecurity, an equalization between the more and less fortunate at all levels." Thomas. H. Marshall, *Citizenship and Social Class* (Cambridge: Cambridge University Press, 1950), pp. 102–103.

[84] See the discussion in Kostakopoulou, *The Future Governance of Citizenship*, pp. 28–30.

declarations recognizing civil rights to all human beings, thereby creating tension between the national and international dimensions of citizenship. According to Marshall, citizenship is inherently international because parallel standards of equality can be created in different nation-states, as happened in Europe in the last century. It comes as no surprise that nationals somehow see their foreign neighbors as peers, since most substantial sources of identification, like lifestyle and economic standing, have been met to the same extent by all of them. If citizenship is a set of rights and duties, we have also *latitudinal* citizenship(s) which cuts across national borders and gathers together people with the same culture, with the same income, job, religion, language, or even the same ethnicity.[85] From diplomacy to business, from religion to sports, people find their "fellow citizens" across borders when they unite in the pursuit of shared causes and interests. And this happens at the bottom of the socioeconomic pyramid as well: with low-class employees in fast-food chains, migrant plantation workers, or even laborers who solidarize as they are exploited in sweatshops, which is the case analyzed by Ahiwa Ong. Her account is particularly focused on economics, but I hold that the concept of "latitudes of citizenship" is a useful device while confronting transnational memberships of other forms also. In Ong's analysis, "latitudes of citizenship" are more of a description of contemporary anthropological realities. But in my view, they cast light on the possible status of global citizenship that to some extent has already been realized, even if often without a conscious effort. Global citizenship is a "latitudinal" citizenship that coexists with national citizenship: the human rights regime should cement a solid membership in a world community where a minimal standard of human rights is accepted and met, while other issues are resolved in a national and local fashion and give rise to communities centered on different aspects of life. Each of us enjoys membership in a diversity of layers or dimensions and communities. So for example a politician, a professor, a trader, and a refugee are all part of transnational communities that, despite not directly impacting citizenship and not creating a citizenry themselves, can heavily influence the "longitudinal" citizenship, namely citizenship as membership in a nation-state: through lobbying, through their organizations, through spontaneous solidarity and exchanges.

---

[85]"Globalization has intensified the connections between external and internal lines of differentiation, leading to a transvaluation of social capital and norms of labor, a patterning I call latitudes of citizenship. Specifically, the space-making technologies of economic liberalism have expanded external borders to include supranational spaces and noncitizens/ transmigrant figures who create economic extensions of the American nation[. . .] I use latitude as an analytical concept to suggest the transversal processes that distribute disparate forms of citizenship in sites linked by the capital-accumulating logic that spans different spheres of worth across the world. Latitude suggests transversal flows that cut into the vertical entities of nation-states, and the conjunctural confluence of global forces in strategic points that are linked to global hubs[. . .]" Aihwa Ong, in *People Out of Place*, p. 56. The concept of citizenship as an institution exposed to the continuous tension between a "right to be different" and a "right to be equal" which gave the title to this chapter is also inspired by a quote by Renato Rosaldo cited by Ong. See ibid., pp. 53–54.

3.2.11 Rethinking "Special Ties"

Iris Marion Young's "social connection model" suggests a possible source for the ties of global citizenship.[86] She endorses a distinction between duty and responsibility while remaining normatively demanding, as it suggests responsibilities are no less compelling than duties but are characterized by a variety of possibilities to be carried out.[87] As sketched in the first chapter, the responsibilities implied by human rights are enormous and broad-ranging and it is difficult to identify which are to be addressed first if an individual together with her society is to face the demands of justice, and especially of global justice, without being overburdened. Young singles out four parameters to discern responsibilities: power, privilege, interest, and collective ability.[88] Individuals are trans-nationally connected by normative relations of a particular strength (1) if they have the power to influence the lives of others, principally as regards human rights; (2) if they benefit from injustices, whether they consented to them or not; (3) if they are directly interested in bringing about changes or (4) if they are capable of collective actions.[89–92]

---

[86] I. M. Young, "Responsibility and Global Justice."

[87] "On the one hand, a duty specifies a rule of action or delineates the substance of what actions count as performing the duty. A responsibility, on the other hand, while no less obligatory, is more open with regard to what counts as carrying it out." Ibid., pp. 126–127. For this distinction Young relies on Joel Feinberg, "Duties, Rights, and Claims," in Joel Feinberg, *Rights, Justice and the Bounds of Liberty* (Princeton: Princeton University Press, 1980).

[88] "I suggest that persons can reason about their action in relation to structural injustice along parameters of power, privilege, interest, and collective ability." Young, "Responsibility," p. 127.

[89] "An agent's position within structural processes usually carries with it a specific degree of potential or actual power or influence over the processes that produce the outcomes. Where individuals and organizations do not have sufficient energy and resources to respond to all structural injustices to which they are connected, they should focus on those where they have a greater capacity to influence structural processes." Ibid.

[90] "Where there are structural injustices, these usually produce not only victims of injustice, but persons who acquire relative privilege by virtue of the structures." Ibid. Note that on Young's account empowered and privileged persons do not necessarily coincide.

[91] This element is what Young calls "interest": "Different people and different organizations usually have divergent interests in the maintenance or transformation of structures that produce injustice. Often those with the greatest interest in perpetuating the structures are also those with the greatest power to influence their transformation. Those who are victims of structural injustice often have a greater interest in structural transformation. Earlier I said that one of the distinctive things about the social connection model of responsibility is that victims of injustice share responsibility with others for cooperating in projects to undermine the injustice. Victims of injustice have the greatest interest in its elimination, and often have unique insights into its social sources and the probable effects of proposals for change." Ibid., p. 128.

[92] "Sometimes a coincidence of interest, power, and existing organization enables people to act collectively to influence processes more easily regarding one issue of justice than another. That is not always a reason to give priority to that issue, for such ease of organization may be a sign that the action makes little structural change. Nevertheless, given the great number of injustices that need remedy, the relative ease with which people can organize collective action to address an injustice can be a useful decision principle" ibid., p. 129.

Correspondingly, it is possible to trace "latitudes" of citizenship linking the empowered and the powerless, the privileged and the disadvantaged, and trans-national communities gathered for a common cause, the socially influential and the marginalized. This also illuminates the definition of citizenship itself. The normative relations that compose it are "equal" not in the sense that they affect each member in the same way, but rather in the sense that they create a reasonably substantial equality as an outcome, and that they hold in the same way when the same configuration is presented. A wealthy adult holds stricter duties than a poor child, because equality, in the global inasmuch as in the local system of norms, is to be achieved holistically. Such an understanding of justice is coherent with the ordinary experience that many systems whose components are in themselves relevantly different are capable of producing an almost equivalent "amount" of justice: "There are many ways up Mount Fuji," claims a Japanese proverb. In the same way, different societies and civilizations can organize very differently to reach human excellence and justice.

Spelling out a full account of global justice and global citizenship, though, implies also an attempt at harmonizing local systems to a certain degree. This can be achieved by considering the "latitudinal" impact that national and international actors have beyond the framework of the nation-state. The four elements of Young's account should also be considered in their historical depth. Power, benefit/privilege, interest, and capability are to be considered historically: for instance, a benefit received through a(n unjust) historical process – say, colonialism – should still be considered at present, as its effects are still felt. Even in a completely different account, such as Robert Nozick's principles of distributive justice, the historical dimension is strongly present.[93] In conclusion about latitudinal citizenship, there are at least three kinds of normative ties and relations to be considered. Some are normative relations between fellow citizens, some others between all human beings, and there are also specific relations between, say, the citizens of an ex-colonial empire and those of the ex-dominions.[94] Yet these considerations should not lead to destructive revanchism only. A historical perspective should be open toward all its horizons: the account of global citizenship I am offering here is therefore understandable only in relation to its "possible future."

---

[93]Robert Nozick, *Anarchy, State, and Utopia* (New York: Basic Books, 1974).
[94]Even leaving aside the most obvious examples such as the British Commonwealth, in which these relations are institutionalized, in many other cases similar politics are already been enforced. Consider the reparation agreement for the WWII genocide between Germany and Israel, or US special policies promptly granting refugee status to Cubans and Vietnamese. On historical responsibility and the relationships between US foreign policy and immigration policy, see Juan Gonzalez *Harvest of the Empire: A History of Latinos in America* (New York: Viking, 2000), and the documentary with the same name.

Chapter 4

The Right to Freedom, World Citizenship, and Global Peace

> Freedom is the only original right, belonging to each human being simply by virtue of his or her humanity. –Immanuel Kant[1]

> If I had no fear of using too solemn words, I would say that democracy, as a form of government characterized by the existence and the observance of rules that permit conflict resolution without making it necessary to resort to violence, as a foreshadowing, however imperfect, of the ideal society wherein the liberty of each is compatible with the liberty of all, is our destiny. –Norberto Bobbio[2]

> Is it possible to be worthy predecessors of our futures? Arduous as it may be, this is a commitment that the philosophy of emancipation requires from the responsibility of men and women like those we have become. –Salvatore Veca[3]

> There is nothing definitive on earth. What we take to be definitive is but a transition as another, and it is good that it be so[...] –Benjamin Constant[4]

---

[1]Immanuel Kant, "Doctrine of Right," pt. 1 of *The Metaphysics of Morals*, in *Practical Philosophy*, ed. and trans. Mary J. Gregor (Cambridge: Cambridge University Press, 1996).
[2]Norberto Bobbio, cited in Salvatore Veca, Cittadinanza. Riflessioni filosofiche sull'idea di emancipazione (Milano: Feltrinelli, 2013).
[3]Salvatore Veca, *Cittadinanza. Riflessioni filosofiche sull'idea di emancipazione* (Milano: Feltrinelli, 2013).
[4]Benjamin Constant, *Mélanges de littérature et de politique* (Paris: Hachette Livres BNF, 2014).

Freedom and Borders, 105–126

4.1 Perspectives for Citizenship

In the foregoing chapter, I offered general definitions of what citizenship is: an abstract and general "content" of citizenship, a more or less invariable definition underlying all the historical and geographical transformations of this institution. In this sense, this was rather a "concept" than a "conception" of citizenship, to rely on Rawls' language.[5,6] Two other elements are instrumental to the continuation of the argument. Citizenship, as mentioned, is an ensemble of normative relations: fundamentally, of rights and duties (but possibly, also of responsibilities and the like). These relations need not be always institutionalized as law: this is more or less relevant depending on whether we are considering just the legal form of citizenship or also its psychological, sociological, cultural, and more properly ethical aspects.[7] Political theory and philosophy could take into account to different degrees all of these. Citizenship, though, is not freestanding: this institution, and especially its "conceptions," and its realizations, need justification and refer to something that is not intrinsic in the concept. The concept(ion) of citizenship does not fluctuate in a void: otherwise, it would hardly be understandable, and relevant. Etymologically, as recalled, citizenship refers to the *city*, the place to which this membership was related and within which it was also exercised. It is only for a few centuries that history has become a history of vast nation-states: formerly, it had been characterized by city-states, empires, and other entities such as confederations and leagues with varying levels of integration and autonomy.

Besides the *definition*, or *content*, of citizenship analyzed before, therefore, the concept can be understood, explored, and criticized by reference to its *requirements*. Citizenship is a (legal, moral, political, civil, and cultural) condition and to gain access to it one must meet some prerequisites. The two prevailing ways are so-called *ius sanguinis* and *ius soli.* "Right of blood" and "right of soil" are two simplistic labels used to state whether national membership is based upon having been born to parents entitled to nationality in turn, or to having been born on the national soil, no matter from whom. In reality, citizenship is often a combination of both, and other criteria apply, especially for naturalization procedures, such as merit, marriage, residence, cultural integration, *ius nexi* (Ayelet Schachar), or even "citizenship by

---

[5]My usage of the word "definition" is flexible: I rely more on the second Wittgenstein's understanding of "linguistic games," with their thread of continuities that elude sets of individually necessary and jointly sufficient conditions, than on stricter logic/positivistic models.

[6]Rawls, *A Theory of Justice*, 5.

[7]Objective citizenship does at the very least include *practices*. This is part of the reason why I used the word "community" instead of "institutions": the duties of a community involve those of establishing institutions, but go even beyond. So does objective citizenship and citizenship itself.

investment" or *ius doni* (Christian H. Kälin).[8,9] During naturalization, the intentions and specific circumstances (e.g. employment, uninterrupted residence in the country, plans to go abroad, etc.) are also taken into account. It is apparent that in both major cases – *ius sanguinis* and *ius soli* – citizenship is essentially a birthright: in the former it is hereditary, in the latter it is not. Through those two accesses, the majority of people become one or the other state's national. *Ius sanguinis* is, generally speaking, more common in the world, thus reflecting the ancestral idea of citizenship as a blood tie, but a large majority of states adopt some combination of the two criteria with an addition of other factors (time spent in the country, clean records, etc.).

There are strong initiatives in place to end statelessness, as citizenship is a fundamental human right: the Global Alliance to End Statelessness, supported by UN agencies, has the goal of ending statelessness by 2030. Moreover, denaturalization (the deprivation of citizenship) has become a less frequent practice in recent decades and centuries.[10]

Saying that nationality and nationalism still determine the attribution of membership would be very simplistic, especially when considering the range of variations that hold in practice. Many former colonies and former imperial metropoles especially are impressively diverse, and their legislation reflects their conditions and history. Having granted this, it is true that national belonging still plays a significant role in the attribution of citizenship, as it is apparent from the blood ties that grant it or make its acquisition quicker. But nationality itself is no longer considered a good *rationale* upon which citizenship is exclusively to be based, at least in pluralistic and diverse liberal democracies. The rationale is the third factor of the model I am sketching and possibly the most relevant one since it influences both the content of citizenship and its requirements. The *rationale* can be very difficult to identify since it may be based on traditions, practices, and what is considered a commonsensical interpretation of the legislation under such circumstances.[11] A *rationale* dictates the criteria for granting citizenship, but it also defines the kind of normative relations included in citizenship. It can be partly ideological – dependent on the national

---

[8]Shachar, Ayelet. (June 30, 2011). "Earned Citizenship: Property Lessons for Immigration Reform". *Yale Journal of Law and the Humanities*, 23. Available at SSRN: https://ssrn.com/abstract=1865758.

[9]Christian H. Kälin, *Ius Doni: The Acquisition of Citizenship by Investment* (Zurich: Ideos Verlag AG, 2016).

[10]Gibney, Matthew J. (2013). "Should Citizenship Be Conditional? The Ethics of Denationalization". *The Journal of Politics*, 75(3), 646–658.

[11]In general here I focus on *legally enforced* normative relations, but a realistic account of citizenship should consider all the relevant aspects. For instance, speaking a certain language might not be necessary by law; (consider the case of English in the US), but it happens that in fact it is impossible to integrate in a society and to achieve full integration without knowing it. These are social constraints which interact with the legal system, but which are also worthy of being considered in themselves.

ideology – and partly legal/political – dependent on the country's constitution and laws. Of course, the two dimensions are intertwined. Furthermore, in any given society, different rationales for citizenship could be upheld and even institutionalized at the same moment.

Consider, for example, a Middle Eastern state where *Shariah* is observed, and it is almost impossible to naturalize unless one is not a Muslim. Alternatively, a pluralistic Western democracy in the Americas where some groups are historically considered to be constitutive to the national identity. Or again, an ethnically homogenous country in the Far East. Each of these sees citizenship as a different institution, with a different relationship with national history, language, culture, religion, and ideology, and the *rationale* for citizenship helps to devise and administer its requirements (how one becomes a citizen) and its content (the bundle of rights and duties citizenship consists in). *Bumiputera* in Malaysia; naturalization procedures and practices in Saudi Arabia, Pakistan, or Iran; the *Juche* ideology in North Korea, or *Drukpa* Buddhism in Buthan are only the most transparent examples that display rationales of citizenship. The rationale in Western liberal democracy may be more contested, composed, and difficult or impossible to state briefly and explicitly but that does not mean that there is no rationale at all.

For another, historical, example: in a 19th to mid-20th century European nation-state, nationality (a romantic-like conception of the nation) was typically understood as the identity providing a rationale for the acquisition of citizenship. The institution of citizenship was meant to strengthen the bonds among a nation, or race, and to help it develop a state in which it could freely rule and express its particular vocation, character, and culture. From this nationalistic self-conception descended requirements of citizenship to protect it: descent, blood ties, and marriages according to *ius sanguinis*. Finally, the *content* of citizenship consisted of a set of normative relations which, as already explained, could well be asymmetrical: for example, some citizens are allowed to enroll in the national army, but are not granted access to higher education and voting, or vice versa. In the case sketched (1) the *rationale* is some conception of nationalism, (2) the *requirements* are those of a strict *ius sanguinis* and direct affiliation, and (3) the *content* of citizenship is a "web" of normative relations shaped in such a way to mirror, protect and improve the national identity and its influence on the world, e.g. by serving in the army, paying taxes that are partly used to increase national power and grandeur or to fund ceremonies celebrating national traditions, or again to study and illustrate prevalently the national culture or to assist fellow-nationals, and so on.

What is, then, the *essence* of citizenship? We could be tempted to answer that it is its general and abstract character, that is, a compact of rights and duties that fits both the institutional arrangements of a society and the corresponding bundles of normative relations holding toward fellow nationals. In this case, the *essence* of citizenship would be its *content*. But at a deeper level, the essential in citizenship is actually its *rationale*, that is, *goal, and purpose*. As I have specified, that is the guiding force: it is the rationale that explains why ethnic Germans can naturalize, why Jews from all over the world can become citizens of Israel through the *aliya* according to the Law of Return, and why citizenship of the United States is instead not predicated on ethnicity or religion. If the *requirements* are decided by the *rationale*, so is the *content* of citizenship: it is the national ideology of Germany, Israel, and the US that makes it so that some citizens are entitled to free healthcare or obliged to serve in the military and so on.

Historically and at present, rationales for citizenship have been of a dizzying complexity. Culture, and especially political culture is very complex and composite, and political ideals (as in the case of the French Revolution) or philosophies (as for Stoicism, or the most cosmopolitan exponents of the Enlightenment) and religions (like Christianity or Islam) have frequently been in tension with nationalistic ideals and institutions. In any given nation-state, these and others can coexist and conflict, as do, for instance, laws and institutions from a previous era with a society that has been transformed since they were formulated. Nonetheless, all of them have often been conflated if not confused with the triumph of the national interest.[12] Sometimes, such or similar concerns are still influential and sometimes embedded in state laws despite clearly exceeding the dimension of the nation-state.

Ius soli is sometimes only apparently alternative to ethnic homogeneity, as geography often serves as an effective proxy. Therefore, the naturalization of minorities is relatively controllable, not just by setting criteria that act as barriers: the first means to control citizenship is by controlling immigration. Permanent legal residence is often the first step toward naturalization: by denying the status of legal resident it is possible to exclude a person from citizenship almost indefinitely.[13] In reality, immigration policies can facilitate entrance for some ethnic groups, either directly or indirectly. But until very

---

[12]As regards the foregoing examples: the cause of rights of man and citizen with Napoleon's dictatorship and French Empire; Stoicism with the Roman order as conceived by emperor Marcus Aurelius; Christianity with a number of European monarchies, from the Hapsburg's "Apostolic Majesty" to the British monarch, the *defensor fidei* (Defender of the Faith).

[13]"Who we let in to the nation as immigrants and allow to become citizens defines who we are as a people. Conversely, looking at who we ban from entry, and for whom we create obstacles to integration into society and to membership in the community of citizens, also reveals how we imagine ourselves as a nation – that is, as a group of people with intertwined destinies despite our differences." Leo Chavez, *The Latino Threat. Constructing Immigrants, Citizens, and the Nation* (Stanford: Stanford University Press, 2008), p. 10. In the US, until the 1965 Immigration and Nationality Act, entrance to the country was allowed to quotas of migrants mirroring the past composition of the population (in fact, they were proportional to the ethnic composition of the preceding decades). US children born to at least one illegal immigrant parent make up about 8% of all births (source: Pew Hispanic Center). In the EU the development of the Union implies, willingly or not, that the right to free movement results in a right to free migration and settlement reserved for the peoples of the member states, which are ethnically and culturally close.

recent years, the racial and nationalistic concern was recognizable even *among* the members of the national community, with *de jure* or de facto different classes of citizenship available to the major ethnic groups and the most marginalized ones.[14]

Of course, things are much more complicated than it seems on the surface. First of all, nationality can be defined in various ways: as allegiance to a particular culture rather than as sharing some physical characteristics and blood ties. Contemporary democratic politics disregards this "cultural ethnocentrism" no less than classic nationalism, but it is much more difficult to define and identify it. A state is governed in different ways and by different people at different times, but often even at the same time in any of its components, there are conflicting views, so that it is difficult to say that the policies expressed are explainable by direct reference to nationalism. In a system under the rule of law and with checks and balances, it is often the case that the welfare agency is more "cosmopolitan" while the immigration control is more "nationalistic"... or even the other way

---

[14]This was the condition of Jews until the complete repeal of discriminatory laws, only some 60–70 years ago depending on the country. In some cases, it is not easy to determine whether citizenship for Jewish people was precluded or not. Beside the extreme cases of denaturalization, like those of Nazi Germany and Fascist Italy, many states established public discrimination or tolerated private ones, therefore betraying the concept of citizenship as a "right to be equal." Even after the end of WWII, when antisemitism was weakened by the discovery of the Holocaust, Jews were indirectly hindered from gaining access to citizenship, say in the US, by the immigration quotas limiting entrances from Eastern Europe. In private contexts, discrimination was sometimes explicit, especially at the highest levels: Princeton restricted the percentage of Jewish students to 2% in 1924, while African Americans were excluded altogether until 1945 (Jerome Karabel, *The Chosen. The Hidden History of Admission and Exclusion at Harvard, Yale and Princeton* (Boston: Houghton Mifflin, 2005). Laws on immigration, naturalization or deportation, and also private regulations, are but the most blatant forms of screening citizens: practices and norms are mutually influenced. A similar case can be made for Afro-American, or for Romani peoples. The fact that those people are considered equal once that they gain entrance to the body politics is not sufficient to prove the liberal state supposed "blindness" on racial or similar matters because they still can be forbidden from entering in a first place. In this case, their rights can be equally recognized but their "right to have rights" (or at least, leaving aside the question of exceptionally grave violations, their "right to have access to national rights") is undermined. The enduring, however informal, connection between nationality and full citizenship is still recognizable in representation. If citizenship is "the right to rule and be ruled," to recall Pocock's formula, a citizenship that is not expressed through the democratic institutions is not complete. In 2013 Italy, for example, where the non-national population was about 8%, and roughly one out of seven–eight babies was born to at least one non-national parent, there were only about five MPs of foreign origins in a group of 945, roughly the 0.5%.

round. Managerial efficientism, conservative bureaucratism, etc., can all play a role in the matter.

In contemporary states *ius sanguinis, ius soli,* and all the practices of naturalization are probably understandable more as guided by a *meta-rationale,* a second-order justification. By this I mean that the traditional way to acquire new citizens and to expand the body politic is maintained despite being considered somehow arbitrary: from a liberal-democratic point of view, assuming equality of all persons, it is hard to attach intrinsic moral relevance to the fact of being born to Jamaican instead of Albanian parents. But even if *this* criterion is contingent, the existence of *a* criterion is considered necessary: a state institution needs a procedure through which it becomes possible to identify and form citizens.[15] This is the pragmatic-instrumental approach of liberal nationalism that maintains some aspects of nationalism to put it to the service of liberal values. Spatial proximity (*ius soli*) is of course convenient for wielding sovereignty, while blood ties and personal relationships (*ius sanguinis*) strengthen mutual commitments and affections. All these elements will play an important part in the so-called instrumental justification of citizenship (and "special ties" in general) that I will borrow from Robert E. Goodin later on and which I hold to be relatively sound. Even if too much homogeneity seems to jeopardize a minimal pluralism on morally neutral and controversial matters, and perhaps even minority rights, too much heterogeneity, whatever its constituents, is also problematic. It is difficult to imagine a political community that works well despite its members' speaking a variety of different languages (and, most importantly, lacking any shared language or code), having diverse if not completely opposite moral views, belonging to ethnic groups of distant origins and having been gathered together from remote and isolated countries. The troubles and the costly achievements of multicultural and multiethnic states are telling evidence that these fears are not unfounded, even for advocates of postnational citizenship. Yet one can envisage an even more fragmented state. Those cosmopolitan thinkers who have suggested replacing traditional requirements with a system called *ius nexi,* namely the recognition of vital relations, independently from the place of birth and from descent, in practice would risk ending up supporting the traditional *ius sanguinis-ius soli* model since

---

[15]This tenet of political philosophy (the need for a polity of a certain kind) is exemplarily voiced by Walzer: "the idea of distributive justice presupposes a bounded world within which distribution takes place: a group of people committed to dividing, exchanging, and sharing social goods, first of all among themselves" *Spheres of Justice,* p. 31. There must be some criterion to identify *this* criterion: an "Ur-criterion," or fundamental criterion, if we want, that everything else in politics presupposes. Even a thought experiment where citizenship is conceded casually, or to all, maintains such a criterion: while the former case is similar to a lottery, the second is close to universal citizenship.

these tend to coincide, however imperfectly. The place and the people who accompany one for the beginning of one's life are generally of great importance to determine one's relations.[16]

It follows from this that nationalistic, centuries-long rationales for citizenship are not justified in themselves. It is not that they justify the way a state community is formed, but the very opposite: the existence of efficient nation-states capable of enforcing members' (and sometimes even outsiders') rights justifies the preservation of *some* requirements guaranteeing the state's survival. To some extent, they justify the underlying rationale of traditional and national citizenship, but at the same time, they look for a broader and higher criterion to criticize it. They also compel to revise the rationale whenever it appears inadequate in light of their standards. This criterion cannot be but the same holding for supranational organisms and the international community itself: peace and observance of human rights.[17] Therefore it is, in the end, the aim of peace that gives legitimacy and restrains the national rationale of citizenship to the point of forcing it to evolve in a continuous tension. From Hobbes to Kant, "perpetual peace," or at least the containment of the *bellum omnium contra omnes,* can be seen as the source of legitimacy for the sovereign and the end that should animate any confederation of states' constitution. Therefore, domestic peace might work as a core rationale for national citizenship, as global peace should do for international citizenship. It is also easily arguable that there is, at any rate, a strong relationship between the two: even when leaving momentarily aside the question of distributive justice, minimal respect for human rights at home and abroad should be integrated if they are both to be granted some strength. Again, I am here relying particularly on Waldron's argument that institutional legitimation streams from the defense of essential rights, as a matter of "natural duty."

Global citizenship has therefore *peace* as its *rationale, humanity* as its only *requirement*, and the *human rights/human duties regime* as its *content*. It seems that none of these is, in turn, specifically defined: since I have said something about (human) rights while analyzing further the idea of "humanity" goes much beyond the purpose and the possibility of this book, I shall now focus on the idea of peace.[18]

---

[16]See again Ayelet Shachar, *The Birthright Lottery. Citizenship and Global Inequality* (Cambridge: MIT Press, 2009); Rainer Bauböck, "Stake-holder Citizenship: An Idea Whose Time Has Come?" in *Delivering Citizenship. The Transatlantic Council on Migration* (Verlag Bertelsmann Stiftung: Gütersloh, 2008). Joseph H. Caren's "social membership model" is, I hold, closely related to this idea.

[17]Those are of course not the *unique* aims of national and international communities. But I think it would be on the other hand indefensible to claim that peace and respect of human rights are secondary elements in politics.

[18]I do believe that a philosophical anthropology would be needed to develop this point further. For the moment, I would be content with saying that I consider humanity to be defined biologically, by the mere belonging to the species *Homo Sapiens Sapiens.* There are no other "prerequisites" to be satisfied for being "human."

4.2 The Concept of Peace and Its Relation to Freedom

The concept of peace is probably more frequently questioned in political sciences than in political philosophy, at least in contemporary times.[19] This has not always been the case in the history of thought, as peace occupied a rather important place in the political theory of Plato, Aristotle, Augustine, Aquinas, Hobbes, and, most famously, Kant (in his contribution on *Perpetual Peace*). Nowadays peace is frequently considered a topic in pacifism and peace studies, or as a "dialectic concept" in opposition to war.[20] And yet it has a central role in international relations, international law, and domestic politics. In Monnet's speech, which I recalled at the end of the first chapter, the concern for peace was the strongest argument for superseding sovereignty as classically understood and for the ensuing establishment of the European Union: "There will be no peace in Europe, if the states are reconstituted on the basis of national sovereignty. . . ."[21] In the preamble of the Universal Declaration, "recognition of the inherent dignity and of the equal inalienable rights" is held to be the "foundation of freedom, justice, and *peace* in the world" (emphasis added). In this way, peace is joined to two central concepts of political philosophy, freedom and justice. As evidenced by the previous quote, peace is also in tension with sovereignty, another "thick" concept that in practice sets the confines of the rights and duties collected in the institution of citizenship. The concept of peace is intrinsically bound to the very principle of a social polity, to the "realm of justice" subtracted from the original state of war and disorder.[22]

What I call the *negative* concept of peace is thus the mere absence of war, the absence of large-scale violations of human rights that prevent the tranquil and

---

[19]I refer in particular to "peace researches" such as those to which Johan Galtung significantly contributed. Even if I deem Galtung's distinction between positive and negative peace (the former "absence of violence, absence of war," the latter "the integration of human society," see "An Editorial", in *Journal of Peace Research*, issue 1, volume 1, 1964) very useful, I am not building directly on it. I am also, of course, drawing from Berlin's distinction between positive and negative freedom (Isaiah Berlin, "Two Concepts of Liberty", in I. Berlin, *Four Essays on Liberty* (London: Oxford University Press, 2002). There are some overlaps with both the schemes (for example, the definition of negative peace I employ is almost identical to Galtung's).
[20]Andrew Fiala, "Pacifism", *The Stanford Encyclopedia of Philosophy* (Fall 2010 Edition), Edward N. Zalta (ed.). http://plato.stanford.edu/archives/fall2010/entries/pacifism/.
[21]See chapter 1, section 3, note 69.
[22]"Peace" is a word of Latin origin (*pax*), related to the word "pact" (*pactum*) and to the idea of "uniting, joining together" (see Latin *pagina*, English "page," in the sense of "ensemble fastened, joined together"). In a contractualist conception, "Peace" refers to what we can philosophically translate as the "original, sovereign contract," the primeval, archetypical (and possibly imaginary) oath of allegiance to the community, which is renewed and sanctioned in everyday life. The German word *Friede, Frieden* is instead related to the English "friend" (German *Freund*) and, less obviously but perhaps more importantly, to *frei, Freiheit* ("free," "freedom"). In German, therefore, the concepts of freedom and peace that are paired in the Universal Declaration are even etymologically coupled.

harmonic development of human societies. Of course, war is its opposite: in particular, however not exclusively, war in the sense of a deliberate attack of a sovereign state against another, and the condition that ensues. But *positive* peace is not the mere absence of war, but rather the free development of ordered political relations and communities. In this sense, while bellicose nationalism is of course a force that threatens negative peace, reasonable cultural and institutional diversity, and even a "positive" patriotism, is supportive of positive peace. There must be parties to agree on positive peace, while there can be but one (victorious) party as a consequence of the destruction of negative peace. The two concepts are distinguishable, at least to some extent, and a situation of negative peace can coexist with an absence of positive peace.[23] Negative peace requires some restrictions to freedom since not all possible actions are to be performed if it is to be secured; on the other hand, positive peace is better pursued through freedom itself: the development and flourishing of human communities need the removal of barriers of many kinds. The one concept implies some measure of homogeneity (at least in accepting only peaceable means of cohabitation); it is rather static and cooperative. The other concept permits variety and transformation, it is dynamic and independent. A complete concept of peace without further specification implies both these meanings despite a certain tension between the two. Nonetheless, just as it is obvious that positive and negative peace are different, it is as evident that they are related, as positive peace without negative peace is simply inconceivable. States and persons need be *equal* in respect of each one's obligation to respect negative peace, but they are *free* as regards the achievement of positive peace.

4.3 Peace, Freedom, and Equality

Freedom is one of the core concepts of political theories. It is one of the most recurrent terms in our "dictionaries of morality."[24] True, justice has been authoritatively described as the "first virtue" of political institutions, but in Rawls' own theory, this does not mean that freedom ranks only second.[25] Rawls' first principle of justice guarantees that all the full "equal basic liberties" compatible with the same liberty for all are distributed to each citizen.[26] Rawls' attention to "fairness" helps us see some of the requirements of the "equality" that defines citizens who have a right to it: it is *equality of freedom*. Equal "basic goods" and opportunities, on the positive side, but also equal responsibilities, on the negative, identify more and more precisely a certain citizenry, a group within it, a subset of this group depending on the degree of focus. One of the "crucial notions for a normative theory of citizenship" is in fact the "fair

---

[23]As in the famous speech of Calgacus reported by Tacitus in *Agricola* 30: the Romans make a desolation and call it peace. Absence of war is consistent with oppression and imperialism. Actually, negative peace has often been an ideological excuse for oppression and imperialism, including in modern times.

[24]Salvatore Veca, *Cittadinanza. Riflessioni filosofiche sull'idea di emancipazione* (Milano: Feltrinelli 2013).

[25]Rawls, *A Theory of Justice*, p. 3.

[26]Ibidem, pp. 42–43.

equality of fundamental opportunities."[27] I believe that this ideal holds even in respect of the international community. Positive peace implies that each citizenry (supposedly granting an "equal equality of fundamental opportunity" to its members) must have the same extent of freedom of development in front of other states and communities. In this sense, far from being at odds with it, peace requires sovereignty and presupposes it. There might be different "spheres of citizenship" that define equality and freedom by different distributive principles. And the very nature of the particular liberty or good necessary for endowing a citizen with "fundamental opportunities" puts further restrains on the way this particular matter is to be dealt with.[28] States can be different in everything, from the way they allow the people to participate in government, to the way they distribute drinkable water. Yet as a look at the world reveals, in these very diverse ways they can achieve sufficiency and excellence in fulfilling human and other rights and duties. Notably, neither of these goods and the corresponding rights and liberties – not participation in government and certainly not distribution of drinking water – can be achieved individually.

From this cultural and national diversity in organizing collective life, it follows that different "standing floors" for relative equality give rise to different "spheres of citizenship."[29] Despite the close relation between the concept of peace and that of freedom, I think that employing both, in addition to paying due attention to the "moral dictionary" inherited from our public political culture, enables us to consider not only one agent's or one state's individual freedom in their own perspectives but also the *relations* that are necessary to ensure it. Peace is a political condition for freedom, both in the positive and in the negative sense of the two.[30] One's freedom is enhanced by one's community positive peace, and protected by negative

---

[27]Veca, *Cittadinanza*, p. 94. Cf. "My interest in the measurement of freedom[...] arises out of the idea that justice consists, in part, in a distribution of freedom that is either maximal or in some sense fair – in other words, that justice means, in part, 'maximal freedom' or 'equal freedom' or 'a minimum of freedom for all' or something of the sort, or perhaps some combination of these principles." Ian Carter, *A Measure of Freedom* (Oxford: Oxford University Press, 1999), p. 4. I cannot engage at present in a fuller explanation of what "fundamental opportunities" mean. They may refer to human rights, understood as "basic capabilities," like in Sen's approach: Amartya Sen, "Equality of What?" in *The Tanner Lectures on Human Values,* I, pp. 197–220. Sen considers his argument "essentially an extension of the Rawlsian approach in a non-fetishist direction" (p. 219).

[28]"The regulative principle for anything depends on the nature of that thing." Rawls, *A Theory of Justice*, p. 29.

[29]Yishai Blank. (2007). "Spheres of Citizenship". *Theoretical Inquires in Law*, 8(2), 411–452.

[30]It could be thought that the two concepts have only accidental connections at first sight. And yet, in addition to the etymological observations I recalled in note 18, it may be interesting to note that according to the Oxford Dictionary they have some overlap. "Peace" means *"freedom* from disturbance, tranquility" (emphasis added), and only as a secondary reference it has to do with "a state or period where there is no war or a war is ended." One could feel tempted to fix some stipulatory translation between the two, and therefore reducing one term to another in order to define it more precisely. But I am not sure it would be possible, and such effort is unnecessary here.

peace between communities. This helps us understand more clearly what is empirically obvious, namely that only in a condition in which states abstain from violating other state's and other peoples' rights and individual human rights in general (negative peace) each and every state is capable of securing respect to human rights internally (understood as negative freedom enjoyed by each citizen). *Extra rem publicam nulla libertas* ("there is no liberty out of society"), and no freedom without peace. On the other hand, positive peace as, say, is developed through treaties provisioning cooperation and trade-offs of goods and services, increases positive freedom of choice at the individual level. International cooperation against terrorism ensures one's freedom from interference in one's movement; international cooperation on food sharing and trading enables one to better one's health and well-being, one's choice, and also one's knowledge and enjoyment of foreign flavors. These examples are meant to illustrate that integration of freedoms does not mean their decreasing: freedom is not a zero-sum game on conditions that some restrictions on each part are respected. Integration between freedoms magnifies freedoms, once the core and essential freedoms (negative peace) are respected.

Again, it seems that while freedom is "free-standing" and original as a concept, *peace has to do with the mutual and harmonic interaction between different freedoms and different agencies exercising them.*[31] Equality is, in turn, a condition of similarity, of fairness of distribution, but abstract and rigid equality is not strictly necessary.[32] Granted, *equal agents* (and agencies) seem to require *equal freedom* to interact *peacefully*, while agents who are unequal need a relatively unequal "amount"[33] of freedom. In international relations, without denying the obvious imbalances of power, wealth, demography, etc., equal respect for every human being, for the communities they formed, and for their sovereignty is all that is needed for peace.

Thus, when I claim that both global and national citizenship should have peace as their rationale (or meta-rationale) I mean that both the equality of freedom ensured by the human rights regime and the "inequalities" of freedom, or better the different and diverse ways in which freedom is exerted, along national and local particularism, must be harmonized to their mutual benefit.

---

[31]At least for the usage I am doing with the concept here.
[32]Think of the relation between parents and their children: peaceable and yet unequal (especially as regards freedom) until a certain age. Relationships between states can also be asymmetrical yet mutually satisfactory. Against the concept of "abstract equality" see Raymond Geuss' reworking of Marx's lesson: *Philosophy and Real Politics*, pp. 76–80.
[33]See Ian Carter, *A Measure of Freedom*.

4.4 The Defenses of National Citizenship

Despite the significant quantities and qualities of cosmopolitan and "cosmopolist"[34] arguments, there are still some strong cases for national citizenship to be considered. I shall now focus on two examples of this kind and consider their compatibility with, and relevance for, some form of international or global citizenship. None of them implies abandoning the claim for a global citizenship *lato sensu*, but they both put different constraints on the way it can be envisioned. The first is a defense of the ethical significance of nationality by David Miller, and the second is a vindication of the legitimacy of special ties by Robert E. Goodin.[35,36] Many other views and theories could be invoked: for example, a more radically cosmopolitan account than the one presented here or arguments for global democracy. Yet the radicality of the present argument should not be underestimated, and I have already sketched some reservations concerning accounts of direct global democracy: at present, I will have to be content with that general line of argument.[37] If one instead focuses on the matters that I stressed the most – say the distribution of coercion, the increase of equal political representation, the development of a global culture that requires a deep knowledge of foreign practices and values, and so on – then it might follow that my suggestions on these aspects imply directly or indirectly many of the crucial requests of cosmopolitanism, depending on how this latter is conceived. But since moderate stances on the legitimacy of nation-states, like Goodin's and Miller's, are prevalent within and without academia, and thanks to their convergence with some of my points, I shall address these here.[38]

---

[34]By the word cosmopolitan I refer, in line with the scholarship, to the thinkers who are in favor of a universal community, no matter if it is already realized or achievable in the close future. By the neologism "cosmopolist" I refer to those who believe that a global polity is existing as a matter of fact, completely or partially at any rate. The latter doctrine is more influenced by historical, sociological and anthropological accounts, but it can be seen also in a purely philosophical perspective. In fact, it implies an analytic conceptualization of the notion of "polity" that pertains to political philosophy. It is roughly possible to schematize as following: cosmopolitans are those who argue for the existence or the moral necessity of *cosmopolitai* (πολῖται, Greek for "citizens"); cosmopolists are those who argue for the existence or the moral necessity of a *cosmopolis* (πόλις, Greek for "city"). The two concepts are related but not synonymous. There can be global political actors of various kinds, and yet no global political community, and vice versa.

[35]David Miller, "The Ethical Significance of Nationality", *Global Justice: Seminal Essays,* editors Thomas Pogge and Darrel Moellendorf (Saint Paul: Paragon House, 2008), pp. 235–253.

[36]Robert E. Goodin, "What Is So Special about Our Fellow Countrymen?" Ibid., pp. 255–285.

[37]See note 60 in chapter 2.

[38]I focus on seminal essays by both, since these present their views in a synthetic and straightforward way, and because I have discussed David Miller's broader work at length elsewhere (especially in my Ph.D. thesis *The Migrant Crisis and Philosophy of Migration: Reality, Realism, Ethics*, available online).

4.4.1 A Defense of Nationality in the Perspective of Ethical Particularism

While contemporary philosophy predominantly embraces universalism, David Miller prefers an *ethical* standpoint.[39] In his lexicon, influenced by the displacement of morality from the central place in ethics by Bernard Williams, this perspective opens the door for the justification of some special commitments, like national attachments, that are otherwise hardly legitimatized.[40] Nonetheless, he does not mean to defend particularism in itself, as to show how this is a plausible view. He holds, in fact, that universalism is capable of explaining special ties only by indirectly deriving them from universal principles and therefore deprives them of effective motives for respecting them. On the one hand, he sees the Rawls-Hart approach as by far the most systematically developed and widely accepted in present political theory; on the other hand, he recognizes the salience of some communitarian critiques to it.[41,42] On these theoretical bases, Miller holds that nationality is ethically significant. Thus, he must, in the first place, define what nationality actually *is*. Miller sharply distinguishes nationality from membership in a state. He refers to the undeniable facts that nationalities extend themselves far beyond state borders or, contrariwise, are only a "source of identity" among others for a state's population.[43] Miller also provides some real examples.[44] Then he suggests as the main difference between nations and ethnic groups that a nation "should enjoy some degree of political autonomy," while an ethnic group has "no political aspiration."[45]

There is, to my eyes, a tension between those distinctions: since a state is by definition a political institution, the sort of "political aspiration" intrinsic in Miller's concept of a nation seems to be either impacting on a state (so that the

---

[39]"The view I have called ethical universalism may at first sight seem simply to *be* the ethical point of view"; "[universalism] is so prominent a feature of contemporary ethical culture." Miller, "The Ethical Significance," p. 237, 251.

[40]Bernard Williams, *Ethics and the Limits of Philosophy* (London: Fontana, 1985).

[41]Rawls, *A Theory of Justice*, H. L. A. Hart, "Are There Any Natural Rights?" in Quinton, A. (ed.) *Political Philosophy* (Oxford: Oxford University Press, 1967).

[42]The sources explicitly mentioned by Miller here are Alasdair MacIntyre, *Is Patriotism a Virtue?* (Lawrence: University of Kansas, Department of Philosophy, 1984); Michael Sandel, *Liberalism and the Limits of Justice* (Cambridge: Cambridge University Press, 1982) and especially Michael Walzer, *Spheres of Justice* (Oxford: Martin Robertson, 1983).

[43]For a contrasting view see Kwame Anthony Appiah: "I can only say what I think is wrong here if I insist on the distinction between state and nation[. . .] Nations never preexist states[. . .] But all the nations I can think of that are not coterminous with states are the legacy of older state arrangements – as Asante is in what has become Ghana, and as the Serbian and Croatian nations are in what used to be Yugoslavia," *Cosmopolitan Patriots,* in Martha C. Nussbaum with Respondents, *For Love of Country: Debating the Limits of Patriotism*, ed. Joshua Cohen (Boston: Beacon Press, 1996), p. 27.

[44]Miller provides an example of an ethnic group ("Italian-American," p. 246.) and some of nationalities (American and British, see note 39). Perhaps some are questionable: for example, is "American" a nationality in the same sense as "British"?.

[45]Ibidem, p. 247.

state itself becomes very important, even if not sufficient, as regards national identity) or irrelevant.[46] Miller rejects the classic nationalistic claim that "every nation should have its own sovereign state," but this way the kind of political claims advanced by a nation that renders it a nation in Miller's terminology is left unspecified. However, this is not the core of Miller's argument to be considered here. Miller speaks generally of an "ethical relevance" of nationality. And in the end, nationality is in Miller's words "an essentially subjective phenomenon, constituted by the shared beliefs of a set of people." The confusion between ethnicity, nationality, and citizenship is due, in my opinion, not to political philosophy (even less to some individual political philosophers) but to political reality as such and in particular to the lasting importance of institutions like nation-states and their ideologies.[47,48]

Turning from the definitions to the core of Miller's argument, it is important to notice that it claims nationality relies more or less on a myth.[49] Miller quotes at length Anthony Smith's description of the two processes of nation-building. In some cases, there is a predominant ethnic culture that is imposed on minorities and therefore elevated to the status of a "national culture." In others, especially for newly created nations, such a culture is completely lacking and it is the result

---

[46]Miller's account is not always perspicuous on the issue. Miller himself opens his essay with an example meant to illustrate the ethical relevance of *national boundaries*, and the example literally reads as such: "We do not [. . .] hesitate to introduce welfare measures on the grounds that their benefits will be enjoyed only by Americans, or Britons, or whomever." (p. 235). And yet I have sincere difficulties in conceiving of any liberal government approving welfare benefits by declaring they are reserved for one *nationality* only. They would easily apply only to *citizens,* but this is not what Miller is saying, since he himself distinguishes sharply between national identity and membership in a state (citizenship). This is one of the reasons why, to the contrary, I avoided distinguishing between citizenship and nationality so far. In legal–political lexicon the two words can even refer to the same object or have some overlap, as happens in Article 15 of the Universal Declaration. It is there stated that each individual has a right to a nationality, and that no one can be arbitrarily deprived of nationality. If nationality was defined in Miller's terms, this would not make any sense. There is no way of depriving one of a "subjective phenomenon," or "myth," whether arbitrarily or not. This Article instead clearly addresses statelessness, i.e. "citizenship-lessness" For additional clarification on this distinction, see the Introduction.

[47]On ethnicity and nationality: they come from two words, "natio" and "ἔθνος" that refer basically to the same concepts of nation, people, group of humans, race (especially after Homer, according to the Liddell-Scott-Jones Greek/Latin- English lexicons, consulted online in date 11/21/2013). The confusion in political discourses is thus not incidental.

[48]See the note by Appiah in the previous page, and also section 2.1.6 and the quote by Jones reported there.

[49]"[. . .]for it is characteristic of nations that their identities are formed not through spontaneous processes of ethnic self-definition but primarily according to the exigencies of power-the demands of states seeking to assure themselves of the loyalty of their subjects. Nationality is to a greater or lesser degree *a manufactured item*[. . .] nations require histories that are to a greater or lesser degree '*mythical*' (as judged by the standards of impartial scholarship)," Miller, p. 243, my emphasis.

of a process of invention.[50] However, according to Miller, the mythological nature of national identity is not sufficient to diminish its ethical relevance and the possibility of defending it rationally through the "bottom-up" approach of ethical particularism. Attachment is valuable in itself. The example advanced by Miller helps clarify this point: if a family is based upon the belief in common blood ties, and suddenly it is revealed that the people supposed to be their parents' children were in fact confused at the hospital immediately after birth, the mutual affective boundaries do not cease to exist overnight. The *constitutive* beliefs, in contrast to the mythical *background* beliefs, are, in Miller's words, "all in order."[51] This implies that national affection, as family ties, has in Miller's eyes intrinsic value. And in support of such a claim, he sets forth both a negative and a positive argument. The negative argument is that ethnic ties, with which national ties are usually contrasted, are themselves as fictitious as national ties. But, on the contrary of the latter, ethnic ties are entirely *defined* by descent. The consequence is that when common descent is exposed as a sort of serious fable, the relevance of ethnicity should fade much more irremediably than that of nationality. From this negative argument, one infers the positive social functioning of nationality, which has proved capable of displacing more local and inconsistent boundaries. The independent positive argument, though, is that nationality functions "at the collective level" as "the equivalent of autonomy at the individual level": nationality provides individuals and communities with a shared past (be it reliable or not) and most importantly with a shared perspective future. Collective identity and self-understanding are therefore the valuable goods attached to national loyalty. It is important to stress, though, that Miller has nothing to say to those who feel that they lack a sense of common allegiance: "crudely speaking, either one has loyalties or one has not."[52]

Miller is not arguing for the creation of nationality. He is rather attempting to defend *a fact* from a theoretical standpoint. And to accomplish this purpose, he sketches some arguments for defending the ethical relevance of national boundaries while accepting the claims of universalism also. These additional arguments can be roughly summarized in this way: a particular principle of distributive

---

[50]Anthony D. Smiths, *The Ethnic Origins of Nations* (Oxford: Blackwell, 1986). Smiths speaks of a "ideological myth of origin and descent" (p. 147). It is here important to stress that this myth has a surprisingly firm grip on reality, since, for example, by the laws of *ius sanguinis* citizenship *and* nationality *are* coupled, and are both related to biological characteristics.

[51]Miller, p. 244. I believe Miller's example is misleading. To name but one issue, the affections that develop in the case of the family are due to shared experiences. One has been nurtured, protected, cheered by one's parents, irrespectively of whether they may turn out not to be the biological parents. Relationships between fellow nationals are usually much looser and potentially less positive.

[52]Miller, p. 248. The "negative argument" for nationality starts from the previous page.

justice could be, say, that of giving each according to his or her needs.[53,54,55] But first of all we have to define "each," namely to specify the members of a community who must be entitled to the redistribution.[56] And then, we have to address specifically the correct "needs," which is possible only if these are well-defined by more precise social coordinates. In conclusion, there is no defining principle competing with nationality according to Miller. The choice is between the nation and smaller communities: tribes, families, regions, and the like. This would hold irrespectively of the specific principle of distributive justice that is invoked. According to Miller, one is to face the alternative between giving ethical relevance to rationality or giving up claims of distributive justice.[57]

How does Miller's argument affect the account of global citizenship that is sketched here? According to it, "there is nothing strictly incoherent in seeking to extend its range [that of distributive justice] to cover the whole globe." But, as I said while considering the essays on the matter by Blake, Nagel, and Sangiovanni, global citizenship does not require an extension of *distributive* justice as such, at least, not beyond a minimal threshold. Even if there might be some door open for at least a less strict principle of distribution, global citizenship should be essentially concerned with fundamental rights. Redistribution would be problematic only in so far as it gets in the way of ensuring everyone has enough to live decently. However frequently overlapping in practice, distributive justice and the establishment of an effective human rights regime are two distinct goals. It is important to stress that the development of this latter regime does not require a denationalized or postnational citizenship, but rather an international citizenship that can peacefully coexist with the present model of citizenship if appropriately modified. This is to some extent harmonic with what Miller says about nationality and ethnicity. If "there is no reason why ethnic identity and national identity cannot peacefully coexist, one nesting inside the other," all the more national identity will be compatible with a more substantial *human* identity that expresses itself in political institutions proportionate to its relevance.[58] Not only individual

---

[53] According to Miller "These strategies are not incompatible, though particularists will of course view the second [those based on universal reason] as an irrelevance" (p. 247).

[54] Miller recalls also the possibility of a sophisticate defense of a double-principled approach in which the universal rational criterion is the ultimate and dominant, but not the unique, rationale: see Philip Pettit, "Social Holism and Moral Theory". *Proceedings of the Aristotelian Society*, 86 (1985–1986), pp. 173–197; P. Pettit and Geoffrey Brennan. (1986). "Restrictive Consequentialism". *Australian Journal of Philosophy*, 64, 438–455. Miller is skeptical on the possibility of developing a moral psychology capable of solving the problems of such a "dualistic" approach (Miller, p. 249).

[55] Miller, pp. 249–250.

[56] And again, it seems to me that it is not *nationality* but *citizenship* that defines the legal or physical borders within which distributive justice is exercised. Perhaps it is possible that Miller is conflating national and state membership here.

[57] This is why, according to Miller, libertarian anxieties about nationalism and socialism are often coupled. See Friedrich A. Hayek, *The Mirage of Social Justice*, vol. 2 of *Law, Legislation and Liberty* (London: Routledge and Keegan Paul, 1976), pp. 133–134.

[58] Miller, p. 246.

autonomy and collective autonomy can coexist: even different collective autonomous agencies can coexist together like individuals in that harmonic integration
of liberties that I previously defined as peace.[59]

4.4.2 A Defense of Special Ties in the Perspective of Moral Universalism

Robert Goodin sees his view as compatible with Miller's claims.[60] Nonetheless,
he chooses a different theoretical framework and even a radically alternative
terminology. For example, Goodin prefers not to distinguish between "state" and
"nation," "citizenship" and "nationality," just as I have done in this book.[61] On
closer scrutiny, this choice is not accidental, nor is speaking of "special duties"
instead of say, "national duties," "familiar duties" etc. In Goodin's eyes, all those
distinctions would be misleading, since singling out individual responsibilities is a
useful and perhaps even necessary way of discharging universal duties as such.
Goodin presents these duties in the form of a "particularist's challenge."[62] *Prima
facie,* particular obligations seem to defy the major models for reasoning provided by moral philosophy, from Kantians to utilitarians. And yet there is no
doubt that these special ties hold: if one were to face the choice between saving
one's mother from a burning house, or rescuing a famous philanthropist at the
cost of the mother's life, kin would almost invariably prevail. In this way, Goodin
reverses the outcome of a thought experiment originally advanced by William
Godwin to defend an "impartial" moral philosophy. The moral significance of
special ties is therefore accepted by Goodin at the outset. It follows that "[n]
othing in this argument claims that one's nationality is a matter of
indifference."[63]

Goodin focuses on another aspect of special ties which is frequently over-
looked in philosophical debates as well as in ordinary conversations: special ties
usually impose special *duties* that are much stricter than those holding for people
in general. He lists many examples drawn from international and national
legislation: it really seems that citizens' *negative* duties are curtailed, as much as
their *positive* duties are commonly strengthened.[64] There is no need to weigh

---

[59]It is important to criticize and qualify this assimilation of individuals to states, that is, the
so-called "domestic analogy" (see Hidemi Suganami, *The Domestic Analogy and World
Order Proposals* (Cambridge: Cambridge University Press, 2009)). Of course, states do not
act and cannot act like individuals, and a "world state" as a hypothesis is unrealistic,
worrying, and inadequate to solve problems of human rights and global justice. If assumed
uncritically, the analogy should cut both ways: a global state could be as unjust as a
nation-state. The analogy instead holds if one wants to suggest, as I do, that just as
individuals can be free despite the existence of equally free individuals, so states can be
free and sovereign without preventing others from achieving the same goal.
[60]Goodin, "What is so Special," note 50.
[61]See "What is so Special," note 1.
[62]Goodin, pp. 263–265.
[63]Ibid., p. 274.
[64]Ibid., pp. 265–267.

whether the former exceeds the latter or vice versa. The strengthening and increasing of positive duties are by themselves sufficient to rebut two typical ways of justifying special ties and to identify their underlying principle and refute it also. The "magnifier" model implies that special duties are a mere magnification of general duties: one has, toward his or her compatriots, the same duties one has toward aliens, their intensity excepted which, in the case of nationals, is greater.[65] This is not enough to explain why, in the case of negative duties, for example, that of abstaining from collecting taxes, the opposite is true. Neither is the "multiplier" model capable of explaining this.[66] Even if, in the case of special duties, some new duties were to start existing, this should not affect already existing duties to the point of diminishing or even eliminating them.

When examined more carefully, both ways of reasoning reveal to be examples of the model of society as a "mutual-benefit" association.[67] This model claims that reciprocity is the foundation of special ties: one is a legitimate member of a society if one's contribution is proportional to the gains. It is all too easy for Goodin to set forth counterexamples. One is that of resident aliens: they usually work for the host country, they are sometimes eligible for conscription, and yet it seems that their benefits do not match their participation. One even more convincing case against the "mutual-benefit" model is that of congenitally handicapped members. They are not able to contribute proportionately to the expense they request, but all the possible justifications for helping them seem to disrupt the coherence of the model or to be highly incompatible with our moral intuitions and political practices (e.g., the idea that they are benefited only indirectly due to their parents' or their friends' contribution and only proportionally to this).[68] The positive part of Goodin's theory is that special ties are to be understood as "assigned responsibilities."[69] His proposal is to consider special duties as "not very special, after all": they are instead "derivative from general duties."[70,71] This means not simply that general duties are the only ones existing at root but also that special duties are to be overridden by them, at least in some circumstances. Goodin describes two examples that work well in illustrating the case: without a lifeguard, people who come across someone in danger of drowning may not be able to swim well enough or interfere with each other's intervention. In a hospital, too, it is

---

[65]Ibid., pp. 267–268.
[66]Ibid., pp. 268–269.
[67]Ibid., pp. 270–272. "Yet if those models are to fit the elementary facts about duties toward compatriots[. . .] they must fall back on a sort of mutual-benefit logic that provides a very particular answer to the question of how and why the magnification or multiplication of duties occurred[. . .] that is not an altogether happy result."
[68]"That membership is nonetheless denied to those who confer benefits to the society demonstrates that the society is not acting consistently on that moral premise. Either is it acting on some other moral premise or else it is acting on none at all (or none consistently, which morally amounts to the same)." Ibid., p. 272.
[69]Ibid., pp. 272–276.
[70]Ibid., p. 271.
[71]Ibid., p. 272.

necessary to appoint one doctor, or one group of doctors, to one patient, instead of dividing all the staff's time equally between each patient. National ties, according to Goodin, "perform much the same function."[72] If someone is left without a system or a community capable of enforcing one's rights, it is the "residual responsibility" of all to establish or offer one.[73] But what gives states their legitimacy is that they pursue moral goals that preexist them.

There are some weaknesses to Goodin's account. I believe that general/universal duties so construed – as intellectual and impersonal duties, so to speak, which are chiefly recognized through reason – lack motivating force. Ontogenetically and phylogenetically, that is, from the points of view of individual and historical development, special ties precede general and universal duties. There are also instances where the distinction between the two collapses: when one heeds to one's conscience is the duty special or universal? Furthermore, Goodin conceives of "local" or "special" communities simplistically. As stated with respect to human rights, they are not merely "communities of implementation" but also "communities of interpretation" or even "communities of definition." Some general rights and duties, at the very least, require local circumstances, ideologies, etc. not only to be implemented and applied but also to be interpreted: in some cases, it would be correct to claim that such rights come into existence only through the community. More fundamentally, I believe Goodin's account to lack – just like most contemporary moral/ethical/political accounts, including by nationalists – an anthropological dimension: to fail to grasp the way in which one can identify with a community as well as with humanity so that the distinction between one's good and one people's or the whole world's becomes absurd. As special and universal duties (and rights) would be one and the same thing.

When leaving these problems aside, as we should do now, my account of citizenship is largely compatible with Goodin's argument. More generally, Goodin's argument shows the compatibility and complementarity between special ties and universal duties, including thus between national and global citizenship. I shall now list the characteristics of Goodin's approach that I take to be the most salient. First, it is a *duty-based approach*.[74] But the duties it analyzes are mainly *collective duties*: it is obviously illogical to require a single person to be a lifeguard of a shore unless she herself is to work full-time as a lifeguard, which implies

---

[72]Ibid., p. 274.

[73]Ibid., p. 275.

[74]"Let us start, then, from the assumption that we all have certain general duties, of both a positive and a negative sort, toward one another" (Goodin, p. 272). Of course, it does not seem that Goodin is putting duties before rights (and neither am I). He thinks, like me, that since citizenship consists not only of special rights (that the mutual-benefit model would be capable of explaining) but also of special duties, this is the most appropriate perspective on the question.

someone else is saving food etc.[75],[76] Likewise, national and human rights require collective efforts. And yet these duties are influenced by *naturalistic criteria* and are somehow similar to Waldron's *"natural duties."*[77],[78] Like these, the *general duties can override the special ones* if the two sets are clashing, but there is no reason to believe that they displace the other in principle.[79] On the contrary, Goodin shows the "genesis," morally if not historically, of particular ties from the necessity of discharging general duties. Why is Goodin investing so much on duties instead of rights? Because in this essay he is inquiring about what I call *objective citizenship*. He puts aside the subjective level, the set of rights each citizen is endowed with. The question in fact is not "Why am I to privilege fellow citizens?" but "How are *we* to enforce the most indisputable rights?[80]" The answer needs to be "by appointing not only this or that person, but a whole organized community to do so," up until organizing the entirety of humanity toward our common, universal good, i.e. through objective national and global citizenship. This cannot be achieved through managerial or, even worse, despotic top-down ruling: it can only be done by harmonizing positive peace and freedom and by tempering them by the boundaries of negative freedom and peace. There is therefore no wonder that the definition of citizenship Goodin mentions dovetails with the ones I advanced earlier.[81] *Objective citizenship is the appointee to the*

---

[75]"I also argue that one of our more important duties is to organize political action to press for our community as a whole to discharge these duties, rather than necessarily trying to do it all by ourselves." Goodin, note 61.

[76]But if there is no lifeguard, the person has a duty to help people in difficulties. Similarly, if people are suffering because they lack institutions or because their institutions are inefficient in protecting their rights, we and our states have a duty to step in and establish and substitute those (see the third-fourth fundamental duties in the first chapter). See Goodin, notes 53, 55. Of course, the qualifications I specified in Chapter 1 while mentioning the UN Charter and R2P apply here.

[77]Here is perhaps where it lays more space for nationality in the cultural sense, and for other geographic, linguistic and social elements related to nation-building: "There are all sorts of reasons for wishing national boundaries to be drawn in such a way that you are lumped together with others 'of your own kind'; these range from mundane considerations of the ease and efficiency of administration to deep psychological attachments and a sense of self that may thereby be promoted," Goodin, p. 274.

[78]"Those general injunctions get applied to specific people in a variety of ways. Some are quasinaturalistic. Others are frankly social in character." Goodin, p. 273. This distinction is salient in my approach. Global citizenship could be distinguished from national citizenship also by considering how natural are the duties and rights implied by it. In this sentence, Goodin is pointing to the way duties are assigned. But it is possible to argue that these duties are themselves more or less natural or social in character.

[79]P. 272. But see the example of saving one's mother from the building in flames.

[80]Goodin does not specify the sort of rights he refers to, but the examples he uses (a person drowning, doctors assisting someone in a hospital, refugees, alien residents) show that he concerns himself mainly with basic rights like human rights.

[81]"Citizenship is merely a device for fixing special responsibilities in some agent for discharging our general duties vis-à-vis each particular person. At root, however, it is the person and the general duty that we all have toward him that matters morally" p. 276.

enforcement of each citizen's rights. And the political consequences of his arguments are close to mine too: we all have *a duty to provide everybody with substantial citizenship, citizenship that includes the most basic human rights,* and, in Goodin's view as in mine, this is among the most urgent goals to be pursued.[82,83]

---

[82]"[. . .] the state's special responsibility to its own citizen is, at root, derived from the same considerations that underlie its general duty to the refugee," ibidem.

[83]"[. . .] the derivative special responsibilities cannot bar the way to our discharging the more general duties from which they are derived. In the present world system, it is often – perhaps ordinarily – wrong to give priorities to the claims of our compatriots." Ibid.

Chapter 5

Conclusion: From Parts to Whole

God loves from Whole to Parts: but human soul Must rise from Individual to the Whole. Self love but serves the virtuous mind to wake, As the small pebble stirs the peaceful lake; The centre mov'd, a circle strait succeeds, Another still, and still another spreads, Friend, parent, neighbour, first it will embrace, His country next, and next all human race. –Alexander Pope (cited and discussed by Sissela Bok)[1]

5.1 Spheres of Freedom: "From Part to Whole"

The foregoing examples show how it is possible to reconcile national and global citizenship from different philosophical standpoints. Both authors, though, acknowledge that the ethical influence of nationality is not necessarily positive. The counterpart to Miller's view that the nation functions as the collective equivalent of individual autonomy is that it can also mimic egoism. The pursuit of national identity can override universal human values and jeopardize both individual and collective liberties. In fact, the main problem with nationalism is its exclusivism, which Miller does not cover thoroughly. But if, on the one hand, it is obvious that nationality plays a positive role when, among other appreciable outcomes, it strengthens internal bonds and facilitates solidarity and redistribution, it is on the other hand all too clear that when the importance of nationality is exaggerated it removes from sight different and perhaps more significant kinds of considerations. As sufferers of totalitarian regimes experienced, and as the victims of colonial empires that played one ethnic group against the other knew all too

---

[1] Sissela Bok. "From Part to Whole". *Boston Review*, 01.10.1994.

Freedom and Borders, 127–134

Copyright © 2025 Dario Mazzola.
Published by Emerald Publishing Limited. This work is published under the Creative
Commons Attribution (CC BY 4.0) licence. Anyone may reproduce, distribute, translate and
create derivative works of this work (for both commercial and non-commercial purposes), subject to
full attribution to the original publication and authors. The full terms of this licence may be seen at
http://creativecommons.org/licences/by/4.0/legalcode
doi:10.1108/978-1-80117-990-420241005

well, nationality can serve the cause of unfreedom through *divide et impera* ("divide and rule").[2]

The problem with nationality and exclusion is not, of course, that some people are denied access to the "subjective" experience of believing to be the offspring of a common past and the forerunners of future progress. If it is true that the *background* myths of national origins sometimes contribute to strengthening, or are only a byproduct of, the *constitutive* and valuable practices of special affection, other times these very bonds act as obstacles against nonnational and supranational developments. Myths can easily become dogmas, and dogmas can fuel intolerance.

Human rights are affected only in the gravest cases: arts, sciences, sports, personal relations and many other spheres of human life can be jeopardized when the concern for national identity is given an undeserved urgency. To explain this, it is sufficient to reverse Miller's example: familial affection *can* be diminished by the suspect that a child or a parent is not actually biological: this is the plot of countless novels and tragedies. It is important to notice that, differently from the case made by Miller, there would be many instances in which whether myths of common origins prove true is relevant.

The problem with nationalism, in other words, is not that nationality and national forms of citizenship should be replaced by global citizenship. The problem is thinking and acting as though there were no grounds for the equal endowment with the compact of rights we call (national or global) citizenship other than nationality. It is, in other words, the *confusion* between nationality and citizenship itself, between national practices and human rights, between the cause of a nation, or of its country, and that of humankind. In this latter case, if my interpretation of Agamben's argument on the "state of exception" and the "Arendt's paradox" is correct, "constitutional faith" would paradoxically legitimize a "war of civilization" and support not only "cosmopolitan patriotism," but nationalism with global ambitions and an ideologically cosmopolitan flavor.[3]

The cause of human rights *cannot* be conflated with the cause of this or that individual nation-state. But this also implies the more counter-intuitive implication that when we claim allegiance to our country in opposition to others, its commitment to equality or freedom does not suffice to explain why. These are not one country's defining prerogatives. There are of course cases in which it is more reasonable to hold allegiance to a state, or to a coalition of states, because of the pragmatic recognition that this or those are in fact favoring the advancement of human rights, or the "least worst." The Second World War is probably one of the best examples of this possibility, but in the majority of cases, the "axis of evil" will cut across states, and not coincide

---

[2]See for instance Aleksandr Solzhenitsyn, *Gulag Archipelago*, trans. Harry Willetts, foreword by Anne Applebaum (New York: Harper Collins, 1992) volume III chapter 11 pp. 249–284. Ethnic divisions get in the way of breaking free from a *gulag*.
[3]On this crucial concept see for example the reply to Nussbaum by Benjamin Barber in *For Love of Country*, pp. 30–37.

with one or some of them. Even during the Second World War, eugenics, racial discrimination, colonial domination, and in some cases, totalitarian oppression cast many shadows on the heroes fighting the villains. Human rights and a state's or a nation-state's identity *cannot be yoked in principle.* This would generate a kind of political messianism reminiscent of Napoleon or the Crusades. One's allegiance to a state can be justified only by the state's commitment to the protection of fundamental rights when reasonably conceived, but this should hold toward *every humane state.* One's *national* allegiance to the state one is a citizen of needs a different and additional justification. When on the surface we have an opposition between patriotism and human rights, what we have in fact is one sole conflict or dilemma about the ultimate injunctions of justice. In fact, it is consistent with our moral intuitions that in case of open conflict between national practices and human rights, as in Nazi Germany, the general and deeper allegiance to humanity should prevail. A national project can be morally salvaged only when it does not make itself incompatible with humanity. It is therefore important to avoid the confusion between allegiance to *the* state, which must be grounded in human rights, and allegiance to *a* state under all and every circumstance.

Special national rights, duties, practices, and traditions are thus justified, but only in so far as this hierarchy is respected. Only *natural duties,* in the sense that Waldron gives to this term, can justify the substantial and general allegiance to the state; only *national duties,* and other implications of citizenship in this or that nation-state, justify one's affiliation to one's individual nation-state. The two forms of relations are not only hierarchically ordered but often substantially different: national rights are at best *instantiations* of human rights, as one's individual and specific free expression can be an instantiation of the right to freedom of expression.

The confusion between national identities and the defense of justice in itself is mirrored in the debate over citizenship, a debate that current conditions make so urgent in many Western countries. But this debate is set on disputable premises, namely on those of states that defend their citizens' rights *independently*, as though all these rights were on an equal footing, and as though non-nationals were of no importance for the state itself. Conversely, many cultural issues – such as the right to wear the *hijab* – are securitized as if they had to do with oppression and terrorism. Nation-states are not separated universes. Not only they *are* affected by the conditions of human beings in general: but they *should* also share the legitimation provided by *natural duties* (again, in the sense given to these by Waldron). More gravely, issues of human rights, and the lack of objective global citizenship, are confused with issues of national rights and local citizenship when we confront the tragedies of mass migration and asylum flows, from the Mediterranean to the Sonora desert. These phenomena are symptoms of a world that is structurally destabilized and unjust and result in the failure of the peaceful integration of national and individual freedom. Their toll can be quantitatively compared with the greatest tragedies of history, such as the

Atlantic slave trade.[4] This shows what is at stake, but it is relevant also for another reason here: the current "citizenship gap" has to do with inequality of fundamental rights and of economic prospects, which are inextricably intertwined.

The dilemmas we are left to face as citizens of democratic "non-dominating" countries are: is it possible to endure a system of differentiated citizenship that allows phenomena like these? Is there a contradiction between each *national citizenship*'s internal legitimation and its proving incompatible with the guarantee of equal rights for all (*global citizenship*) a few meters from of the national borders, or even inside them? Is national citizenship working for global citizenship in these cases and improving the capacity of the collectivity to react to rights violations? When we assess our country's legitimacy in view of its respect for human rights, do we also consider its policies toward other countries, including private actors that are permitted to elude taxes, exploit and pollute as long as these happen abroad?

Citizenship is best understood if its maximal meaning is recalled: being a citizen essentially does not mean to have this or that set of rights, but to have rights at all. The establishment of an international and even intercontinental standard in human rights protection has at one time developed and obscured the significance of citizenship. And the irreflexive conflation of national rights with human rights has worked in the same way. There is nothing new in distinguishing national practices from human rights. Similarly, there is nothing new in constructing a civilization in which different nationalities can coexist while retaining their unique characteristics. They may perhaps give origin to a better civilization, a broader "nationality" over time. The ancient *Ecclesiastical History of the English People* informs us in the very first chapter that "This island at present[...] contains five nations: the English, Britons, Scots, Picts, and Latins, each with its own particular dialect."[5] History is full of "hyphenated" identities like the Anglo–Saxon nation or the Austria-Hungary empire. As successfully argued by Miller, one of the most relevant merits of the nation is that it surpassed the parochial identity of ethnicity. But this would be no merit at all if there was not a deeper, underlying presupposition in favor of a *global* ethical conscience. If the merit of national citizenship over tribal ethnocentrism is its inclusiveness, why stop there? The nation, even in Miller's account, is a positive achievement only if it allows to overcome morally

---

[4]According to Patrick Manning, as many as 1.5 million died in about five centuries while being deported to the other side of the Atlantic Ocean for slavery. The death rate per year is therefore comparable to that of contemporary flows (Patrick Manning, "The Slave Trade: The Formal Demographics of a Global System" in Joseph E. Inikori and Stanley L. Engerman (eds.) *The Atlantic Slave Trade: Effects on Economies, Societies and Peoples in Africa, the Americas, and Europe* (Durham: Duke University Press, 1992), pp. 119–121). But of course migrations across the Mediterranean and from Mexico to the US is only a tiny part of the movement from the less to the more developed countries (see Benhabib, *The Rights of Others*, pp. 4–7; cf. also *People Out of Place*, p. 6).

[5]David and Hilary Crystal, *Wordsmiths and Warriors: The English Language Tourist's Guide to Britain* (Oxford: Oxford University Press, 2013), chap. 4.

indefensible divisions. It becomes an obstacle, though, if it prevents from pursuing, or even from envisaging, a political system compatible with the inherent dignity of any and each human being. In many countries there are heated debates about the special liberties of some regions or people, debates that sometimes come to the point of discussing secession. Those who want to invent or restore some local state shaped according to an "identity" rediscovered or reinvented are sometimes dismissed as supporters of medieval tribalism. It is important to note that there are almost no grounds for such a dismissal unless we consider citizenship as a *process* that moves from egoistic, familistic, tribalistic, and finally nationalistic pretensions toward a fairer and morally more consistent ideal of universal "siblinghood." But there is no reason to think that this centuries-long process has reached its end. If this were the case, we would be bereft of any hierarchical order to judge particularistic claims: Italian and European identity are left to compete with Milanese, Bavarian or, why not, also Roman Imperial identity. If citizenship is to mirror any pre-existing national identity, and national identity cannot be in turn nothing but the "subjective phenomenon" described by Miller, then there is no large difference between claiming to belong to an actually recognized group or to a national group of a mythical past. There are also particularly feeble reasons to argue that states of the scale they are now are the best arrangement for self-determination. However, the reality is that citizenship cannot be a merely backward-looking process.

In many processes of state-building the main ideal focus was not nationalization but rather unification: *e pluribus unum* ("out of many, one"). This ideal is still desirable, not in the sense of sanctioning one national cause as superior to the other, and therefore entitled by "destiny" to subdue nonnationals for egoistic advantage. This was as extreme nationalism put it, but this is not the ideal of unification *in itself.* Unification may imply, as the European motto suggests, "unity in diversity." Also, it should be unity in freedom, as citizenship within each individual democratic state is supposed to be. A desirable unification in itself means "only" the positive integration between different "liberties," or rather between different free agents, be they one country's government, one country's nationals, or even stateless and displaced people. In other words: it means peace, a condition that is far from being secured by present international disparities (in power, wealth, in cultural and diplomatic influence).[6] The many peculiar ways that this unification could take, from an "Anarchical Society" to a "Community of a Shared Future," should be determined only by a truthful understanding of human nature, the nature of international relations, and the need to eliminate present injustices. There is nothing

---

[6]It is eerie to return to this note 10 years after I wrote its previous version and read what I had written in 2013: "we are still lacking a proportionate procedure to deal with conflicting interests without the threat of direct or indirect international domination. As long as this state of affairs persists, the threatening possibility of a "world war" will not be either eliminated (which is hardly conceivable of) nor limited as strictly as possible and desirable."

destructive in requiring substantiality for global citizenship, as there was nothing, destructive in establishing the United Nations or the European Union.[7] National identities are *not* to be eradicated by their integration into a broader sphere. On the contrary, the threat of engulfment by "McWorld" has delayed if not devastated the prospects for global progress in the recent past.

Historically, families were neither substituted nor abolished by ethnic clans nor individual identity by families, and the establishment of the nation-state maintained both. In many cases, the definition of the limits of each sphere proves useful, and not detrimental, to their preservation. It is easier for a nation to disappear at present when the human rights regime and objective citizenship are not substantial enough to secure its members' fundamental rights than in a stronger international community that considers nationality to be relevant, but not overriding the common good.[8] The pragmatic remark that there is no such thing as a cosmopolitan community at present is also not to be overstated. True that this may be, depending on the requirements one set for a "community," again it is not to be forgotten that culture is, as Dora Kostakopoulou defines it, a process, a project, a practice.[9]

As mentioned with regard to the "domestic analogy," analogies in this sphere work only if they are very loose. The world community certainly needs to be as different from a unified nation-state as the EU is, and probably much more. As was the case with ethnic groups, nations, and families, it is expected that the international regime of objective citizenship functions in a specific fashion: it certainly needs to be *horizontal* rather than *vertical* in the free and equal relationships between sovereign states. Furthermore, this can be only the counterpart of a development of human rights theories and practices whose complexity exceeds by far any individual's political reasoning and imagination. And this is perhaps one of the most urgent and important world dialogues to engage in, as an alternative to the "clash of civilizations," which is often artificially intended for reasons that have nothing to do with culture.

---

[7] The two organisms are admittedly *very* different. The world does not present the cultural and socio-economic similarities that facilitated European integration. Nor would it be necessary to develop such an institution over every region or across regions. Yet the UN are still too conditioned by their origins right after WWII, and need a radical reform to reestablish free and equitable relations between countries (especially considering the Global South). This reform will only be possible if a number of conditions are met. There is an internal process to be started within the UN itself – and proposals abound – but there is also a need for the establishment and working of other, supportive international bodies with the same goal. Finally, an honest and objective reassessment by states that inherited the disproportionate influence of colonial empires is also a requirement for a comprehensive and effective transition toward a more just world order.

[8] It is possible to argue that it is the present state of international deregulation that jeopardize identity rather than conscious cosmopolitanism: see Benjamin Barber, *Jihad vs. McWorld* (New York: Times Books, 1995).

[9] I believe that the uniformity one finds in Europe could possibly be greater than in some large multinational states.

What is presently at hand, though, and needs stating and stressing once more, is that the global horizon of political development is not antagonistic and all the less opposite to the thriving of the nation-state. Most leading philosophers writing on cosmopolitanism agree on that.[10] It would be very unrealistic and harmful for any cosmopolitan vision to forget, or even worse to oppose, loyalty to a nation and to a country. Once again, it would be as if the state contested one's affection for one's own family or neighbors. This is a litmus test for the reasonability of its authority. There can of course be occasional tensions between these institutions, but the normal dynamic is that of mutual cooperation: the state is strengthened by sound social ties like those provided by a favorable social environment.

Human experience has an inner impulse to move "from part to whole": from individual well-being to socialization, from socialization to universalization.[11] This is why we would not contradict our national identity and the allegiance to our states by establishing a more substantial cosmopolitan citizenship: the very opposite, we would contradict these affiliations and their principles, all so vital to human thriving, by not striving after its establishment. Each culture has a unique understanding of, and tension toward, universality. In the worst cases, this is perhaps part of the reason why sometimes cultures find it so difficult to withstand the very existence of alternatives and even try to resolve the challenge of pluralism by annexation. In the past this legitimized nationalism, but it is important to recognize that in recent times we have come closer to a situation when only one state retained full sovereignty.[12] So a very partial and peculiar form of "global sovereignty" has been limitedly realized already, and what we need, through the dialectic process I recalled in Section 1.2.2, is not to bring something to existence but to rectify and develop what exists. This is because, if we have global sovereignty, we cannot settle into a condition of global subjects. The passive entitlement to human rights is not enough: the enforcement of these very rights requires active citizenship to avoid domination. The main purveyor of this empowerment can be the state only, but this does not imply for it to be the sole form of

---

[10]See a few examples from the responses to Martha Nussbaum contained in *For Love of Country:* "The nation [...] *is* arbitrary, but not in a way that permits us to discard it in our moral reflections[...] Nations matter morally [...] as things desired by autonomous agents [...] There is, then, no need for the cosmopolitan to claim that the state is morally arbitrary in the way that I have suggested the nation is." Kwame A. Appiah, pp. 28–29; "If Sheldon Hackney wants to recreate a sense of such patriotic rhetoric among ordinary Americans, he surely is more likely to strengthen than to imperil the civic fabric and the American commitment to cosmopolitan ideals," Benjamin R. Barber, p. 33; "In sum, we do not have to choose between patriotism and universal reason; critical intelligence and loyalty to what is best in our traditions, including our national and ethnic traditions, are interdependent" Hilary Putnam, p. 97.
[11]"Without learning to understand the uniqueness of cultures, beginning with one's own, it may be impossible to honor both human distinctiveness and the shared humanity central to the cosmopolitan ideal," Sissela Bok, "From Part to Whole", in *For Love of Country*, p. 44. See ibidem the quote from Tagore.
[12]This according to Sebastiano Maffettone, *Giustizia globale* (Milano: Il Saggiatore, 2006), p. 57.

mediation between the local and the global. The attainment of global peace, namely the positive integration of national and individual liberties in a way that they do not restrain but sustain each other, is certainly worth some effort, experimentation, and risks. If not historically, states are theoretically justifiable only for the sake of greater freedom. But in the present conditions of the world, it is again for each human being's freedom that substantial international citizenship has become necessary. Coherence with the past and courage in front of our possible futures require us to step across this border also.[13]

---

[13]On the anthropological and existential meaning of frontiers-crossing see Salman Rushdie, *Step Across This Line,* Tanner Lecture on Human Value delivered at Yale University, February 25–26, 2002.

Bibliography

Books and Essays

J. N. Adams. (2003). "Romanitas and the Latin Language." *Classical Quarterly*, *53*(1), 184–205.

Giorgio Agamben, *Il potere sovrano e la nuda vita* (Torino: Einaudi, 1995).

Giorgio Agamben, *State of Exception*, trans. Kevin Attell (Chicago: University of Chicago Press, 2005).

Wayne Ambler. (1987). "Aristotle on Nature and Politics: The Case of Slavery." *Political Theory*, *15*(3), 390–410. http://www.jstor.org/stable/191210

J. An and J. Sun. (September 22, 2022). "Translation Strategy of Legal Terms With Chinese Characteristics in Civil Code of the People's Republic of China Based on Skopos Theory." *PLoS One*, *17*(9), e0273944. https://doi.org/10.1371/journal.pone.0273944

Benedict Anderson, *Imagined Communities: Reflections on the Origin and Spread of Nationalism* (New York: Verso, 1991).

Daniele Archibugi and David Held (eds.) *Cosmopolitan Democracy: An Agenda for a New World Order* (Cambridge: Polity Press, 1995).

Hannah Arendt, *The Origins of Totalitarianism* (New York: Harcourt Brace, 1971).

Hannah Arendt, "Zionism Reconsidered", in Ron H. Feldman (ed.) *The Jew as Pariah: Jewish Identity and Politics in the Modern Age* (New York: Grove Press, 1978), pp. 131–192.

Hannah Arendt-Karl Jaspers, *Correspondence: 1926–1969*, ed. Lotte Kohler and Hans Saner, trans. Robert and Rita Kimber (New York: Harcourt Brace Jovanovich, 1992).

Hannah Arendt, *Eichmann in Jerusalem: A Report on the Banality of Evil*, Rev. and Enl. edn. (New York: Penguin Books, 1994).

Aristotle, *The Politics of Aristotle*, trans. into English with introduction, marginal analysis, essays, notes and indices by B. Jowett (Oxford, Clarendon Press, 1885), 2 vols.

Christopher Arnold, "Analyses of Right", in Eugene Kamenka and Alice Erh-Soon Tay (eds.) *Human Rights* (London: Edward Arnold, 1978).

Benjamin Barber, *Jihad vs. McWorld* (New York: Times Books, 1995).

Geoffrey Barraclough, *The Origins of Modern Germany* (Oxford: Blackwell, 1962).

Rainer Bauböck, "Stake-holder Citizenship: An Idea Whose Time Has Come?", in *Delivering Citizenship. The Transatlantic Council on Migration* (Gütersloh: Verlag Bertelsmann Stiftung, 2008).

Hugo Bedau, "International Human Rights", in T. Regan and D. van de Weer (eds.) *And Justice for All* (Totowa, NJ: Rowman & Littlefield, 1983).

Ruth Benedict, *The Chrysanthemum and the Sword: Patterns of Japanese Culture* (Boston: Houghton Mifflin, 1989).

Charles Beitz, *Political Theory and International Relations* (Princeton: Princeton University Press, 1999).

Charles Beitz. (2001). "Human Rights as a Common Concern." *American Political Science Review*, *95*(2), 269–282.

Charles Beitz, *The Idea of Human Rights* (Oxford: Oxford University Press, 2011).

Seyla Benhabib, *The Rights of Others. Aliens, Residents and Citizens*, (Cambridge: Cambridge University Press, 2004).

Seyla Benhabib, *Another Cosmopolitanism* (Oxford: Oxford University Press, 2006).

Isaiah Berlin, "Two Concepts of Liberty", in I. Berlin (ed.) *Four Essays on Liberty* (London: Oxford University Press, 2002).

Walter Berns, *On Patriotism*. (Washington: Bradley Lecture, American Enterprise Institute, September 16, 1996).

Michael Blake. (2001). "Distributive Justice, State Coercion, and Autonomy." *Philosophy and Public Affairs*, *30*(3), 257–296.

Michael Blake, *Justice, Migration, and Mercy* (Oxford: Oxford University Press, 2020).

James Bohman. (August, 2009). "Living Without Freedom. Cosmopolitanism at Home and the Rule of Law." *Political Theory*, *37*(4), 539–561.

Eugene Borza, *In the Shadow of the Olympus: The Emergence of Macedon* (Princeton: Princeton University Press, 1990).

Ernst-Wolfgang Böckenförde, *Constitutional and Political Theory: Selected Writings*, eds. Mirjam Künkler and Tine Stein (Oxford: Oxford University Press, 2017), Vol. II, p. 45.

Donald E. Brown, *Human Universals* (New York: McGraw-Hill, 1991).

Donald E. Brown, "Human Universals", in *The MIT Encyclopedia of the Cognitive Sciences* (Cambridge: MIT Press, 1999), pp. 382–384.

Alison Brysk (ed.), *Globalization and Human Rights* (Berkeley: University of California Press, 2002).

Allison Brysk and Gershon Shafir (eds.), *People out of Place: Globalization, Human Rights, and the Citizenship Gap* (New York: Routledge, 2004).

Joseph H. Carens, "Aliens and Citizens: The Case for Open Borders", in *Global Justice: Seminal Essays* (Saint Paul: Paragon House, 2008), pp. 211–233.

Ian Carter and Mario Ricciardi (eds.) *L'idea di libertà* (Milano: Feltrinelli, 1996).

Ian Carter, *A Measure of Freedom* (Oxford: Oxford University Press, 1999).

Leo Chavez, *The Latino Threat. Constructing Immigrants, Citizens, and the Nation* (Stanford: Stanford University Press, 2008).

Michael D. Coe (February 27, 1994). "The Language Within Us." *The New York Times*. https://archive.nytimes.com/www.nytimes.com/books/98/12/06/specials/pinker-instinct.html?scp=1&sq=The%2520Language%2520Instinct&st=cse

Joshua Cohen. (2004). "Minimalism About Human Rights: The Most We Can Hope For?" *The Journal of Political Philosophy*, *12*(2), 190–213.

Joshua Cohen and Charles Sabel. "Extra Rempublicam Nulla Justitia". *Philosophy & Public Affairs*, *34*(2), 147–175.

Noam Chomsky and Michel Foucault, *The Chomsky-Foucault Debate On Human Nature* (New York: The New Press, 2006).

David and Hilary Crystal, *Wordsmiths and Warriors: The English Language Tourist's Guide to Britain* (Oxford: Oxford University Press, 2013).

Lawrence S. Cunningham (ed.) *Intractable Disputes About the Natural Law: Alasdair MacIntyre and Critics* (Notre Dame (IN): University of Notre Dame Press, 2009).
Mario De Caro and Benedetta Giovanola. (January, 2017). "Social Justice, Individualism, and Cooperation: Integrating Political Philosophy and Cognitive Sciences." *Teoria*, *37*(2), 53–63.
Eric R. Dodds, *The Greeks and the Irrational* (Berkeley: University of California Press, 1951).
Burton Dreben, "On Rawls and Political Liberalism." In Samuel Freeman (ed.) *The Cambridge Companion to Rawls*, Cambridge Companions to Philosophy (Cambridge: Cambridge University Press, 2002).
Nah Dove. (2018). "Aristotle as Realist Critic of Slavery." *History of Political Thought*, *39*(3), 399–421.
Jan Eckel, *The Ambivalence of Good: Human Rights in International Politics Since the 1940s* (Oxford: Oxford University Press, 2019).
Albert A. Ehrenzweig and Barna Horvath. (1954). "Review of *Inquiries into the Nature of Law and Morals*, by A. Hägerström, K. Olivecrona, & C. D. Broad." *The American Journal of Comparative Law*, *3*(1), 116–119. https://doi.org/10.2307/837139
Peter Garnsey, *Thinking About Property: From Antiquity to the Age of Revolution* (Cambridge: Cambridge University Press, 2008).
Kwame Gyekye, "African Ethics", in Edward N. Zalta (ed.) *The Stanford Encyclopedia of Philosophy* (Fall 2011 Edition). https://plato.stanford.edu/archives/fall2011/entries/african-ethics/
Joel Feinberg, *Social Philosophy* (Englewood Cliffs: Prentice Hall, 1973).
Joel Feinberg, *Rights, Justice and the Bounds of Liberty* (Princeton: Princeton University Press, 1980).
François de Salignac de La Mothe Fénelon, *The adventures of Telemachus, the son of Ulysses* (Manchester: Johnson, 1847).
Moses I. Finley, *The World of Odysseus* (New York: Viking Press, 1954).
Michel Foucault, *The Foucault Reader*, ed. Paul Rabinow (New York: Pantheon Book, 1984).
Philippa Foot, *Natural Goodness* (Oxford: Clarendon Press, 2001).
Michael Freeden. (2005). "What Should the 'Political' in Political Theory Explore?" *The Journal of Political Philosophy*, *13*, 113–134.
David Frydrych. "The Theories of Rights Debate." *Jurisprudence*, *9*(3), 566–588. https://doi.org/10.1080/20403313.2018.1451028
David Frydrych. (2020). "The Case Against the Theories of Rights." *Oxford Journal of Legal Studies*, *40*(2), 320–346.
Johan Galtung. (1964). "An Editorial." *Journal of Peace Research*, *1*(1).
Chiara Giaccardi and Mauro Magatti, *La globalizzazione non è un destino. Mutamenti strutturali ed esperienze soggettive nell'età contemporanea* (Roma: Laterza, 2001).
Raymond Geuss, *Philosophy and Real Politics* (Princeton and Oxford: Princeton University Press, 2008), pp. 60–70.
Raymond Geuss, *Reality and Its Dreams* (Cambridge: Harvard University Press, 2016).
Matthew J. Gibney. (2013). "Should Citizenship Be Conditional? The Ethics of Denationalization." *The Journal of Politics*, *75*(3), 646–658.
Carol Gilligan, *In a Different Voice* (Cambridge: Harvard University Press, 2003).
Giorgio Napolitano, *Una e indivisibile, Riflessioni sui 150 anni della nostra Italia* (Milano: Rizzoli, 2011).

Mary Ann Glendon, *Rights Talk: The Impoverishment of Political Discourse* (New York: Free Press, 1991).

Mary Ann Glendon, *A World Made New: Eleanor Roosvelt and the Universal Declaration of Human Rights* (New York, Random House, 2001).

Robert E. Goodin, "What Is So Special About Our Fellow Countrymen?" in Thomas Pogge and Darrel Moellendorf (eds.) *Global Justice: Seminal Essays* (Saint Paul: Paragon House, 2008), pp. 255/285.

Juan Gonzalez, *Harvest of the Empire: A History of Latinos in America* (New York: Viking, 2000).

James Griffin, *On Human Rights* (Oxford: Oxford University Press, 2008).

Jürgen Habermas, "Kant's Idea of a Perpetual Peace, With the Benefit of Two Hundred Year's Hindsight", in *Perpetual Peace: Essays on Kant's Cosmopolitan Ideal* (Cambridge: MIT Press, 1997), pp. 113–153.

Peter Harvey, *An Introduction to Buddhist Ethics: Foundations, Values and Issues* (Cambridge: Cambridge University Press, 2012).

Oona A. Hathaway. (2002). "Do Human Rights Treaties Make a Difference?" *The Yale Law Journal, 111*(8), 1935–2042. https://doi.org/10.2307/797642

Herbert L. A. Hart, "Are There Any Natural Rights?", in A. Quinton (ed.) *Political Philosophy* (Oxford: Oxford University Press, 1967).

Herbert L. A. Hart, *Essays on Bentham* (Oxford: Oxford University Press, 1982).

Horace, *The Odes and Carmen Saeculare of Horace*, trans. John Conington (London: George Bell and Sons, 1882).

Friedrich A. Hayek, *The Mirage of Social Justice, Vol. 2 of Law, Legislation and Liberty* (London: Routledge and Keegan Paul, 1976).

Wesley Hohfeld, *Fundamental Legal Conceptions*, ed. W. Cook (New Haven: Yale University Press, 1919).

Eric J. Hobsbawm, *The Age of Empire, 1875–1914* (New York: Pantheon Books, 1987).

Eric J. Hobsbawm and Terence Rangers (eds.) *The Invention of Tradition* (New York: Cambridge University Press, 1983).

Eric J. Hobsbawm, *Nation and Nationalism Since 1780. Programme, Myth, and Reality* (Cambridge: Cambridge University Press, 1992).

Simon Hope. (2023). "Perfect and Imperfect Duty: Unpacking Kant's Complex Distinction." *Kantian Review, 28*(1), 63–80. https://doi.org/10.1017/S1369415 422000528

Samuel P. Huntington. (March/April, 2004). "The Hispanic Challenge". *Foreign Policy.*

Michael Ignatieff, *Human Rights as Politics and as Idolatry* (Princeton: Princeton University Press, 2001).

Michael Ignatieff, "Human Rights, Sovereignty, and Intervention", in N.Owen (ed.) *Human Rights and Human Wrongs: The Oxford Amnesty Lectures 2001* (Oxford: Oxford University Press, 2003).

Isocrates, *Isocrates With an English Translation in Three Volumes*, by George Norlin (London: William Heinemann Ltd., 1980).

Werner Jaeger, *Paideia: The Ideals of Greek Culture*, trans. Gilbert Highet, Vol. III, The Conflict of Cultural Ideals in the Age of Plato (Oxford: Oxford University Press, 1986).

W. I. Jennings, *The Approach to Self-Government* (Cambridge: Cambridge University Press, 1956).

Peter Jones, *Rights* (London: Macmillan, 1994).

Immanuel Kant, *Perpetual Peace*, ed. Lewis White Beck (Indianapolis: Bobbs-Merrill, 1997).

Immanuel Kant, "Doctrine of Right", pt. 1 of *The Metaphysics of Morals*, in *Practical Philosophy*, ed. and trans. Mary J. Gregor (Cambridge: Cambridge University Press, 1996).

Jerome Karabel, *The Chosen. The Hidden History of Admission and Exclusion at Harvard, Yale and Princeton* (Boston: Houghton Mifflin, 2005).

Christian H. Kälin, *Ius Doni: The Acquisition of Citizenship by Investment* (Zurich: Ideos Verlag AG, 2016).

James T. Kloppenberg, *Reading Obama: Dreams, Hope, and the American Political Tradition* (Princeton: Princeton University Press, 2010).

Dora Kostakopoulou, *The Future Governance of Citizenship* (Cambridge: Cambridge University Press, 2008).

Cécile Laborde. (October, 2002). "The Reception of John Rawls in Europe." *European Journal of Political Theory*, *1*, 133–146.

Thornton Lockwood. (2021). "Aristotle's Politics on Greeks and Non-Greeks." *The Review of Politics*, *83*(4), 465–485. https://doi.org/10.1017/S0034670521000462

Guojie Luo, "Introduction", in *Traditional Ethics and Contemporary Society of China* (Berlin: Springer, 2023).

Alasdair MacIntyre, *After Virtue: A Study in Moral Theory* (Notre Dame: Notre Dame University Press, 2007).

Alasdair MacIntyre, *Is Patriotism a Virtue?* (Lawrence: University of Kansas, Department of Philosophy, 1984).

Alasdair MacIntyre, *Dependent Rational Animals. Why Human Beings Need the Virtues* (Chicago: Open Court, 1999).

Alasdair MacIntyre (De Nicola Center for Ethics and Culture). Plenary Session of the 2021 Notre Dame Fall Conference. https://www.youtube.com/watch?v=V727Ac OoogQ. Accessed February 4, 2024.

M. Mannoni. (2019). Hefa Quanyi: "More Than a Problem of Translation. Linguistic Evidence of Lawfully Limited Rights in China." *International Journal for the Semiotics of Law*, *32*, 29–46. https://doi.org/10.1007/s11196-018-9554-0

Jacques Maritain, *The Peasant of the Garonne, An Old Layman Questions Himself About the Present Time*, trans. Michael Cuddihy and Elizabeth Hughes (New York: Holt, Rinehart and Winston, 1968; orig. 1966).

Thomas H. Marshall, *Citizenship and Social Class* (Cambridge: Cambridge University Press, 1950).

Thomas R. Martin, *Ancient Greek From Prehistoric to Hellenistic Time* (New Haven: Yale University Press, 1996).

Alasdair MacIntyre, *Three Rival Versions of Moral Enquiry. Encyclopaedia, Genealogy and Tradition* (Notre Dame: University of Notre Dame Press, 1990).

A. Matulewska. (2019). "Legal and LSP Linguistics and Translation: Asian Languages' Perspectives." *International Journal for the Semiotics of Law – Revue Internationale De Sémiotique Juridique*, *32*(1), 1–11. https://doi.org/10.1007/s11196-019-09602-x

Dario Mazzola, "Aristotelian Ethics and Darwinian Biology: Perspectives on Human Nature", in Sante Maletta and Damiano Simoncelli (eds.) *Practical Rationality and Human Difference* (Sesto San Giovanni: Mimesis International, 2023).

John Mearsheimer. Interview With (Australian Former Deputy Prime Minister) John Anderson. https://www.youtube.com/watch?v=huDriv7IAa0. Accessed December 8, 2023.

James McGilvray, "Chomsky Versus Pinker on Human Nature and Politics", in A. Edgley (ed.) *Noam Chomsky. Critical Explorations in Contemporary Political Thought.* (London: Palgrave Macmillan, 2015). https://doi.org/10.1007/978-1-137-32021-6_7

Christopher Menke, "Dignity as the Right to Have Rights: Human Dignity in Hannah Arendt", in M. Düwell, J. Braarvig, R. Brownsword, D. Mieth (eds.) *The Cambridge Handbook of Human Dignity: Interdisciplinary Perspectives* (Cambridge: Cambridge University Press, 2014), pp. 332–342.

Frank Michelman. "Parsing 'A right to Have Rights.'" *Constellations*, *3*(2) (October), 200–209.

David Miller. (2008). "Immigrants, Nations and Citizenship." *The Journal of Political Philosophy*, *16*(4).

Andrea Moro, *The Boundaries of Babel: The Brain and the Enigma of Impossible Languages* (Cambridge: MIT Press, 2008).

Mangesh V. Nadkarni, "Ethics in Hinduism", in *Ethics for Our Times: Essays in Gandhian Perspective* (2nd edn.) (Oxford: Oxford University Press, 2014).

Thomas Nagel. (2005). "The Problem of Global Justice." *Philosophy and Public Affairs*, *33*(3), 113–147.

Joseph Nevins, *Operation Gatekeeper and Beyond: The War on "Illegals" and the Remaking of the U.S.-Mexico Boundary* (New York: Routledge, 2002).

Robert Nozick, *Anarchy, State, and Utopia* (New York: Basic Books, 1974).

Peter Nyers. (2003). "Abject Cosmopolitanism. The Politics of Protection in the Anti-Deportation Movement." *Third World Quarterly*, *24*(6), 1069–1093.

Martha C. Nussbaum, "Non-Relative Virtues: An Aristotelian Approach", in Martha C. Nussbaum and Amartya Sen (eds.) *The Quality of Life* (Oxford: Oxford University Press, 1993).

Martha C. Nussbaum with Respondents, *For Love of Country: Debating the Limits of Patriotism*, ed. Joshua Cohen (Boston: Beacon Press, 1996).

Martha C. Nussbaum, "Patriotism and Cosmopolitanism", in Joshua Cohen (ed.), *For Love of Country? Debating the Limits of Patriotism* (Boston, MA: Beacon Press, 2002), pp. 2–17; 145 (notes).

Claus Offe. (1998). "Homogeneity and Constitutional Democracy: Coping With Identity Conflicts Through Group Rights." *Journal of Political Philosophy*, *6*(2), 113–141.

Joel Olson and Luis Fernandez. (2011). "To Live, Love and Work Anywhere You Please." *Contemporary Philosophical Theory*, *10*, 411–419.

Ahiwa Ong, *Neoliberalism as Exception: Mutations in Citizenship and Sovereignty* (Durham and London: Duke University Press, 2006).

Andreas Osiander. (2001). "Sovereignty, International Relations, and the Westphalian Myth." *International Organization*, *55*(2), 251–287. http://www.jstor.org/stable/3078632

David Owen, "In Loco Civitatis: On the Normative Basis of the Institution of Refugeehood and Responsibilities for Refugees", in Sarah Fine and Lea Ypi (eds.). *Migration in Political Theory: The Ethics of Movement and Membership* (Oxford: Oxford Academic, March 24, 2016). https://doi.org/10.1093/acprof:oso/9780199676606.003.0013. Accessed February 5, 2024.

Philip Pettit. (1985–1986). "Social Holism and Moral Theory." *Proceedings of the Aristotelian Society, 86*, 173–197.

Philip Pettit and Geoffrey Brennan. (1986). "Restrictive Consequentialism." *Australian Journal of Philosophy, 64*, 438–455.

Philip Pettit, *Republicanism. A Theory of Freedom and Government* (Oxford: Oxford University Press, 1997).

Steven Pinker, *The Blank Slate: The Modern Denial of Human Nature* (London: The Penguin Press, 2002).

John G. A. Pocock, "The Ideal of Citizenship Since Classical Times", in R. Beiner (ed.) *Theorizing Citizenship* (Albany: State University of New York Press, 1995), pp. 29–52.

Hilary Putnam, *The Collapse of the Fact/Value Dichotomy and Other Essays* (Cambridge: Harvard University Press, 2002).

Jonathan Quong, "Introduction", *Liberalism Without Perfection*, online edn., January 1, 2011 (Oxford: Oxford Academic, 2010). https://doi.org/10.1093/acprof:oso/9780199594870.003.0001. Accessed December 30, 2023.

John Rawls, *A Theory of Justice* (Oxford: Oxford University Press, 1971).

Joseph Ratzinger and Jürgen Habermas, *The Dialectics of Secularization: On Reason and Religion* (San Francisco: Ignatius Press, 2007).

Joseph Raz, *The Morality of Freedom* (Oxford: Clarendon Press, 1986).

Peter Riesenberg, *Citizenship in the Western Tradition: Plato to Rousseau* (Chapel Hill: University of North Carolina Press, 1992).

Jean Jacques Rousseau, *The Social Contract and Discourses*, trans. G. D. H. Cole (London: Everyman, 1913).

Salman Rushdie, *Step Across This Line*, Tanner Lecture on Human Value delivered at Yale University (February 25–26, 2002).

Michael J. Sandel, *Liberalism and the Limits of Justice* (Cambridge: Cambridge University Press, 1982).

Michael J. Sandel, *Justice. What's the Right Thing to Do?* (New York: Farrar, Straus and Giroux, 2010).

Andrea Sangiovanni. (2007). "Global Justice, Reciprocity, and the State", *Philosophy and Public Affairs, 35*(1), 3–39.

Andrea Sangiovanni, *Humanity Without Dignity, Moral Equality, Respect, and Human Rights* (Harvard: Harvard University Press, 2017).

Saskia Sassen, *Territory, Authority, Rights: From Medieval to Global Assemblages* (Princeton: Princeton University Press, 2006).

Carl Schmitt, *Politic Theology: Four Chapters on the Concept of Sovereignty*, trans. G. Schwab (Chicago: University of Chicago Press, 2005).

Amartya Sen, "Human Rights and Asian Values", in *Sixteenth Morgenthau Memorial Lecture on Ethics and International Affairs* (New York: Carnegie Council on Ethics and International Affairs, 1997).

Amartya Sen, "Equality of What?" in *The Tanner Lectures on Human Values, I* (Salt Lake City: University of Utah Press, 1986), pp. 197–220.

Amartya Sen. (Fall 2004). "Elements of a Theory of Human Rights." *Philosophy and Public Affairs, 32,* 4.

Amartya Sen, Piero Fassino, and Sebastiano Maffettone, *Giustizia globale*, With a Foreword by Ingrid Salvatore (Milano: Il Saggiatore, 2006).

De Consolatione ad Helviam Seneca, *Loeb Classical Library 254,* trans. John W. Basore (Cambridge, MA: Harvard University Press, 1932), p. 442.

Ayelet Shachar, *The Birthright Lottery. Citizenship and Global Inequality* (Cambridge: MIT Press, 2009).

Ayelet Shachar. (June 30, 2011). "Earned Citizenship: Property Lessons for Immigration Reform." *Yale Journal of Law and the Humanities, 23.* https://ssrn.com/abstract=1865758

Ataullah Siddiqui. (1997). "Ethics in Islam: Key Concepts and Contemporary Challenges." *Journal of Moral Education, 26*(4), 423–431, https://doi.org/10.1080/0305724970260403

Anthony D. Smiths, *The Ethnic Origins of Nations* (Oxford: Blackwell, 1986).

Aleksandr Solzhenitsyn, *Gulag Archipelago*, trans. Harry Willetts, foreword by Anne Applebaum (New York: Harper Collins, 1992), Vol. III.

Samuel Stoljar, *An Analysis of Rights* (London: Macmillan, 1984).

Hidemi Suganami, *The Domestic Analogy and World Order Proposals* (Cambridge: Cambridge University Press, 2009).

Charles Taylor, *A Secular Age* (Harvard: Harvard University Press, 2007).

L. Thomas-Walters. (2021). "The Complexities of Translating Legal Terms: Understanding Fa (法) and the Chinese Concept of Law." *Melbourne Asia Review*, 6. https://doi.org/10.37839/mar2652-550x6.18

Thucydides. *Historiae in Two Volumes*, eds. H. Stuart Jones and J. E. Powell (Oxford: Oxford University Press, 1942)

Salvatore Veca. (2002). "John Rawls o della filosofia politica del XX secolo." *Notizie di POLITEIA, XVIII, 68,* 3–5. ISSN 1128-2401.

Salvatore Veca, *La filosofia politica* (Milano: Feltrinelli, 2007).

Salvatore Veca, *L'idea di incompletezza. Quattro lezioni* (Milano: Feltrinelli, 2011).

Salvatore Veca, *Cittadinanza. Riflessioni filosofiche sull'idea di emancipazione* (Milano: Feltrinelli, 2013).

Jeremy Waldron, *Nonsense Upon Stilts: Bentham, Burke, and Marx on the Rights of Man* (London: Methuen, 1987).

Jeremy Waldron, "Special Ties and Natural Duties", in Thomas Pogge and Darrel Moellendorf (eds.) *Global Justice: Seminal Essays* (Saint Paul: Paragon House, 2008), pp. 391–419.

Michael Walzer, *Spheres of Justice* (Oxford: Martin Robertson, 1983).

Max Weber, *General Economic History* (New Brunswick: Transaction, 1981).

Leif Wenar. (2005). "The Nature of Rights." *Philosophy and Public Affairs, 33,* 223–253.

Bernard Williams, *Ethics and the Limits of Philosophy* (London: Fontana, 1985).

Iris Marion Young. (2004). "Responsibility and Global Justice: A Social Connection Model." *The Journal of Political Philosophy, 12*(4), 365–388.

Josh Zumbrun. (November 3, 2023). "Is Globalization in Decline? A New Number Contradicts the Consensus." *The Wall Street Journal.*

Danilo Zolo, *Globalisation: An Overview* (Colchester: ECPR, 2007).

Newspaper Articles

Guerre en Ukraine: Emmanuel Macron appelle à un « sursaut » pour assurer la « défaite » de la Russie". *Le Monde* avec AFP, Published February 27, 2024.

Quando i Savoia parlavano francese", in *Corriere della Sera* (October 2, 1996), an interview of journalist Troiano Antonio with historian Silvio Lanaro.

Giovanni Maria Bellu, "Il cimitero del Mediterraneo: in dieci anni ventimila annegati", in *Repubblica* 11/19/2005.

Maria Eloisa Capurro and Andrew Rosati. "Taxing the Super-Rich Is Brazil's G-20 Plan for Climate, Hunger." *Bloomberg*, 18.04.24.

Piero Cingari. "US Magnificent Seven Rival Europe's Top Four Economies: A Sign of Overvaluation?" *Euronews*, 06.02.24.

Ana Gonzalez-Barrera, Mark Hugo Lopez, Jeffrey S. Passel, and Paul Taylor, "The Path Not Taken. Two Thirds of Mexican Legal Immigrants Are Not US Citizens", Pew Hispanic Center (Washington: Pew Research Center, 2013).

Steven Mazie. (February 19, 2013). "Equality of Opportunity. Obama's Rawlsian Vision." *The Economist*.

Aila Slisco, "NATO Will Be Drawn Into War With Russia if Ukraine Loses: Lloyd Austin", *Newsweek*, Published February 29, 2024.

Websites

https://thedailyomnivore.net/2014/08/21/human-universals/

Entries of the Stanford Encyclopedia of Philosophy

Christopher Bertram, "Jean Jacques Rousseau", in Edward N. Zalta (ed.) *The Stanford Encyclopedia of Philosophy* (Winter 2012 Edition). http://plato.stanford.edu/archives/win2012/entries/rousseau/

Ian Carter, "Positive and Negative Liberty", in Edward N. Zalta (ed.) *The Stanford Encyclopedia of Philosophy* (Spring 2012 Edition). http://plato.stanford.edu/archives/spr2012/entries/liberty-positive-negative/

Andrew Fiala, "Pacifism", in Edward N. Zalta (ed.) *The Stanford Encyclopedia of Philosophy* (Fall 2010 Edition). http://plato.stanford.edu/archives/fall2010/entries/pacifism/

Michael Forster, "Johann Gottfried von Herder", in Edward N. Zalta (ed.) *The Stanford Encyclopedia of Philosophy* (Fall 2008 Edition). http://plato.stanford.edu/archives/fall2008/entries/herder/

Robert Johnson, "Kant's Moral Philosophy", in Edward N. Zalta (ed.) *The Stanford Encyclopedia of Philosophy* (Winter 2013 Edition). http://plato.stanford.edu/archives/win2013/entries/kant-moral/

Dominique Leydet, "Citizenship", in Edward N. Zalta (ed.) *The Stanford Encyclopedia of Philosophy* (Fall 2011 Edition). http://plato.stanford.edu/archives/fall2011/entries/citizenship/

James Nickel, "Human Rights", in Edward N. Zalta (ed.) *The Stanford Encyclopedia of Philosophy* (Spring 2014 Edition), forthcoming. http://plato.stanford.edu/archives/spr2014/entries/rights-human/

Paul Redding, "Georg Wilhelm Friedrich Hegel", in Edward N. Zalta (ed.) *The Stanford Encyclopedia of Philosophy* (Winter 2013 Edition). http://plato.stanford.edu/archives/win2013/entries/hegel/

Leif Wenar, "Rights", in Edward N. Zalta (ed.) *The Stanford Encyclopedia of Philosophy* (Fall 2011 Edition). http://plato.stanford.edu/archives/fall2011/entries/rights/

Leif Wenar, "John Rawls", in Edward N. Zalta (ed.) *The Stanford Encyclopedia of Philosophy* (Winter 2013 Edition). http://plato.stanford.edu/archives/win2013/entries/rawls/

Institutional Websites

Home – Global Alliance to End Statelessness (statelessnessalliance.org). Global Citizenship Observatory (GLOBALCIT) – Globalcit.

Italy – Ministero dell'Interno: Concessione della cittadinanza. http://www.interno.gov.it/mininterno/export/sites/default/it/temi/cittadinanza/sottotema002.html

U.K. – Border Agency: British Citizenship. http://www.ukba.homeoffice.gov.uk/britishcitizenship/

U.S. – Department of State: Certificate of Noncitizen Nationality. http://travel.state.gov/content/travel/english/legal-considerations/us-citizenship-laws-policies/certificates-of-non-citizen-nationality.html

U.S. – Departments of Homeland Security: Customs and Borders Protection. http://www.cbp.gov

Umberto Eco, "L'italiano di domani", speech delivered on February 11 2011 before the President of the Republic for the anniversary of the Unification of Italy. http://www.quirinale.it/qrnw/statico/eventi/2011-02-lett/doc/Eco.pdf

UNESCO and the Universal Declaration of Human Rights. https://www.unesco.org/en/udhr#:~:text=UNESCO%20was%20the%20first%20UN,in%20a%20spirit%20of%20brotherhood

UN – Drafters of the UDHR. https://www.un.org/en/about-us/udhr/drafters-of-the-declaration#:~:text=In%20February%201947%2C%20a%20group,Secretariat%27s%20Division%20for%20Human%20Rights

Index

Printed and bound by CPI Group (UK) Ltd, Croydon, CR0 4YY

29/10/2024

14582690-0005